How To
Get Lost
And Found
In London

Dedicated to Jim, Kim and Jay
Our Traveling Brothers & Sister

How To Get Lost And Found In London

by John and Bobbye McDermott

ORAFA Publishing Co., Inc.
Honolulu, Hawaii, U.S.A.

First Published 1988
Dual Editions:
Orafa Publishing Company, Inc.
  1314 So. King Street, Suite 1064
  Honolulu, Hawaii 96814
  U.S.A.

Hunter Publishing Inc.
155 Riverside Drive
New York, NY 10024

Library of Congress Cataloging in Publication Data

John and Bobbye McDermott
  HOW TO GET LOST AND FOUND IN LONDON
  Includes Index
  1. London — Description and travel — 1988 Travel Experience
  Books. II. Title 87-91328

ISBN: 0-912273-17-8, Hawaii and Overseas
ISBN: 1-55650-018-1, Continental USA and Canada

Typeset by Crossroads Press, Hawaii
Printed by Fairfield Graphics, Pennsylvania

Books Of The Series
  HOW TO GET LOST AND FOUND IN AUSTRALIA
  HOW TO GET LOST AND FOUND IN CALIFORNIA & OTHER LOVELY PLACES
  HOW TO GET LOST AND FOUND IN THE COOK ISLANDS
  HOW TO GET LOST AND FOUND IN FIJI
  HOW TO GET LOST AND FOUND IN OUR HAWAII
  HOW TO GET LOST AND FOUND IN NEW JAPAN
  HOW TO GET LOST AND FOUND IN LONDON
  HOW TO GET LOST AND FOUND IN *UPGRADED*—NEW ZEALAND
  HOW TO GET LOST AND FOUND IN TAHITI

Contents

LIST Of MAPS

Maps by Ken Chapman, New Zealand

Introduction

London is a theater.

The past and present elements of the London documentary surround you in the city. The fortresses and walls against enemies. The temples and churches for the gods. The monuments for great victories. The memorials for the dead. The playgrounds of the kings and the prisons for the condemned.

Against this scenery was played every drama. The goriest of murder stories, the raunchiest of sexual farces, the most sugarcoated of coronations and wedding romances. Power, lust, greed, idealism, hatred, insanity, bravery, humor, affection and love were intermixed in the cast of characters producing real life plots beyond the imagination of a fiction writer.

All part of a true, tumultuous, storybook past.

History.

The great difference of history in England compared with other countries is the stardust of royalty; most important, a royalty which still exists—politically powerless but psychologically influential.

England, especially London, without its royalty and attendant pomp and circumstance would just be another country, enrapturing and picturesque, to be sure, but so are Bavaria and Switzerland and Swaziland.

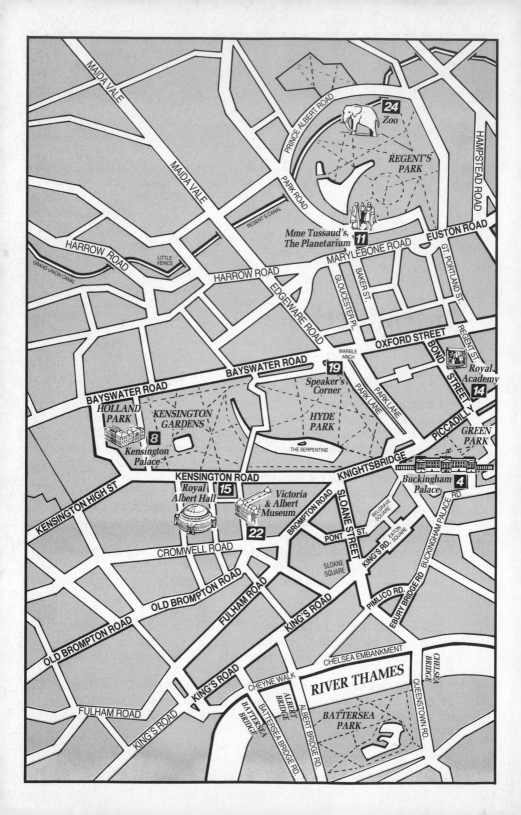

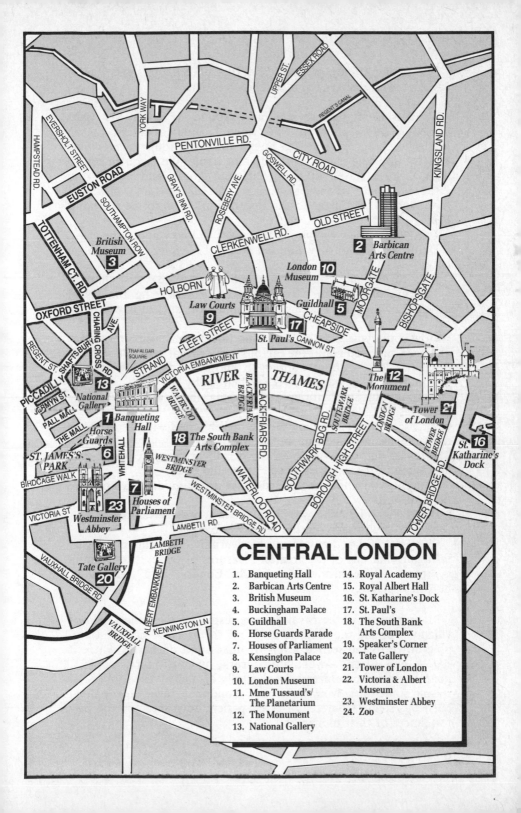

CENTRAL LONDON

1. Banqueting Hall
2. Barbican Arts Centre
3. British Museum
4. Buckingham Palace
5. Guildhall
6. Horse Guards Parade
7. Houses of Parliament
8. Kensington Palace
9. Law Courts
10. London Museum
11. Mme Tussaud's/
    The Planetarium
12. The Monument
13. National Gallery
14. Royal Academy
15. Royal Albert Hall
16. St. Katharine's Dock
17. St. Paul's
18. The South Bank
    Arts Complex
19. Speaker's Corner
20. Tate Gallery
21. Tower of London
22. Victoria & Albert
    Museum
23. Westminster Abbey
24. Zoo

The Leading Lady in the theater that is London is the Queen. Live-in royalty makes the difference.

London is an ancient stomping ground of mine. My visits started in 1945, after the war, when I came to the city as an artillery captain on leave to attend drama school, a mark-time exercise until the troops could be sent home. On frequent return trips, I have stayed at many different hotels and poked into different corners of the city, seen wonderful plays and, always, I have made a pilgrimage to the Regent Park Zoo to see the polar bears.

I thought I knew everything there was to know about the city.

Doing a book on *My London* would be a piece of chocolate cake.

As it turned out, I didn't know enough to write a first chapter.

Looking at London with new eyes, experiencing the visual evidence of the past, I became more and more sucked into English history.

How could you tour the State Apartments in Kensington Palace and hear and read about the famous quarrel that took place in the Queen's Closet without wanting to know the details? What was the quarrel? Who was involved? When? Why?

Digging out such stories and sharing them was one of the pleasures of the visit.

Why visit the Banqueting House in Whitehall without knowing the momentous event that took place there?

Research into the Anglo-Saxon period brings you back again and again to the name of Bede, Venerable Bede.

"Surely, you know about Bede," said one guide to a knowing flock of Brits.

Bede? Famous? Who was Bede and why was he famous?

Back to the library and the history books.

Every day in London was another learning experience emphasizing again that one of the greatest pleasures of travel is to stand in the place where history was made. London is a treasury of historical places.

Many players in the royal dramas displayed the richest vein of villainy. Among the kings and queens themselves—not even dipping down to the second levels of dukes and duchesses where it *really* got bitchy—were murderers, executioners, rapists, homosexuals, womanizers, the mentally disturbed and robbers.

One sometimes wonders if the Londoner talent for patient queueing stems from centuries of patient tolerance for the performances of their monarchs.

You cannot tour London without realizing the great progress, physically, that has been made since 1945 when it was so war scarred and burned. Her wounds hardly show now.

It has always been a city with many elements of charm. The colonnaded Georgian buildings. The graceful Wren spires. The bridges over the Thames. The many parks and gardens, large and small, that dot the cityscape relieving the buildings of red brick and white stone with swards of green and mosaics of colorful flowers.

You wake up and the first sound you hear at dawn is the sound of birds singing. In a city of more than seven million people!

The second sound on weekdays will be the sound of jackhammers.

Subway stations (The Underground, or more commonly called the Tube) are being rebuilt all over London. Buildings are coming down, new buildings are going up. Run-down flats are being gutted and replaced with upmarket apartments for the new generation of Yuppies and wealthy foreigners who want a *pied-a-terre* in the city and for whom price is not important.

New restaurants open every day.

New hotels open every year.

Old restaurants and hotels are constantly being upgraded.

Since the 1956 Clean Air Bill passed, the smoggy fogs of yesterday are gone and so are the blackened buildings. Public buildings such as the Houses of Parliament have been scrubbed and sandblasted and now can be seen in their original glory.

There are some expected negatives.

London is not a clean city. Litter is almost everywhere. Prime Minister Thatcher knows it. The press harps on it. Nothing gets done about it.

Nevertheless, London has long been everyone's favorite city. In today's travel-oriented world, the result is a tourist-packed city. Over 24 million a year.

The most familiar sight on the London street is a visitor studying a map and peering right and left before stopping the first person— another tourist—and asking for directions. If not looking at maps, the tourists are licking ice cream cones.

The ladies have overlapped, double hammerlock grips on their purses.

A strong majority are wearing running shoes.

Expect to hear every accent and every language.

Prices are in keeping with the rest of the world. They are high. However, you can do London on the cheap.

You can eat in fast food shops.

You can stay in hostels, bed-and-breakfast houses and low cost—not easy to find—hotels.

You can walk and not spend a farthing on transportation. Although Metropolitan London covers 670 square miles, you can walk from the Tower of London on the east side of the city to Holland Park beyond Kensington in less than three hours. The core of London is not that big.

On the other hand, you can spend a fortune without great effort.

A hundred pounds each for dinner? Four hundred pounds for a room? Care to drop ten grand at a casino? Easy to do in high-rolling London.

The biggest problem in London is time.

There are so many things to see and do.

Take the "Albertropolis" cluster of buildings in Kensington as a single example. The Victoria & Albert Museum, the incredible Science Museum, the Natural History Museum, and the Geological Museum all are within a hundred yards of each other.

You could spend several lifetimes in any one of them and never see the Changing of the Guard.

In offering the London we see and love to readers, we visit the famous historical places in London where everyone goes, backed with a little historical color of the events and profiles on the players. And references if you want to learn more. (I can hear the Lady Navigator: "Just a little. Just a little.")

After establishing the period of the Romans and the physical boundaries of The City they defined with their protective walls, we look at London area by area going from east to west, following the chronological growth of the city.

Originally, the idea was to examine London's various major periods of development, by era if not by ruler. But the Anglo-Saxons didn't leave anything and the Great Fire of 1666 destroyed Elizabethan and Shakespearean London.

We have visited most of the important museums and galleries and offer our preferences for quick touring.

Naturally, theaters and restaurants and accommodations are examined in some detail and we refer you to guidebooks we found helpful.

The Lady Navigator has devoted her unbridled energy and boundless enthusiasm to the research of shopping in London. She never had a job she enjoyed more. I had to stop her with a knee-high tackle from writing a complete book.

The parks and palaces of London are not overlooked. London would not be London without these green rugs and glamorous edifices sprinkled around the neighborhoods.

We have walked everywhere: on conducted walks, self-guided walks, exploratory walks, walks in the rain and, occasionally, walks under sunny skies. London is a walking town.

We have floated up and down the River Thames, the *raison d'etre* for London.

One of the most enjoyable chapters to research was "Get Out Of Town: Day Trips And Overnighters." We share our trips and talk about others. So much of England can be explored in a day trip, returning to London to sleep.

We have concluded the book with basic knowledge. How to get in from the airport. Where to change money. That kind of thing. You might want to start there.

Two objectives always guided us beyond that of giving you a book that is a pleasure to read. We want to fan your interest in boarding a plane or ship to share our London. Secondly, we want to share with you what we found most enjoyable so that you will have a better idea of what you want to do and see after you arrive. If we can increase your enjoyment of London, we will have succeeded.

London itself is the greatest of theaters.

Make your reservations early.

A Dialogue

Lady Navigator: Remember, you are not writing a history of England.

Answer: Right.

L.N.: I mean, who cares if Monmouth was the bastard son of Nell Gwynn or Lucy Walters?

A: Right.

L.N.: People want to know where to eat and where to get cheap theater tickets.

A: Right.

L.N.: More pasta and fewer dates.

A: Right. **In the beginning there was Caesar—.**

L.N.: Oh, honestly.

Act One

1. The Founding of London

In the beginning there was Caesar.

Goaded by the raids of tribes from England on the northwest reaches of Gaul (France), part of the Roman empire, the legions of Julius Caesar embarked on a punitive expedition in 56BC to teach the northern barbarians a lesson, gain a new territory and, give Caesar a chance to report to Rome with the glory of a fresh victory.

He disembarked with 12,000 legionaries and was surprised by the vigor with which the British chariots and cavalry met his troops in the Channel Coast surf. Endangered of losing their eagle, the symbol of honor, the hardened legionaries slashed and stabbed their way to shore and established a beachhead. But never much more than that.

Caesar withdrew but returned the following year, 55BC, with 30,000 legionaries and 2,000 cavalrymen.

He landed in Kent, stormed across the country—unopposed—crossed the Thames River and engaged the most important British king in an easily won battle. He took a number of hostages, subjected the natives to tribute and again retreated across the channel to Gaul.

For almost a hundred years the tribes of England were left to fight among themselves.

In 43AD the Romans, under Aulus Plautius, returned with 40,000 men, successfully fought their way through the country, again crossed the Thames and, at a prearranged rendezvous, waited for their emperor, Claudius. Claudius led the victory march to *Camulodunum* (Colchester). Having established his victory, Claudius returned to Rome after sixteen days and left Aulus Plautius in command of the new territory.

1

Plautius set up his headquarters at a place high enough on the tidal river that his boats could safely negotiate without grounding. Here he also found two gravel hills to provide firm foundations for fortress walls and buildings on either side of the Walbrook Stream.

A bridge was erected across the river bringing the focus of new roads into the settlement, then called *Londinium*.

A small blip in the establishment of the new Roman province occurred in 60AD when the king of the Iceni tribe died. The Romans saw this as the opportune moment to assume total control of the heretofore peaceful, independent—if subordinate—kingdom paying tribute.

The king's wife—spelled *Boudica* in the Museum of London brochure and *Boudicca* in other spellings and *Boadicea* in Latin—tried to establish her position as queen but the Romans ignored her, raped her daughters and took over the kingdom. She was humiliated. A woman scorned. Beware.

Boudica rallied her people and stormed the Roman stronghold at Chichester and eventually sacked Londinium, slaughtering 70,000 in the process.

Of course the avenging Romans returned, put her entire tribe to the sword. The valiant queen, so the legend goes, took her own life.

Her memorial stands at the northeast entrance to the Westminster Bridge, a bronze chariot with scythes at the wheels, flanked by bare bosom attendants, and commanded by Queen Boudica.

Initially, only a small fort protected the governor and his staff. Then about 200AD in order to protect their critical port of Londinium, they built a massive wall just over a mile in length and 18-feet high around the city.

Within this London Wall—as it would become called—the Romans built a splendid palace for the provincial governor, and a gigantic basilica which contained the town hall, forums, public bathhouses and temples.

For almost four hundred years Londinium flourished as the capital of the Roman province.

But in 410AD the Roman Empire was in trouble and Emperor Honorius was unable to support the British province as his northwest borders on the Continent collapsed.

The resident Romans tried to stay on but gradually Londinium was practically deserted until its rebirth as a Saxon market town in the latter part of the 5th century.

Although the foundations of Londinium now lie buried under six yards of dirt and rubble, many symbols of the first fortress city remain including the names of the gates where roads intersected the wall: Aldgate, Bishopsgate, Newgate, Ludgate.

To appreciate the Roman period fully, the visitor should first visit the Museum of London, adjacent to the Barbican Centre. Closest tube station is the Barbican on the Circle Line.

The Museum of London is relatively new, built in 1984 to show the evolution of the capital city. It should be on the top of every first-time visitor's list.

The Museum of London takes you on a time-warp voyage and lets you play the roles of many people who walked the streets of London. The Romans, the Anglo-Saxons, the Vikings, the Normans, the Elizabethans, the Stuarts, the Georgians.

The exhibits, arranged chronologically, start with Ice Age animals that once could have stalked up and down Piccadilly—a woolly mammoth, a musk ox, reindeer, a straight tusk elephant, even a hippopotamus—and end with the 1930 lifts (elevators) from Selfridges department store.

On the entry level you learn the story of the Roman invasion and 400 year occupation.

The River Thames and its importance to the development of London is laid out before you. Evidence, says the museum, indicates that the Thames was a route for Celtic settlers from Gaul and Anglo-Saxons from Germany as early as 2000BC.

The early Britons were farmers. They made domestic tools and pottery and mass produced bronze war implements. Iron daggers were made near London from 500BC to 300BC by which time there were established trade routes between southeast England and northern France via the Thames estuary. A model of a prehistoric boat is shown with eighteen rowers.

Perhaps it was the field testing of their war instruments in Roman Gaul that goaded Caesar into the initial invasion.

On this same level you learn about the Roman invasion, the initial settlement and the Roman way of life.

The museum displays many Roman artifacts uncovered in the city and even the remains of a Roman barge found only in 1962. It had been submerged in the preserving silt near Blackfriars

Bridge. The barge had sunk loaded with ragstone, a building material from the area of Kent.

Buy the excellent brochure "Londinium" which contains a map of the Roman city overlaying the present city, pictures of re-covered artifacts, and illustrations showing Londinium as it once was.

If you are a dedicated adventurer, also buy a guidebook entitled *The London Wall Walk* (£1.50) and take off on a self-guided two-hour stroll. The booklet gives a map of the wall walk and illustrates 21 stops en route, each marked by informational blue plaques.

Another way to appreciate Londinium is to take an escorted walk with a licensed archaeologist or historian. (As part of a daily Information Services, *The Times* publishes a list of guided walks.) Citisights, I read, had a walk called "Roman London." I decided to meet the tour at the Museum of London.

On second thought I called Colin Oates, one of the archaeological guides, and asked if he were available for a private tour.

Yes, was the answer.

How much, was the question.

Fifteen pounds, was the answer.

Could anybody arrange for a private tour for the same amount?

Yes, was the answer.

Luxury. I could ask all the questions I wanted without being muscled out of the way by a tweedy lady from Manchester.

We met outside the Museum of London entrance and proceeded just south on a walk overlooking remains of walls.

Colin Oates had been a guide on a previous walk. A graduate archaeologist presently studying for a higher degree, his face, stature and easy bounce reminded me of Mickey Rooney. He had a voice that could be heard five blocks away. In heavy traffic.

"At one time it was thought that the Celts lived in the area of London itself," he boomed, "but there has never been hard evidence of anything more than just camping forays. Picnics if you will.

"London was founded by the Romans.

"We are now standing on the west hill of the original Roman town. Over to the east was another hill on the other side of the Walbrook Stream where the first forum, temple and basilica were built.

"Why did the Romans establish themselves here?" It was Colin's question.

Based on museum visits and reading we ventured an opinion: "Because the Thames narrowed here and would allow the footing for the construction of a bridge and the Walbrook was a supply for fresh water."

"No.

"The basic reason was that the Thames is a *tidal* river. Supply boats coming up the Thames came in with the incoming tide and went out on the outgoing tide. The boats could come up river this far without fear of going aground."

We asked the question that had been bothering us, "We don't understand why the Romans came this far afield in the first place."

"Many reasons," said Colin.

"Britain, even at that time, was a bread basket. It offered ample supplies of corn. Also the Romans, who couldn't make slaves of the their own citizens, had to go beyond their own established provinces for slave labor. They could conscript labor gangs in Britain. Another reason: Britain also had gold, silver, lead, iron. And, not the last consideration, Britain was well known for its hunting dogs."

We descended down the stairs to the remains of walls we could see from overhead.

"Look," said Colin. "This was the first wall built by the Romans for a fort about 120AD. It was, you can see, about three feet thick. Notice this layer of red tile which was inserted about every three feet to stabilize the wall. Then, look. Built right next to it is the wall of 200BC which is another six feet thick and 18 feet high. The outer wall was made of ragstone and the inner wall was filled with rubble.

"In the 12th and 17th centuries, large sections of the wall were repaired or rebuilt. But by the 19th century the wall had largely disappeared.

We walked to another part of the wall where an addition had been built.

"Here is an interesting corner of the fort wall.

"No evidence of the famous Roman aqueducts has been found in ancient Londinium. What was found in the walls were these iron rings. What happened? What happened was that the Romans rigged a system that carried the water in wooden pipes mounted to the walls by iron rings. Naturally, in time the wood rotted away but the iron rings remained.

"This was marshy land and the Romans built drainage trenches to divert the water away from the wall. You might think those drains big enough to hide an enemy but there is an elbow in the conduit preventing anything larger than a lamb to hide within. Ingenious, eh?"

Our next stop was at Wood Street.

"Wood Street is the only Roman Road which still exists. It led in a straight line from the north gate to the south gate."

At the corner of Russian Road and Milk Street Colin stopped before the pub Magog, calling my attention to its curved wall. "The shape of the wall is the same as a former public bathhouse which lies underneath it. The bathhouse included the customary hot and cold plunge pools.

"The bathhouse was just outside the gate of the fort so it probably was used by soldiers. No bathhouses were allowed inside the walls where wooden barracks could have been endangered by bathhouse fires which heated the hot plunges.

"For a time in Londinium there was mixed bathing, but Hadrian put a stop to that scandalous behavior. He decreed alternate day bathing; males on one day, females the next.

"Cheapside, from the word *cheapen* or barter, was a road between the new gate and the old gate. It was a place for vintners, goldsmiths and gem cutters and fast food shops of the day.

"Around 200AD, when the London wall was built, there seems to be a disappearance of merchants from London. Brown earth and gardens appeared where houses once stood, archaeologically speaking. The population dropped from 40,000 inhabitants to around 5,000.

"What happened?

"Well, as the Romans penetrated north, they established new ports and the merchants followed them. But Londinium still remained the capital because the governor of the province stayed here as did the financial procurator."

On Queen Victoria Street in front of the Sumitomo Bank are remains of the foundation of the Temple of Mithras.

We stopped at its edge.

"What's wrong with this setting?" asked Colin.

"It should be fifteen feet underground."

"Right.

"Also it is oriented north and south and it should be east and west. The temple was found when they were excavating for the building of the Bank of Montreal next door. The bank was persuaded, as good subjects, to pay for the relocation of the foundation, stone by stone, to its new exhibition location.

"Note the configuration of this *pagan* temple. The altar which worshipers faced. The chancery steps. The apse. The fount over in the corner.

"The churches of Christianity were modeled along the same architectural lines."

Mithras was the god of light in a Persian religion which came close to being the state religion of the Roman Empire. The Romans adopted many religions, their only restriction being that all religions were subservient to the emperor. Because the Druids, the Christians, and the Jews refused to acknowledge Caesar before their gods, they automatically became the enemies of the Roman state.

"Before the temple was destroyed by the Christians many pieces of sacred sculpture were buried by the temple faithful in the area. It is said that the goddess Diana is buried under St Paul's—where Lady Diana Spencer married the Prince of Wales in 1981."

From the temple we walked over to St Stephen Walbrook which stands on the site of the former Walbrook Stream. The church is closed due to erosion because the underground stream was never confined to a conduit.

"The Walbrook was a sacred stream to the Celts. In it we have found votive offerings, curses written on pieces of lead and curled up and thrown into the stream, styluses—used as writing instruments—in large numbers for some unfathomable reason. Also 107 skulls. No evidence of bodies. Just skulls. There is a story that Boudica cut off the heads of her enemies and threw them into the Walbrook. But 107? And no bodies? More likely it was an act of religion to consecrate the most important part of the dead member of the family to the sacred stream."

On Cannon Street we stood opposite Cannon Street Station, a tall, featureless building.

"When the new station was erected after the war, the foundation of the Roman Governor's Palace was discovered, a magnificent building on forty-two different levels."

"Forty-two levels!" we exclaimed.

"Yes. You have to remember that the palace rose from the riverbank to this elevation. In the tradition of Roman architecture, multiple terraces were created and landscaped with ponds and fountains . . . every luxury befitting a Roman governor.

"The governor was responsible for the community and for the army. The financial procurator was responsible for money. Both reported directly to Rome. The palace of the procurator has never been found.

"The original fort—where we started—was in fact nothing more than a hotel for the soldiers. They were drafted to work as staff in the Governor's Palace."

Down the street we stopped in front of a caged-in hunk of rock.

"This stone is the subject of many myths. Some say it was the Lord Mayor's symbol of power. Others believe it was the cornerstone of the Governor's Palace. A popular version used in some guidebooks is that it is a mileage stone from which all distances from London were measured. The truth is, there is no evidence of it being anything but a desirable piece of rock which people have been chipping at for ages. To protect it, it had to be put behind bars."

The last stop of Colin's Roman guided walk was at the intersection where traffic pours off of and onto the London Bridge with the constancy of ants swarming a morsel of food.

"Where was the original London Bridge?

"It was not until 1982 that the pier base of the bridge was found at the river side of Fish Road. Later, evidence of ancient shops along Fish Road seemed to verify that this was, indeed, the road to the bridge. In 1983 the pier base of the bridge was found on the other side of the river.

"In Roman times the road led straight up from the bridge to the basilica/forum at the time of Trajan—he of the Trajan Column in Rome. The edifice was the largest building west of the Alps. It lasted from about 100AD to 1477."

In 410AD the final act of the Romans in Londinium was approaching. The Emperor Honorius declined to support the Roman province in Britain any longer. A plea for help in 433 by Romans still fighting to hold Londinium was ignored. By 450 the city was blending into the future Saxon empire.

The Roman curtain had come down.

End of Act I.

The First Community

2. The City of London

London is distinctly three cities:

1. The City of London, that "square mile" walled in by the early Romans and generally referred to as "The City," remains an independent political entity administered by its own Lord Mayor and corporation and police force;

2. The City of Westminster which became a second city when Edward the Confessor moved upriver out of the stench of The City to the sweet smell of the country, to build the palace and abbey of Westminster; and

3. Greater London which includes both of the above plus the boroughs surrounding them, a total of some 620 square miles

9

bedding down seven-and-a-half million residents nightly.

Geographically and chronologically, a visit to London should first concentrate on The City, just as the Museum of London does, to gain appreciation for everything from the shape of the River Thames to the gloriously gilded Lord Mayor's coach.

Two of the most attractive and captivating sights, and sites, in England mark either end of The City. At the east end is the Tower of London. At the west end is St Paul's Cathedral.

The Anglo-Saxons, who came to dominate the critical port of London for a period of something over 600 years after the curtain came down on the Romans, didn't write a lot of postcards back home.

The theatre went to dark.

Only two documents have supplied valid history of the era. One was the *Anglo-Saxon Chronicles,* a series of seven chronicles spanning eleven centuries—diary entries mostly—providing sketchy material from 1AD to 1154AD.

The second was the *Ecclesiastical History of the English Nation* covering a period from 597AD to 731AD and providing the only known history of the powerful church, center of much of the country's education and government. It was written, in his 60th year, by the venerable Bede, a monk who had spent almost his entire life in two northern monasteries. The document is considered a masterpiece of historical narration and a source of accurate history. The preface alone was a goldmine of information because it acknowledged all of his widespread sources.

The Anglo-Saxons didn't leave many physical monuments either because they were farmers. Having turned the city inside the walls into a vast farm, they lived in a new community, *Ludenwich,* or The Market Town Outside the Walls.

However, an Anglo-Saxon royal palace and chapel were built inside the walls. This royal residence was maintained until Edward the Confessor, the king until 1066, moved up river to build a new palace and abbey at Westminster. The old palace has never been uncovered although it is strongly suspected to be adjacent to St Alban's Tower on Wood Street.

But the site of the first Anglo-Saxon cathedral is known.

According to Bede, in 604 the first Christian Saxon king, Ethelbert, founded and dedicated the first cathedral of St Paul's.

His action was no doubt inspired by a French wife, Bertha, daughter of the King of Paris. (Ethelbert and Bertha were also responsible for the Cathedral of Canterbury where their figures are engraved in the facade of the southwest entrance to the church.)

Fires, lightning, malicious ransacking have been part of the historical menu of havoc and destruction of several successive buildings called St Paul's.

The largest St Paul's was built by the Normans over more than sixty years. It was a huge building, 72 feet longer than the present St Paul's with a spire 100 feet higher than the present spire.

During the time of Henry VIII and the Dissolution, the High Altar was destroyed and the main nave became a thoroughfare. Tombs were used as counter tops for the sale of goods, horse fairs were held in the middle of church aisles, and the fount was a place for payments of money.

The standard measure of a "foot" as a measure of length came from merchants using the carved foot of one of the cathedral's statues.

Queen Mary restored the splendor of the Cathedral and the Roman Catholic services halted by Henry VIII.

Her successor and half sister, Elizabeth I, having emerged safely from the Tower of London, threw the Catholics out again.

Fifty years after Elizabeth, Oliver Cromwell, the Lord Protector of the Commonwealth and king without title, not only appropriated the £ 17,000 earmarked for Cathedral restoration to pay his troops but also used the Cathedral as a cavalry barracks and rented portico space to peddlers and traders. His troops smashed windows, burned precious wood carvings, and vandalized the statues.

The roof fell in.

The spire had been hit by lightning and had not been replaced.

The cathedral was a shambles.

Enter the hero. Christopher Wren.

Cromwell and his ruling son, Richard, had gone and the wanton wrecking of churches was over. Three years after the return of the monarchy, a young professor of astronomy at Oxford—a "miracle" of youth—was asked to make a recommendation for the restoration of the St Paul's.

"Tear it down," said Christopher Wren, the consultant.

"No," said the authorities.

"Yes," said Fate.

The cathedral was destroyed in The Great Fire of 1666.

Two momentous events happened in back-to-back years, 1665 and 1666.
The Great Plague of 1665 wiped out much of the city's population.
A year later, a candle turned over in a bakery in Pudding Lane and ignited a three-day fire that eliminated all but a fraction of the city.
It also cremated the rats that had caused the plague.
The hygienic lessons learned from the plague banned the return of live animals and slaughter houses to the heart of the city.
The fire removed the wooden structures prompting authorities to decree that future building would be only of stone and brick.
In place of the old St Paul's eventually appeared the masterpiece of Christopher Wren.

When I first saw St Paul's in 1945, it stood miraculously intact within a field of unimaginable destruction.
The remains of surrounding buildings were blackened and broken, jagged walls and bombed out sockets of dwellings. Desolation was everywhere. And yet, here stood that plumpest of targets, the splendid dome of the Cathedral of The City, the second largest dome in the world, second only to St Peter's in Rome, seemingly untouched. Truly, a miracle. (In truth it wasn't that pristine. During the course of the war over sixty incendiary bombs had hit the Cathedral but had been successfully snuffed out by volunteers.)

An earlier miracle was that the building was erected at all.

Do two things. First go into the Cathedral, sit down and drink in its magnificent beauty.
Walk up to the nave and view the gold and mosaic tile walls and ceiling in the distant altar and the choir. Like a vision of a coming of heaven.
Stand beneath the dome and look up-up-up-so-far-up to the Whispering Galley.
What a splendid House of God.
Now, before you get involved in the history of the Cathedral or the monuments, before climbing up to the Whispering Gallery and on to the Stone Gallery and the Golden Gallery (another 650

upward steps), go instead to the Crypt and learn about that master genius, Christopher Wren.

The Crypt is bright and well lighted and is filled with many objects of interest. Major among them is the tomb of Horatio Nelson in a black sarcophagus, a reject tomb if you will. Originally carved for Cardinal Wolsey, who didn't rank such magnificence at the time of his demise, and then suggested and refused for Henry VIII, the sarcophagus was finally used to entomb Britain's greatest admiral, he who defeated the French fleet at Trafalgar and set the course of England's greatest years of glory and conquest by dominating the high seas.

But that is not why we are here.

Go beyond the tomb of Nelson to the large wood model of a proposed Cathedral in the middle of the room. Read the plaques on the walls around the model describing the stages of design which led to the present church.

In 1663 a commission was formed to study the best means of restoring the dilapidated and disgraceful Cathedral. Young Christopher Wren, then 31, was appointed to that commission. An astronomer, inventor, mathematician and draughtsman, Wren submitted his own plan for rebuilding the cathedral six days before the great fire destroyed it.

(Ten days after the fire Wren also offered a plan for rebuilding the entire city. The plan was turned down.)

In 1668 he was asked to submit drawings for a new cathedral which had been his idea all along.

He submitted a model of his first design, the Greek Cross.

It was rejected.

Wren then drew and financed the Great Model, his second effort. This is the model in the middle of the room. It cost around £ 600, the price of a three-story house at the time.

But church authorities thought it too reminiscent of Europe, more precisely of Rome and, hence, of Catholicism.

Wren got yet another pink slip.

He resolved never to make another model. A model was too easy to understand, too easy to find fault with.

As Surveyor General to the King's Works, he later submitted a Warrant Design which was approved by the king. Work went ahead "as ordered by his Majesty."

The ecclesiastics were by-passed.

No one knew what the church would look like except Wren. The first stone was laid in 1675 without ceremony, and the final stone put in place thirty-three years later (1708) by Wren's son. Wren, now an old man, had to watch the historic scene from below. Historic because Wren became the first architect—and his associate, Thomas Strong, the first master builder—who lived long enough to see work completed on a structure of such magnificence.

Wren lived to age 91.

A display case in the Crypt guards a few personal items of the man whose architectural impact on London is so admired today along with an etching and a bust of the architect. "He was handsome!" exclaimed a young lady next to me.

The black slab in the southeast corner marks his grave and bears an epitaph written by his son:

> *"Si monumentum requiris, circumspice."*
> "If you would seek his monument, look around you."

Sharing the honor of St Paul's Crypt with Wren are the many tombs or memorials of famous military men including that of the Duke of Wellington, the hero of Waterloo, whose funeral service at St Paul's was attended by 18,000 mourners.

You'll find writers and artists as well in the Artists' Corner: Sir Max Beerbohm, Walter de la Mare and other recognizable names.

Gold plates and chalices and a wealth of elaborate vestments from the Cathedral's treasury are also housed here.

Back upstairs in the Cathedral proper, pay a few bob and take a guided tour. Or at least buy a small pamphlet for a few pence to discover the highlights.

When Wren finished the Cathedral there were no statues. It was not until 1790 that Samuel Johnson and three others were placed near the dome piers, after which time the numbers grew dramatically. Like Westminster Abbey, there is carved marble everywhere.

Note the memorial to Wellington mounted on a horse on the north side. A horse in the church? It so offended parishioners at one time that it was removed, but replaced in 1912.

The High Altar at the east end of the Cathedral—at the East end because it was the custom of the day to place the altar in the direction of Jerusalem—was destroyed by a bomb in 1940. The copy duplicates Wren's original design.

A small charge lets you into the Ambulatory, ambulatory meaning "walking space" on either side of the choir stalls and the high altar.

A funny scene. Amid all of this amassed historical and artistic richness, famous statues and gems of woodcarving and ironwork, where is the largest gathering of awe-struck people?

They are in front of a photo display of the royal wedding of Prince Charles and Lady Diana.

Crowds of people, mostly teen-age girls, cluster before the series of poster-sized color prints, each bearing such impressive labels as The Stage Is Set, Prelude to Pageantry, The Marriage Service, Signing the Register, The Triumphant Departure.

What sets London part? The magic dust of royalty.

Exasperated guide: "Those Italian girls just won't move!"

Note the wreaths and garlands of ever so delicately carved wooden flowers and leaves in the choir stalls, the work of Grinling Gibbons. So is the wood casing for the German built organ.

Note, too, the gates to the choir aisles and the masterful iron railing by Jean Tijou.

Every day, services are sung in the cathedral by the famous St Paul's Choir, 12 Vicars (men) and 36 Choristers (boys) under the direction of the Choir Master, and accompanied by an organist.

The Headmaster and four teachers run the Choir School where the Choristers live and study.

Behind the High Altar is the American War Memorial Chapel commemorating the loss of 28,000 United States servicemen who had been based in Britain. A floor plaque reads: To the American Dead from the People of Britain. Engraved lettering on the altar reads: To the Overseas Members of the Commonwealth and Empire.

On the south side of the choir you will find the statue of John Donne, a Dean of Old St Paul's during the reign of Charles I and a talented poet who wrote the famous lines "Never send to know for whom the bell tolls; it tolls for thee."

This monument survived the 1666 fire by falling through the floor into the crypt below. The urn at the statue's base still bears scorch marks.

Now of course you want to walk to the top of the cupola if you are physically able. Pay the small admission charge, walk 259 steps up to the Whispering Gallery to enjoy the close-up inspection of the life of St Paul painted by Sir James Thornhill, as well as the activities of the ant-sized humans below you.

Listen. You can hear a whisper across the dome's 405-foot diameter. To look outside the Cathedral climb again up to the

Stone Gallery and then higher to the Golden Gallery. On a clear day you can get a great photo of Tower Bridge.

The northwest tower of the Cathedral has thirteen bells; the southwest tower, five.

The final cost of Wren's St Paul's was £ 721,552 plus seven shillings and seven-and-a-half pence. Coal brought into the Port of London was taxed to raise the amount.

Wren, the genius, was paid £ 200 a year during the Cathedral's construction.

Not content with one masterpiece—enough to satisfy most men for their lifetime—Wren was also involved in rebuilding more than fifty other churches in London plus many other buildings. Although his overture to redesign London failed, his mark of genius is everywhere: St Bride's on Fleet Street, St Mary-le-Bow on Cheapside, St James's on Piccadilly.

In time, it becomes pleasantly easy to recognize the delicate Wren touch.

The Tower Of London

To set the stage for the Tower of London you have to go back to the beginning of the long association of England with France. Initiated by the marriage of Bertha, daughter of the King of Paris, to Ethelbert at the beginning of the seventh century, the link continued into the eleventh century with French-born Queen Emma, sister of Richard II of Normandy and mother of Edward the Confessor.

Edward the Confessor, the future saint, was born in England but raised in exile in Normandy. When he returned to England to reestablish the Saxon kings after the rule of the Danes, he brought his Norman friends with him. He stripped his mother of her property, exiled his powerful father-in-law in 1051—*some saint* —then invited to England his French first cousin, William, the Duke of Normandy, the bastard grandson of his mother's brother, and promised him the throne.

However, when Edward died only eight days after completion of his Westminster Abbey in 1066, he was surrounded by in-laws. He repudiated his promise to his French relative, according to Harold Godwinson, the brother-in-law, naming Harold king.

Harold, wasting no time on argument, assumed the crown the same day.

He was not to wear it long.

The king of Denmark and Norway didn't care who wore the crown. He wanted the English title returned to his collection. Within the year, he attacked from the North. At the same time, the Duke of Normandy slid across the channel to claim that which had been promised.

Harold force marched his army north, defeated the Danish army near York, slew their king at the Battle of Stamford Bridge, and turned south to meet the French.

He was too hasty. He should have taken more time, rested his troops, rearmed and allowed others to reinforce his army and retained the advantage of position. Harold took no respite and no rest and, at first contact at Hastings, took on the army of the Duke of Normandy who was a skilled and battle proven leader. As a result Harold's army was decimated at the Battle of Hastings in the autumn of 1066. Harold took an arrow through the eye and was cut down by the Norman cavalry. He had not been a king for a full year.

The Duke of Normandy circled London like a hungry wolf, razing the surrounding countryside, forcing the terrified city to surrender without a fight.

Crowned William I, the Duke would henceforth become known as William the Conqueror.

William I first gained access to the pages of English history books for the Battle of Hastings but he became known for much more.

A strong leader, he brought under single rule the Celts, the Anglo-Saxons, the Vikings and the Normans through a sophisticated organization backed by a take-no-prisoners army.

He introduced the law and order of the Norman system. The *maire* of the French city became the mayor of the English town. Rape was rewarded with castration. Nor was he reluctant to throw bishops out of palaces and earls into prisons.

The English were thrown off the lands which were rewarded, as promised, to his French and Norman supporters. One of his organizational ideas was a survey of the lands, titles, equipment and people within his kingdom. The resultant census, called the Domesday Book, not only gave William a record from which he could draw tribute, taxes, and manpower but also gave him an understanding of the scope of the kingdom which he now controlled.

Brilliant.

The first edition of the Domesday Book can be seen—unless it is on tour as it was when we tried to see it—at the Public Record Office on Chancery Lane which is at the west end of Fleet Street. ("Near the Silver Vaults," says the Lady Navigator. "Everybody knows where they are.")

Even before the Domesday Book was commissioned, William built a fortress on the River Thames just inside the Roman walls to show the natives that this Frenchman from Normandy meant business.

The first building was of wood, replaced with stone in 1240 and then whitewashed.

Known today at the White Tower, it is the core of the Tower of London.

The Tower served successive kings and queens well. Over almost a thousand years, ever expanding, the 18-acre compound has functioned as a royal palace and church, mint and armory, prison and execution grounds, and burial place.

Early on, its security also encouraged its use as a bank by City merchants; that is, until Charles II took "loan" of the entire deposits— £130,000—a fortune at the time. There is no record of his having paid interest or, for that matter, returning the borrowed funds.

The Tower grounds served as site for the Royal Observatory and once the Royal Menagerie was located in the Lion Tower.

The inherent security of the guarded walls made it the perfect repository for the Crown Jewels which, indeed, it still is.

The Tower of London has to be a prime destination for any firsttime visitor to London. Follow the signs from the Tower Hill tube station downhill to the entrance gates. A small entry fee is charged.

> *Go at 9:30AM to avoid the crowds.*
> *Go straight to the Crown Jewels House.*

When I first saw the crown jewels they were in the Wakefield Tower. Now they are in a well guarded subterranean vault.

The ski-lift crowd control system at the vault entrance gives the first clue why you are urged to go early, by-passing all other enticing attractions initially.

Signs posted along the line caution "No smoking. No pushcarts. No prams. No children. No photos. And please drop your chewing gum in this bin."

Inside, you are asked to keep moving. Rather, you are instructed to keep moving continuously past the exhibits of regalia of royal splendor. Well lighted glass cases glitter with gold wine coolers, tankards and giant sized 17th century flagons. Official maces, Swords of State, medals, ribbons and robes of the royal orders for chivalry and valor dazzle. I picked out as the most desirable vestment that of the Order of the Garter, deep velvet blue. Very royal. If you visit St George's Chapel at Windsor Castle, you'll want to remember these robes because, there, the knights are invested and, there, under their coat of arms and banners, they sit in the choir.

You then descend to the subterranean treasury and the Crown Jewels, the guards admonishing "Keep moving please" as each new group enters the darkened room.

"There is a place in back to stand after you've finished your round." He referred to a raised platform behind the queue where visitors may stand to view the jewels as long as they please.

Enclosed in a glass circular case are all the things you wanted for Christmas.

The doll-like tiara of Queen Victoria. The larger crown of the Imperial State emblazoned with an immense ruby worn by Henry V at Agincourt. The crown of Elizabeth fitted with the Koh-I-Noor diamond that was presented to Queen Victoria by the East India Company. The St Edward crown, dating to 1661 and weighing in at five pounds; seen only at coronations, it might have been made from the old crown of Edward the Confessor.

Note, too, the Royal Scepter. Just the thing to use as a putter at the country club if the Star of Africa diamond didn't blind you. The diamond was found 1905, cut in 1910, and is one of the largest diamonds in the world.

(Long ago, when the jewels were stored in one of the towers of the parapet, you bribed the keeper to see the jewels and for an extra penny he permitted you to try on a crown.)

After seeing the Crown Jewels, return to the entry and join a tour conducted by a Yeoman Warders of the Tower of London. It's free (although a tip is appreciated), informative, and lightly humored.

By good fortune we visited the Tower on the Queen's birthday and the guards were dressed in their gorgeous and gaudy scarlet uniforms instead of the usual blues with cape.

The guards are the Yeoman Warders whose regiment dating to the 15th century once served as the Royal Bodyguards. Now the warders are ex-servicemen dressed in Tudor uniforms embroidered with the sovereign's monogram and more popularly called the Beefeaters.

One of the stops of the tour will be the Chapel of St Peter ad Vincula (St Peter in Chains). It is a functioning chapel—Church of England, of course—with services every Sunday, a fine choir, and open to visitors on Sundays. There is no charge to get into the Tower grounds during Sunday morning services. The regular Sunday opening to the Tower grounds is not until 2PM. Crowded. It is when Londoners go.

The church is the burial place for beheaded royalty, or, as our guide pointed out, "where two dukes lie between the queens." Translation: the bodies of the Duke of Northumberland and the Duke of Somerset are sandwiched between those of Queen Anne and Queen Catherine.

When the floor was removed to repair the chapel, the bones of hundreds of bodies were found.

"The good news," said the guard, "is there is no more burial room under the floor."

Outside, on the Tower Green, is the type of beheading block used to decapitate with an ax the eight royals condemned and imprisoned here. All except Anne Boleyn, that is. For Anne, her beloved husband, Henry VIII, imported a swordsman from France for the duty. You can always tell when a husband really cares.

By far the most popular spot for beheadings was Tower Hill, but the bodies were often buried beneath the chapel. The heads were mounted on spikes facing the south entrance of the London Bridge to remind visitors what happened to those convicted of treason.

The White Tower, William the Conqueror's original fort, was Britain's first public museum. It is the repository of a staggering, unrivaled collection of armament started by Henry VIII, expanded by Charles II who opened the Armories to the public and added to through the ages. Rows and rows of suits of armor and swords and pikes in the thousands from all over Europe.

On an upper floor is the Chapel of St John, the oldest ecclesiastical architecture in London. Made of squared stone imported from the town of Caen in Normandy, the chapel is a cool classic of Norman design.

A custom of mediaeval monarchs was to knight a few friends on the eve of coronation in this chapel where they spent the evening then marched in royal procession to Westminster Abbey.

Surrounding the White Tower are numerous towers. Many were prison to the overly ambitious or the disfranchised. Among them was Elizabeth I, daughter of Henry VIII, imprisoned by her older half sister, Queen Mary, who feared that little sister had too much influence with the Protestants and would do her in.

Elizabeth was the only prisoner who entered through Traitors' Gate from the Thames to exit alive.

The child king Edward V and his brother, the Duke of York, were murdered in the "Bloody Tower" by Richard III, it is claimed today.

The continuing improvements to the Tower complex means you can walk the parapet, inspect some of the early towers and look out over the Thames on one side and the fortifications on the other. All good stuff.

The 13th century moat has been filled in and now serves as lawn and garden and even includes a tennis court for the 150 Warders who reside with their families inside the walls. Seeing a line of laundry swinging in the breeze gives the Tower grounds a homey touch.

Roaming the Tower lawns and grounds are the seven famous black ravens. Evil looking creatures. Legend has it that if the ravens disappear, England and the Tower will fall. Not a chance. Their wings are clipped. Besides, why would they want to leave such luxury and tender loving care? They are fed every day and tucked into monogrammed cages every night.

Don't you try to feed or pet them. They bite. And they love

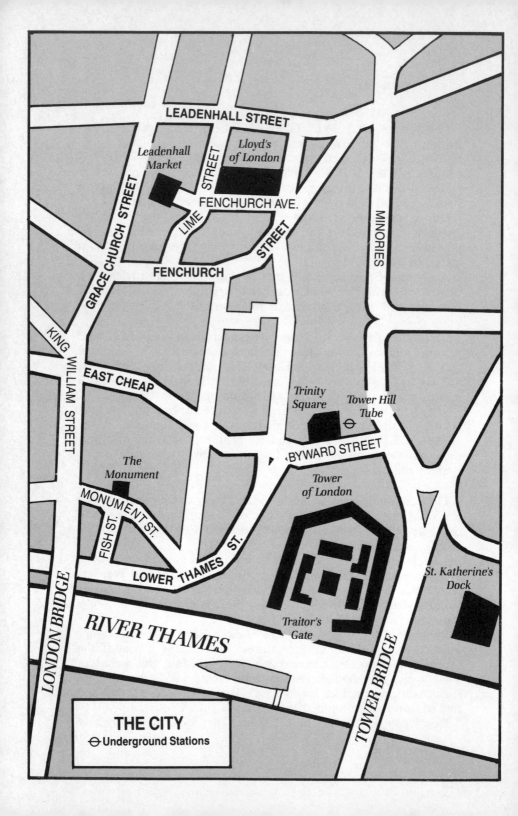

THE CITY
⊖ Underground Stations

ladies' ankles, a Yeoman told us.

Two ceremonies take place daily at the Tower.

The Changing of the Guard at high noon by the same regiment guarding Buckingham Palace.

The Ceremony of the Keys is conducted by the Beefeaters at ten nightly to keep the Tower safe from attack. It is free but you must have a ticket. Write well in advance to the Resident Governor, Queen's House, HM Tower of London, EC3N 4AB. Specify a range of dates for flexibility if your schedule permits. It improves your chances for tickets.

Before leaving the area, take advantage of the sensational views available from the Tower Bridge adjacent to the Tower. A small charge is levied but you walk from one tower to the other tower, high above the snaking traffic on the bridge and boats on the river.

Much detail available, in case you want to build a draw bridge in your backyard.

At one o'clock we were on the glassed enclosed crosswalk of Tower Bridge, the perfect time and place for the waterfront artillery salute in celebration of the Queen's birthday.

Between The Fortress And The Cathedral

The power and the poverty of the old City of London were never very far apart. Nor was the crowding of houses holding each other up, the cruelty of the populace, and the color of the street scene.

When you walk The City east to west from the Tower of London to St Paul's, you see reminders of times past, glorious and grisly, alongside the present, packed with the puissance of international financial controls.

The residents have gone but the punch remains.

For hundreds of years killing in London was a spectator sport. More popular than the sight of pit bulldogs tearing bulls and bears apart (paid admission) were the no-charge public executions staged at Tyburn—where Marble Arch is now—at Smithfield, at Newgate prison and Kensington Common . . . even at St Paul's Churchyard.

London was known as the "City of Gallows."
Hanging days were public holidays.
As late as 1819 there were 200 offenses punishable by death.
At Tyburn, the location of the first permanent public gallows, a triangular structure was engineered whereby twenty-one condemned could hang simultaneously. Huge crowds attended the "Tyburn Fairs." An enterprising entrepreneur erected a grandstand known as "Mother Proctor's Pews" and a good day yielded a fortune to the proprietor.
Samuel Pepys attended a celebrity hanging at Tyburn paying a shilling to stand on a cart wheel for a better view. He estimated an audience between 12,000 and 14,000, relatively small after you read that 100,000 watched the hanging of Henry Fauntleroy who was convicted of forgery in 1824.

Tower Hill, just above the Tower of London, is marked today by a small fenced off patch of green outside the Tower Hill tube station. Before it became Trinity Square Gardens, it was the site of public beheadings . . . but only for notables who had been imprisoned in the Tower of London for treason. A stone in the pavement at the west end of the garden marks the execution spot.
The Earl of Essex lost his head here at the hands of an executioner to whom he had granted pardon for rape.
Sir Thomas More, the Duke of Somerset, Thomas Cromwell, the Earl of Strafford, the Duke of Monmouth, Archbishop Laud were among the many noblemen on Tower Hill's Final Roll Call.
Although the victims may have been titled, the public executions were not what you would call white tie affairs. Spectators brought food and drink with them for a party. Their behavior was riotous, bawdy, ribald, abusive.
Mrs. Booth's spectator stand at Tower Hill afforded a comfort perch for a penny. When Lord Lovat was executed in 1747, just before he laid his head on the block, the stand collapsed killing twelve people. It was recorded that he died smiling with satisfaction.

From Tower Hill walk west on Tower Hill Street to Byward and Great Tower to Eastcheap, turn down Fish Street to reach the isolated pillar of Portland stone erected by an Act of Parliament to commemorate the Great Fire of 1666.
The translation of the Latin inscription on the north panel of the Monument proclaims "In the year of Christ 1666, on 2

September, at a distance eastward of this place of 202 feet, which is the height of this column, a fire broke out in the dead of night which, the wind blowing, devoured even distant buildings, and rushed devastating through every quarter with astonishing swiftness and noise . . . On the third day . . . at the bidding, we may well believe, of heaven, the fatal fire stayed its course and everywhere died out."

At one time the inscription attributed the fire to "Popish frenzy," a tag line later removed.

The column of Portland stone is another Christopher Wren design. Its top is a gilt bronze flaming urn.

You may climb the 311 steps to a gallery viewing platform beneath the urn, now encaged, the result of six people throwing themselves off the column to become statistics. The last entry, a maidservant, was made in 1842.

Note: the Monument stairs are open 9 to 6 in summer and 9 to 4 in winter and 2 to 6 on weekends.

(A minister laid the blame of the fire on gluttony, clearly pointed out by divine signs, he claimed, because the fire started in Pudding Lane and ended at Pie Corner. Farryner's bakery shop on Pudding Lane where the fire started was not making "puddings" at the time. The word comes from mediaeval usage meaning animal guts and entrails.)

From atop the Monument you can get a monumental view of the controversial headquarters of Lloyd's of London. It's a short stroll away and is one of the most joyful, incongruous corners of London.

Walk up Gracechurch Street to the intersection of Leadenhall and Lime Streets to find Leadenhall Market, one of the hundred or so daily street markets of London.

Leadenhall is special, a delightful enclave of tradition. Its 19th century cast iron finery, high vaulted glass roof, stone arches at each entrance, and cupola over a central four-street intersection give it a particular antique poignancy. Especially as it is positioned next to the new Lloyd's of London headquarters, a most futuristic building with exposed exterior pipes and glass elevators climbing its metal sheathing. It looks more like an oil refinery than the home of the world's most famous insurance conglomerate.

In the 1300's Leadenhall was a place where country people sold country produce. The Market evolved into a general provisions market and after the Great Fire it was replaced in 1881 with the arcade buildings that have housed many of the same high quality provisioners ever since. R S Ashby's make their own sausages and sell Scotchbeef; Butcher & Edwards offer grouse, mallard, quail and guinea fowl in season, or hare, venison and wild boar if that is the preference.

Local pin-stripers, Leadenhall's elite Stock Exchange and Lloyd's clientele, bemoan the fact they can no longer inspect their Christmas goose "on the webfoot."

At noon the action pulses around Young's Lamb Tavern where Yuppies stand outside to drink their ale and munch on sandwiches from the deli next door.

Go, join them. Or dine in one of Leadenhall's cafes or the replica of a 17th century coffee house in Lloyd's next door.

Around the corner on Lime Street, you'll find the visitors' entrance to Lloyd's of London, (not to be confused with Lloyds Bank).

What the imagination conjures up is the 17th century face of Edward Lloyd pondering this gleaming 21st century building which bears his name.

Lloyd's Coffee House in 1680 was a gathering place where ship captains, ship owners and merchants buying and selling their cargoes congregated. It was where one learned the latest—the most reliable—news of shipping.

Lloyd's became a place where one could find marine insurance.

The insurance broker originated at Lloyd's Coffee House. Based on the information he gleaned from Lloyd's customers, he would guarantee a cargo against loss—write a policy—then he would take it around to men of wealth, selling portions of it speculatively. High risks. High profits. So long as things went well.

Essentially, Lloyd's still operates that way today. It is a marketplace with no corporate liability and no shareholders.

For over three hundred years, Lloyd's grew in every direction. An ever expanding number of syndicates insured every type of risk.

Headquarters kept changing to keep pace with the growth.

In 1979 a commission to build a new building on the Lloyd's site was given to Richard Rogers and Partners, architects for the controversial Pompidou Centre in Paris, another dazzling display of a child's metal Erector Set magnified to gargantuan size.

At the Tower Three entrance, visitors are lifted to a fourth floor gallery of history where a series of displays explain everything you wanted to know about Lloyd's. And it is absorbing because Lloyd's is so unique and so immense. Over 20 million in insurance premiums pour into Lloyd's every working day from all parts of the world. They are filtered through computerized work stations representing some 370 underwriting syndicates. You can see these open offices in an atrium environment from the visitors' balcony.

Unfortunately, what you cannot see clearly from above is the famous Lutine Bell which rings twice in the event of good news, once for bad news. You can only see the top of its ornate wooden rostrum.

The question I had to ask was why would an insurance society whose reputation rests on dependability, solidness, historic financial stability of its members (stodginess is another way of saying it) adopt such a wild, tinker toy building as home? Particularly in London where stuffiness is akin to sainthood?

The answer was simple. Space was a major criterion. Rogers won the commission, in competition, because his vertical floor plan built around a central atrium put all of the expensive space-eating ducts and pipes for air-conditioning, elevators, utilities outside of the building.

You have to wonder if a "dare to be different" factor didn't also influence their decision. As one of Lloyd's men said about the eyebrows-lifting decision: "We are in the risk business, so why shouldn't we take one more?" International publicity after the headquarters opened confirmed the choice. Visitors far exceed initial projections.

You are in the financial heart of London and, for many, the financial heart of the world.

Thread your way west down Threadneedle Street and stand at the entrance of the Bank Station tube.

You have walked past The Stock Exchange where there is a visitors' gallery but little action since the Big Bang, the day in 1986 when London stockbrokers embraced twenty-four hour computerized buying and selling.

Like Lloyd's, The Stock Exchange grew out of coffee houses. Jonathan's and Garraway's were primary gathering places where brokers and jobbers and clients traded news and monies.

The "bear" in a bear market, widely used today to reflect a

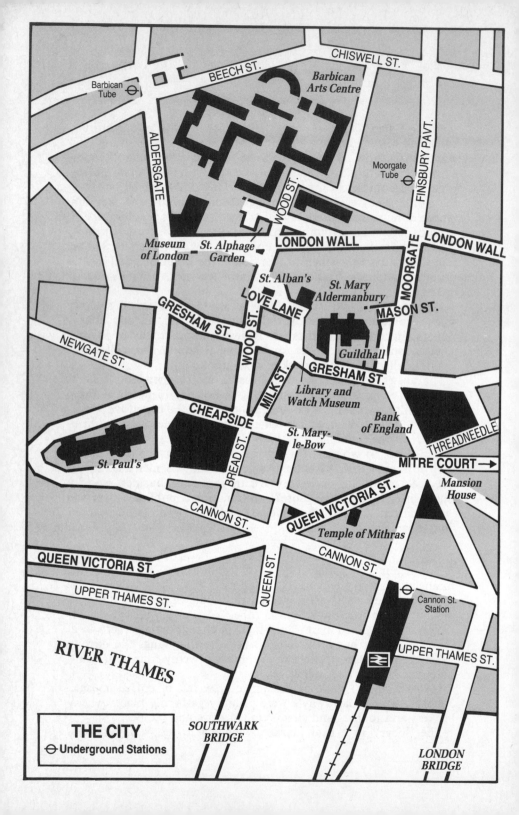

cautious market tendency, derived from those times and the
proverb "You must not sell the bear skin until you have shot the
bear."

Numerous exchanges came and went until all were unified in
The Stock Exchange. About 4,000 members belong to some 275
separate firms. Today the London Stock Exchange has the largest
number of securities listed in the world and has been on its present
site since 1801 and in its present building since 1972.

At the Bank tube station, you stand at an intersection where
seven streets merge. Stop a moment to inspect three fascinating
buildings.

Face north. The largest building of the three, Georgian in style,
is the Bank of England, the "Old Lady of Threadneedle Street"
where you cannot open an account or take out samples.

Face southwest and look at the Mansion House. The Palladium
structure is noticeable for its six giant Corinthian columns. Two
simple staircases on each side lead to a raised portico. This is the
official residence of London's Lord Mayor who serves a one year
term and is required to spend a small fortune from his private
purse to pay for expenses not covered by City funds.

Where the Mansion House now stands was once The Stocks
Market where fish and meat—not stocks and bonds—were sold.
Later it was expanded into a general market surpassing all the
other markets in London. At that time there was a statue in the
market showing Charles II tramping on the head of Oliver
Cromwell who had executed his father, Charles I.

In 1737 the market was moved to Farringdon Street to make
way for construction of the Mansion House.

When the Lord Mayor is sworn into office on the second
Saturday in November, the Lord Mayor's Show begins. His
carriage comes out of storage from the Museum of London and
he is paraded from Mansion House to the Law Courts in the
Strand in a great colorful parade. The following Monday a
traditional Lord Mayor's Banquet is held at Guildhall where the
Prime Minister traditionally delivers a major address.

Now face east. The Royal Exchange was founded of necessity.
The merchants and traders doing business on the streets needed
shelter from the wet and the cold. Modeled on foreign *bourses* it
was, in effect, an office building for people buying and selling—a
trading center—during a time when the naval power and the

financial power of England began to surface. The East India Company, the West India Company the Hudson's Bay Company were given virtually monopolistic control over entire foreign colonies. It was the beginning of . . . *(full capitals)* . . . COMMERCE.

The first exchange opened at the beginning of 1568. Two years later Elizabeth proclaimed it The Royal Exchange.

Queen Victoria opened the present building in 1844 and, following the precedent of Elizabeth I, announced "It is my royal will and pleasure that this building be hereafter called The Royal Exchange."

Take a minute and study the features of this classic building with its massive portico of eight Corinthian columns. Note the pediment above, the figures cut into the limestone. The center figure is, of course, COMMERCE.

In 1939 the Exchange ceased as a general office building and, today, an insurance company occupies part; the rest serves as an exhibition center.

Don't miss the statue of Wellington, the conqueror of Napoleon at Waterloo, facing away from the Royal Exchange. Wellington's dominate facial feature was an enormous nose, a factor not missed by the sculptor. Shortly after its unveiling, a French pedestrian looked at it, smiled and exclaimed jubilantly, "We have been avenged."

Across the street is the Bank of England. It is the country's note issuing authority, controller of the national debt and custodian of the country's gold reserves. (In 1836 a sewer worker found his way into the Bullion Room, told the directors how he did it, and was awarded a large gratuity for his honesty.)

The massive windowless wall on Princess Street gives it the air of a fortress. Notice the figures on the facade and find the Old Lady of Threadneedle Street. The same artist who did the facade figures, Charles Wheeler, also created the bronze doors.

Cheapside leads away from this financial center into the world of the marketplace. Just as it always did.

In the middle of Cheapside is St Mary-le-Bow Church, another Wren masterpiece. The church came by its descriptive name, le Bow, because of the bowed arches of the Norman crypt ceiling.

Once upon a time, it was said a Cockney wasn't a true Cockney unless he were born within the sound of the Bow Bells. The bells signaled curfew in mediaeval times.

Notice the names of the streets as you walk west: Poultry Street, Grocers Hall Court, Old Jewry, Ironmonger Lane, Honey Lane, Wood Street.

Milk Street, which swings into Wood just before Wood comes into Cheapside, was a mediaeval milk market.

The curved shape of the street, a guide said, provided an important archaeological clue to the "Dark Age" Anglo-Saxons who left no dwellings inside the Roman walls.

All the archaeologists could find was two feet of brown earth. They sieved the earth. It revealed nothing.

Could the earth have been brought in by the wind?

Negative.

Perhaps the Thames River deposited it after a giant tidal flood?

Negative.

When samples were analyzed the soil was found to be high in phosphate. And what would have created the phosphate? The spreading of animal manure to enrich the soil.

The interior of London was a vast farm.

Another archaeological clue exists. The Saxon farmers were also known to plow with an instrument called an *ard* in figure-eight patterns. Milk Street is shaped in the same looping figure-eight pattern set by an ard.

The reason why they deserted the city walls is uncertain.

One possible reason was their reported belief that Roman cities were "tombs within walls." Perhaps they were referring to the recurring plagues. Not a bad reason reason for living in the open suburbs.

This whole area is a fascinating enclave within The City and, time permitting, a great place to poke around little courts and alleys. It is an historic section of London featured in many of the Guided Walks.

Before you get sidetracked into such intriguing diversions, come with me to visit a most important historical building in the neighborhood, the Guildhall. Its entrance is on Gresham Street parallel with, but two blocks north of, Cheapside.

The historic room of the Guildhall is an immense meeting hall where Lord Mayors are elected and the Court of Common Council is held with 25 Alderman and 150 Councilmen in attendance.

In 1067—the year after he came to power—William I, the conquering Duke of Normandy, granted the first city charter to the City of London. A Guildhall was mentioned in the records of St Paul's dated 1128. The first Lord Mayor took office on the site in 1193. Much of the present structure has its origin in the mediaeval 15th century.

Incredibly, the 1666 Great Fire went through the building leaving it as "a bright shining coale as if it had been a place of gold or a great building of burnished brass," an eye witness reported. The outer walls remained.

The most famous Lord Mayor was Richard Whittington, elected four times, the first time in 1397. He paid for the Guildhall floor which endures to this day and also for the windows on which his name was emblazoned.

Whittington came to London, the son of a Gloucestershire squire, amassed a fortune as a merchant trader, principally in coal. He initiated many civic projects including the funding of libraries to educate the people, the first being just outside the entrance to the Guildhall. He rebuilt Newgate Prison.

Cromwell, the puritan, thought the window advertising a bit pushy and ordered them smashed.

Today's windows bear the names of every mayor since 1215.

Overhead are the symbols of almost 100 guilds.

In mediaeval times the guilds of London were the masters of their particular trades. Their functions included establishing wages and prices, controlling the number and training of apprentices.

The guilds were also strict about establishing and maintaining high levels of quality control.

In 1319 a butcher was pilloried in the Stocks Market for selling rotten meat and the carcasses were burned under his nose.

Over the years the Guilds assumed the role of a beneficial society for members, assuring them the proper funeral and care of family. Often, members left their estates to their guilds in gratitude.

Officers became ornately uniformed or "liveried" and their organizations were then known as Livery Companies. The twelve largest were known as The City Livery Companies led by the Mercers, traders in fine cloth, the Grocers, who kept tight reign of the spices monopoly, and the Drapers, associated with England's well established wool industry.

The banners below the clerestory windows are those of the twelve City Livery Companies.

The wealth of the guilds and their penchant for lavish dinners almost led to their destruction. Charles II, hungry for money, took away many charters only to sell them back again for substantial fees.

Guilds were forced to back governmental explorations such as the initial attempt to establish a plantation in Virginia in 1610.

Today most of the guilds function as philanthropic organizations; for some it is their only occupation. A few, like the Goldsmiths, are still active professionally in addition to donating over 1 million a year to charity.

But the power of the Livery Companies remains intact and the freedom of The City is reflected in their election of the Lord Mayor.

At the entrance to the hall is the Musicians' Gallery embellished at either end with the mythical giants, Gog and Magog. Once the figures were hollow and therefore lightweight enough to be born through the streets at Festival time. The post-fire gods are carved from solid lime wood.

At the far side of the hall are brass plates set in the floor marking the official measures of lengths of 100 feet and 66 feet and on the south wall set into a plaque are official lengths of one foot, two feet and one yard.

Administration offices for The City are housed in a modern office complex attached to the Guildhall on the east side.

Nearby, between Basinghall Street and Coleman Street, Mason's Avenue helps you cast yourself back to Elizabethan days rather easily.

On one side of the "avenue"—no more than an alley—is a pseudo Tudor-Elizabethan building of plaster crossed with dark wood. No authentic Tudor buildings still stand in The City of London today because they all went to ashes in the Great Fire.

But you can recreate the street scene mentally. Here, see a rut in the payment which allowed for run-off of slop. Everything went out the window: garbage, chamber pots, the whole thing. Chivalry prompted the custom of a gentleman walking on the outside, his lady under the protective roof-line.

A gentleman needed a man-powered sedan chair or a horse-pulled carriage to avoid getting his pumps soiled in the filth.

Buildings were built wall to wall and, in order to get extra space, rooms jutted out over the lane so far that residents in the upper floors literally could lean out of the window and shake hands.

At the end of the alley is Ye Olde Dr. Butler's Head, a pub established by Dr. Butler in 1616. Dr. Butler, physician to James I, was famous for his unique cures. His cure for epilepsy was to fire pistols next to the patient's head. Hence, we surmise, the name of the pub.

Another cure was to throw the patient off the bridge into the freezing water of the Thames. An early form of shock treatment.

Go around to the other side of Guildhall to Aldermanbury Street and enter the Guildhall library. On the left hand side is a small but elegant museum of watches assembled and donated by The Worshipful Company of Clockmakers (formed 1631).

Many delicate small watches. One is in the shape of a two inch skull, the property of Mary Queen of Scots, given to her by Mary Seton. The dial is visible only when the jaw of the skull is lowered. The watch becomes somewhat poignant when it is remembered that the Scottish queen was beheaded on orders from Queen Elizabeth in 1587.

There are enameled watches, marine chronometers, classic grandfather clocks. We marveled at an ingenious German clock dated 1625 with multiple faces and dials for telling time, months, years, saints' days, the hours of daylight or moonlight. There are Verge watches, a silver star watch which belonged to King James VI of Scotland—later James I of England—and so many other timepieces that time has passed by.

If you turn right upon exiting the library and walk a few steps up Aldermanbury Street you will be at the foot of a small park. On a sunny high noon it will be filled with office workers eating sandwiches.

At one time a church, St Mary Aldermanbury, occupied the site. Bombed during the war, its remaining walls were removed stone by stone and reconstructed at Westminster College, Fulton, Missouri as a memorial to Winston Churchill who, speaking at the college, made the first reference to the "Iron Curtain."

Sit a moment and ponder the past.

Bede, the historian, recorded that a 7th century Saxon palace existed in this area. The name Aldermanbury means the "manor house of the governor."

Where did Edward the Confessor live before he moved his palace to Westminster?

Could it have been here?

Is his palace buried under the police station in back of the

Aldermanbury Park?

Or ponder the world of England's greatest playwright, William Shakespeare.

Here is a bronze memorial by Charles J. Allen to the bard and two partners and fellow actors, Heminge and Condell. All lived in this parish. The memorial states that Heminge and Condell "gave to the world without profit" the first folio of Shakespeare plays published in 1623.

Records show that Shakespeare lived in a boarding house owned by Charles Mountjoy near here, walked to the Thames to be ferried across the river to the Globe Theatre at Southwark. His landlord was sued by a son-in-law who claimed he was short-changed on a promised dowry and Shakespeare was called as a witness.

To the west of Aldermanbury Park is Love Street.

Why Love Street?

Because it was the haunt of prostitutes who often worked out of "stews," short for stewhouses or bathhouses.

Henry VIII—of all people—not remembered historically for his virtue, banned the stews from the City. They moved to Southwark, known as the brothel capital of the English world. With all of the high rollers going to Southwark to spend their money, the city fathers complained so effectively the stewhouses were reinstated north of the river.

Prostitutes were commonly found in Shakespeare's plays and in those of his contemporaries.

On Wood Street just opposite Love Street stands the tower remains of St Alban on an island in the middle of the road.

Underneath the tower is possibly the palace chapel of King Offa, an 8th century ruler, who was responsible for the murder of Alban, the first English martyr.

The church was rebuilt several times: in a Gothic style by Inigo Jones before the Great Fire and by Christopher Wren after the fire. Demolished again in the war, today only the tower remains and it is privately owned.

Wood Street itself is unique. It is the last surviving street of the old Roman fortress and was so named because wood was brought in from the north gate.

A blue plaque marks the location of the north entrance to the fort known as Cripplegate, destroyed in the 18th century.

In Anglo-Saxon times, this entrance to London received extra protection because it was so close to the king's palace. Additional fortifications, called *barbican,* were built outside of the first walls.

In August, 1940 the first bomb fell on London a short distance away from Cripplegate. Subsequent bombing reduced to rubble 325 acres of real estate.

In 1958 the property was bought by The City of London and developed into a residential-offices-arts complex. It is called the Barbican. In addition to two 43-story apartment blocks and other buildings housing 6,500 people, there are stores, high rise office structures, and the Barbican Arts Centre, home of the Royal Shakespeare Theatre and London Symphony Orchestra opened by the Queen in 1982. The Centre has a concert hall, two theaters, three cinemas, restaurants, art galleries and exhibition halls.

I find it ironic that the biggest development in the city has been named after the obscure defense system of the Anglo-Saxons, the farmers who left no trace of their civilization.

On the other hand, the project is as stark as any fortress you'll see.

Before leaving the area of Cripplegate, walk south along the overhead rampway about a hundred yards. You are overlooking St Alfege Garden. The old wall documents the eras of its use. From bottom to top you can see the different layers of wall construction, the Roman, Mediaeval and 15th century. The top repair work, dating to 1477, with darker brick set in diamond patterns is more decorative than protective. The "new" wall reflected the City's prosperity in the 15th century.

On the other side of the overhead walk you can touch the remains of the St Alfege hospice where the monks took care of a hundred cripples and blind men. At the time of the Dissolution of the abbeys, convents and monasteries by Henry VIII, these men were turned out into the street.

But for every good monastery like St Alfege, there was a bad one. Fat, corrupt, rich and shamelessly avaricious. You only have to visit Hampton Court built by Cardinal Wolsey a few miles from London to appreciate the financial power of a prince of the church and the unbridled appetite for splendor that accompanied the title. To say nothing of the treasury required to make the splendor possible.

In a city where poverty was rife and hunger widespread, the churches were not always generous nor necessarily loved.

It is popular to think that Henry VIII gave the Catholic Church the sack because the church wouldn't give him permission to marry Anne Boleyn, but more likely it was a calculated economic move.

In London alone there were ten churches and monasteries inside The City walls; another dozen beyond.

Around England there were hundreds of other desirable church properties.

What happy income they supplied Henry VIII over a period of five years of Dissolution, from 1535 to 1540, as he plucked the monasteries and abbeys and convents one by one, sold or gave away the properties in return for allegiance and other favors, and melted down their gold and silver plate.

It changed the face of London and of all England.

The familiar appearance of monks and nuns and friars in London streets ceased.

In place of the church power was the royal power.

In place of the church treasury was the royal treasury.

And, as a bonus, in place of the sonless Catherine of Aragon was the young, black-eyed Anne Boleyn.

Did this cause an uprising of the populace? Not at all.

Return to happier times, to St Paul's.

In the northeast corner of the churchyard is Paul's Cross, an historical meeting place since mediaeval days.

Until the 14th century it was the compulsory meeting place, three times a year, of all the citizens of London. Public announcements, royal proclamations, military victories all were made known from Paul's Cross which Thomas Carlyle called "The Times newspaper of the Middle Ages."

The Cross was a lead-covered wooden pulpit from which distinguished preachers and political orators harangued the crowds.

Henry VIII dictated that every Sunday there would be the "preaching down of the papal authority."

Shakespeare used to frequent the Cross to study the characters in the crowd as role models for his plays even though the preacher might be condemning the sinfulness of the theater.

On the north side of St Paul's is a wide open space known as the Churchyard. This was a principal venue for London's booksellers who rimmed the area. Here printers lived and worked. In addition other booksellers came during the day to buy and sell publications and paper from open stalls.

One of the best known publishers was John Newberry, who

bought scripts from Samuel Johnson and Oliver Goldsmith. He first published children's books. His famous *Little Goody Two Shoes* probably was ghosted by Goldsmith. Newberry sold patent medicines. The best known was Dr James's Fever Powder. It was no accident, then, in the *Two Shoes* story that the heroine's father "died miserably seized with a violent fever where Dr James's powder was not to be had."

The selling of plays was a popular item of the marketplace and Shakespeare also frequented the stalls. His plays were not for sale—he was more interested in completing and selling his sonnets—but he was curious to know what was selling, what was popular because the trend of popular taste determined the plots of his plays.

Thus we read and see Shakespeare going through periods of bloody plays, historical plays, comic plays and tragic plays.

It is incorrect to say that Shakespeare's plays were not in the marketplace. Literary pirates attempted to copy plot and dialogue during performances, an all but impossible task. Action and repartee went too fast. To fill in the wide gaps, the pirate publisher would pay another playwright to write the missing script, one reason, it is argued, that often Shakespeare doesn't sound like Shakespeare.

If you walk up Newgate Street and turn right on Old Bailey to Cock Lane, once a licensed walk for prostitutes, you'll see a gilded cherub mounted over the corner. It marks the location of Pie Corner where the Great Fire was reputed to have stopped.

Or from St Paul's walk down Ludgate and Farringdon Street, the entrance of Fleet Street.

Near the corner is the Old King Lud public house built in 1870.

King Lud, according to legend, was a king in 66BC which a guide pooh-poohed. "There was never such a king. The word's origin is Anglo-Saxon meaning 'to bend low' because if you were on a horse coming through the gate you had to bend over to keep from cracking your head. King Lud. Har!"

Ludgate, like the other gates, also served as a debtors' prison. The most charming tale concerns a Stephen Forester who was imprisoned as a boy. A rich widow seeing him at the window bailed him out and married him. He was elected Lord Mayor in 1454.

There are happy endings.

The Wordsmiths

3. Fleet Street and the Inns of Court

The sign of The City is the pound sterling.

The sign of the "West End" is the sound of music.

In between the two is a no-man's land where the sign of the trade is the word, and more words and still more words.

Fleet Street is the traditional haven of London journalism. Straddling Fleet Street at its western extremity where it becomes the Strand is the traditional *endroit* of the legal fraternity, a sizable domain dominated by the impressive Law Courts and the Inns of Court that stretches from above Holborn to the shores of the Thames.

The area, easy to stroll with the aid of a map, encompasses four major legal societies known as the Inns of Court, the Royal Courts of Justice which with "Old Bailey" and the Central Criminal Court several blocks away, represent the guts of British law.

I had never walked the few blocks encompassing these institutions and had often mused over Gray's Inn, Lincoln's Inn, the Temple, Middle Temple, Inner Temple. What did they mean?

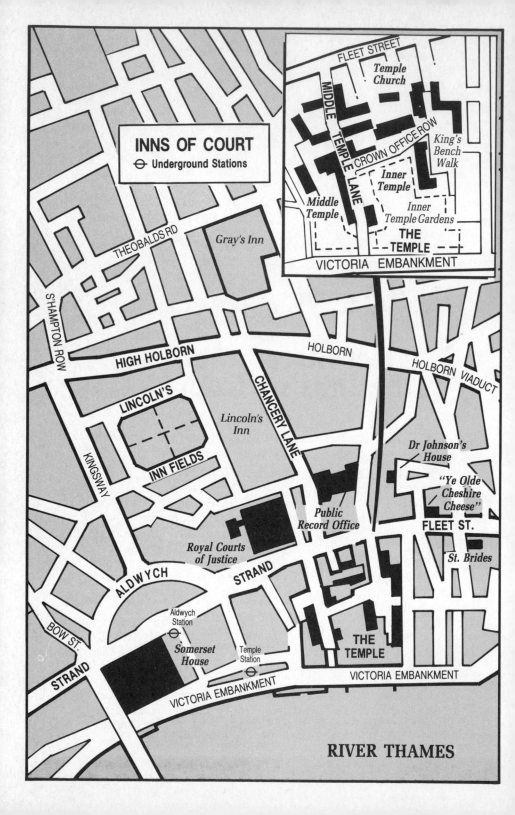

INNS OF COURT

⊖ Underground Stations

FLEET STREET

Temple Church

MIDDLE TEMPLE LANE

CROWN OFFICE ROW

King's Bench Walk

Inner Temple

Middle Temple

Inner Temple Gardens

THE TEMPLE

VICTORIA EMBANKMENT

THEOBALDS RD

Gray's Inn

S'HAMPTON ROW

HIGH HOLBORN

HOLBORN

HOLBORN VIADUCT

LINCOLN'S

Lincoln's Inn

CHANCERY LANE

Dr Johnson's House

KINGSWAY

INN FIELDS

"Ye Olde Cheshire Cheese"

Public Record Office

FLEET ST.

Royal Courts of Justice

STRAND

St. Brides

ALDWYCH

BOW ST.

Aldwych Station

Somerset House

Temple Station

THE TEMPLE

STRAND

VICTORIA EMBANKMENT

VICTORIA EMBANKMENT

RIVER THAMES

But first, let's stroll down Fleet Street which starts in the east at Farringdon Street at the bottom of Ludgate Hill. It was here that London's first daily newspaper started in 1702, the *Daily Courant*. Two centuries earlier the first printing press had been been introduced nearby.

Beneath Farringdon Street is the River Fleet, the name derived from an Anglo-Saxon word meaning "tidal inlet." During an earlier period, wharves occupied this area. A 19th century excavation uncovered a Wren bridge spanning the river which is now subterranean.

Fleet Street, originally Fleetbridge Street, extends up to the Strand and is bordered by mass communications companies—wire services, news bureaus, weekly newspapers and magazines.

The last major daily newspaper pulled out of Fleet Street in 1987 joining the other dailies which had moved to modernized printing plants in less expensive surroundings. But I doubt if the name "Fleet Street" to denote the British press will ever be abandoned.

The most engaging attraction in Fleet Street is the "journalists' church," St Bride's.

The first time I went to St Bride's was on a guided walk. It was a Sunday and the church was closed.

"You know where the traditional wedding cake comes from?

"Here," the guide hastened to answer his own question, "this church. It was designed by Christopher Wren. In 1712 a baker whose shop was across the road and whose daughter was going to be married thought 'What shall I do special for her?'

"He looked up to the beautiful characteristic Wren steeple and said 'Right' then created the first steepled wedding cake.

"St Bride's was mostly destroyed in the war and was restored with funds from journalists on Fleet Street. This has always been their church.

"I'm sorry it is a holiday and the church is locked but come back because the crypt is most interesting. It contains a six-foot-tall Saxon man and skeletons from the 10th, 11th and 13th centuries.

"They found Roman mosaics and wall coverings so it could also have been a Roman mausoleum. What you will be visiting is two thousand years of history and you'll get a small glimpse of the Saxons in London."

I returned, alone, to the church on a day kissed by the first warm sun of spring. Newborn leaves shyly stuck their noses out on otherwise barren limbs and tiny blossoms, pink and rose, sprang from fruit tree buds. One of the delightful surprises of London is the number of fruit trees in small parks which dot the city.

At noon the office workers spend their lunch hours mingling outside of wine bars and pubs, cool summer beverages in hand, reveling in the intoxicating spring air.

"Sweet is pleasure after pain."

Sweeter is spring after an English winter.

That day the Cathedral of Fleet Street was open.

On the evening of December 29, 1940 the city of London was subjected to a fire bomb attack from the Germans. *The Evening News'* front page headline the next day wailed "St Bride's a Blackened Ruin."

Prior to its destruction the church was known to have existed from about 1134. Post-war excavation revealed a Roman ditch, Roman pavement and mosaics, a Saxon tomb, two charnel houses and the remains of seven churches.

The crypt is a museum by itself, revealing Roman fragments and, behind one subterranean altar, a section of Roman pavement. A schematic shows the outline of the church pre-10th century, the location of the Roman mosaic, ditch, pavement and burials tombs, the Saxon tomb, the 10th and 11th century Saxon apse and a 12th century apse.

One learns more here of William Rich, the wedding cake creator. He came to London as an pastry apprentice and attracted a following for his cakes, the secret for which he said was the best French brandy, "even when it costs one guinea a bottle."

Not so generous was Oliver Cromwell. During one six-month segment of his joyless reign, you learn, he curtailed Christmas celebrating, canceled all amusements and permitted no wedding ceremony.

St Bride's was named for a famous Abbess of the Celtic Church—*Brig* or *Brigid* or *Bridget* or *Bride*—who founded a monastic community in Ireland, who may never have left the island but whose missionaries spread her fame as far south as Italy. In her day, she was better known than her contemporary, St Patrick.

One oddity in the crypt is an iron coffin patented in the 19th century under the slogan "Safety for the Dead."

There was an illegal body snatching industry (£ 8 to £ 14 per body) for use in medical school anatomy classes. Infamous in the gruesome trade were Burke and Hare who murdered and then "resurrected" their victims. They were hanged in 1829.

That's right, the purpose of the patented iron coffin was to thwart the body snatchers.

From the time that William Caxton installed the first printing press in the 15th century, Fleet Street continued as headquarters for book publishers who also had booths at St Paul's Churchyard. Consequently, it was an early hangout for scribes of all callings.

On Fleet Street itself (No. 47) is a crusty luncheon hangout for lawyers and journalists, El Vino, where men must wear jacket and tie and women—few in number—must wear a skirt. It was a 1982 Court of Appeal ruling that overturned the chauvinistic eatery's policy of "no women allowed," stating it was against the law for women to be refused a drink at the bar.

Far more historical and in the same neighborhood is Ye Olde Cheshire Cheese, the tavern frequented by Dr Samuel Johnson and others. Low beam ceilings, sawdust on the floor, barren oak tables and benches, roast beef and Yorkshire pudding. And swarms of tourists.

Wander through the back alleys, following the signs, to Gough Square and the Samuel Johnson House. Johnson lived here for thirteen years, from 1746, paying £ 30 a year in rent.

Born in 1709, Johnson was the literary lion of the 18th century.

He attended Oxford's Pembroke College in 1728-29 where he said of himself and colleagues "we were a nest of singing birds."

Timber for the house, American white and yellow pine, was ship ballast. Here, in the attic, he wrote his most famous work, the Dictionary. There were 2,000 copies printed by Andrew Miller in the Strand who said of Johnson upon receiving the last pages: "Thank God I have done with him."

To which Johnson replied: "I am glad he thanks God for anything."

You'll find a first edition copy of the dictionary in the ground floor dining room.

The house has been refurnished in the 18th-century manner and contains a small collection of Johnson memorabilia. There is more than one sketch of Oliver Goldsmith, his writing friend, about whom Johnson said "No man was more foolish when he had not a pen in his hand or more wise when he had.''

James Boswell, whose biography of Johnson assumed more lasting fame than any work by his subject, is also pictured.

Johnson's wife died in this house after which he went to live in several other abodes in same area.

Where An Inn Is Not A Place To Sleep

At the western end of Fleet Street you enter the legal heart of London. It is before The Royal Courts of Justice, more popularly known as the Law Courts, where all non-criminal matters are argued by barristers and settled by judges who are appointed from the ranks of barristers.

Prior to the completion of this centralized legal building the courts sat in Westminster Hall during a defined period of time, then anywhere else that could be found the rest of the year.

Note over the entrance a figure of Christ flanked by King Solomon and King Alfred.

The peek inside the great hall is worth subjecting yourself to the rigorous frisking by attendant guards. "No cameras, please."

You could think that you were in another Cathedral. The vaulted arcade of the Great Hall has the appearance and effect of a great inspiring cathedral. Its ceiling is awesome; 238 feet long and 80 feet high.

You could further imagine that the black robed men swishing importantly past you in their white wigs were high priests.

And so they are. Some high priests are higher than others. A beginning barrister wears a cloak with a rounded collar in back. A Queen's Counsel, or QC, will have fifteen years experience and wear a silk robe with a squared collar.

For ordinary court appearances the barristers wear short white wigs. Full length white wigs are reserved for formal occasions.

The small pocket at the back left shoulder of the black gowns of junior barristers has a long tradition. A client could slip an unsolicited remuneration into it, hoping to move things along.

The museum of legal dress just to the right of the entrance gives you the full story of legal regalia.

Branching off the hall are three-and-a-half miles of corridors leading to more than 1,000 rooms including 60 court rooms. One more statistic: the building used 35 million bricks and the attendant construction nightmares and frustrations led to the early demise of its designer.

Behind the Law Courts on Carey Street is a modern office building housing the Bankruptcy and Companies Courts. In England, the phrase "heading for Carey Street" suggests that the person is spending too much, too fast. Heading for bankruptcy.

An American requiring legal assistance in England needs to know that only a barrister can appear before the Upper Court. Much like an American trial attorney. But, unlike the American system, a company cannot hire the trial attorney (barrister) directly.

The company hires a solicitor who, in turn, negotiates with the Law Clerk of a firm of barristers.

The Law Clerk is like the trainer of a racing stable. He determines which barrister is going to get what work, who needs a rest and who has proven himself on similar tracks, or more correctly, on past cases. The Law Clerk sets the compensation—and takes a percentage. How much percentage? Unknown, but one Law Clerk recently retired at the age of 37.

It's not only a very lucrative job but an enviable one. The Law Clerk, who may hold no more than a high school diploma, is responsible for a troop of highly trained specialists.

If you look at a colored map of this part of London you'll see large patches of green that could be parks. This green real estate encompasses the four major legal centers where barristers are trained, where they fraternize with their peers and superiors, where they are taught by Readers. Each center, not unlike a university campus, contains a library, chapel and a Great Hall where a specified amount of dining is required.

Although the grounds of the Inns can be entered, the Great Halls of the Inns of the Court are the social and business centers of the legal societies and very much off limits to the general public.

Originally, the centers also afforded student accommodations and were called the Inns of Court because they were former manor houses, or "inns" as in hostels.

Today there are four Inns.

North of Fleet Street (into Strand) are Gray's Inn and Lincoln's Inn; south are Inner Temple and Middle Temple.

Gray's Inn can be entered from Holborn High Street through a wide arched Gatehouse to the South Square, a pleasant compound of buildings. The Gothic structure is the Great Hall whose timbers, it is said, came from a conquered galleon of the Spanish Armada, a gift to the Inn from Queen Elizabeth.

Today when Gray's Inn members toast the Queen with "To good Queen Bess," they mean Elizabeth I.

The Earl of Southhampton, Shakespeare's patron and a member here, arranged for the first performance of *The Comedy for Errors* to be staged in the Great Hall.

In the middle of the square is a statue of Francis Bacon, also a member of the Inn, who, besides being a brilliant writer and perhaps a playwright, had a more dubious reputation as one of England's most corrupt politicians. He was quoted as saying, "I may accept a bribe but it will never change my mind."

Bacon is credited with laying out "The Walks," the gardens in the rear of the square. Today a place for strolling; yesterday a secluded venue for dueling. The gardens are open from May to September from noon to 2:30PM.

Chancery Lane intersects Holborn, and by walking south on Chancery you come to magnificent massive oak doors, vintage 16th century, and the Gate House leading into Lincoln's Inn.

The Earl of Lincoln's family crest, a lion rampant, appears above the archway.

Lincoln's Inn is the oldest of the four legal learning centers having been established in the middle of the 14th century.

Ben Jonson, the playwright-to-be, worked as a mason on the chapel for his stepfather with "a trowel in his hand and a book in his pocket."

The list of Lincoln's Inn members is long and illustrious: William Penn, the father of Pennsylvania, John Donne, Walpole, Pitt, Disraeli, Gladstone, David Garrick, John Galsworthy among them.

The Chapel, open weekdays 12:30 to 2:30, was built in 1620-23. The windows illustrate the names of men who have been Benchers, i.e. senior members of the Inn: Cromwell, Canning, Newman, Asquith.

Lincoln's Inn Fields are behind the compound and surrounded by former residences of the titled, the Earl of Sandwich, Lord Coventry, Duke of Newcastle, Earl of Leicester, Earl of Lindsey, Duchess of Portsmouth.

Nell Gwynn gave birth to a son here fathered by Charles II.

The Fields are entered on the east side.

Just off Chancery Lane is the Public Record Office, home of the Domesday Book.

Cross over Fleet Street and into the grounds of the Middle Temple and the Inner Temple. There was formerly an Outer Temple on Essex Street but it has disappeared.

The grounds once were owned by the Knights Templar, an order devoted to the protection of pilgrims en route to Jerusalem and famous for their banner insignia, a large red cross on a field of white, denoting their freedom from any law save that of the Pope. They built churches throughout Europe including a "New Temple" on the banks of the Thames in the 12th century. Temple Church exists to this day.

In time the riches of the Knights Templar aroused the greed in others and their properties throughout Europe were confiscated. In London the knights were thrown into the Tower and their properties given to the Knights Hospitaller who leased space to the lawyers. These were the predecessors of the barristers of the Middle and Inner Temple.

James I granted ownership of the land to the two Inns with the understanding that they would be responsible for the Temple Church.

The Middle Temple is known for its original 1320 Hall. The present building was completed in 1573. Both survived the bombs of World War II.

Besides being a meeting/eating hall, it was the venue for major banquets and parties.

Shakespeare also debuted another play here, *"Twelfth Night,"* on February 2, 1601.

You can cross into Inner Temple from Middle Temple via the Pump Hall or from Fleet Street through Inner Temple Lane. The gateway has been described as one of the best half-timber pieces of work remaining in London.

Dr. Johnson once lived at No. 1 Inner Temple Lane.

The library, chapel and hall of the Inner Temple were demolished during the war.

Facing the Great Hall of the Inner Temple, built in 1955, is the southern side of the ancient Temple Church, the most interesting building among the Inns.

Here, on tombs that have lain there for centuries are stone effigies of Crusader knights. Some have their legs crossed, indicating, a Blue Badge guide told us, that the knights had been on a Crusade.

The Islamic outlines of the Round Church are still very evident. The crypt was a place for secret invitation ceremonies. The walls of the original nave bear grotesque carvings.

A frightening reminder of the punishment by the Knights is seen in the penitential cell built into the wall near the wheel window in the Round Church. Here a noble of Ireland was left to starve in the five-foot cell because he had disobeyed the Master of the Order.

The new part of the church is divided into two congregational sets of pews.

The Inner Temple members sit at the south side under the window bearing their crest and the Middle Temple members sit at the north side under their crested window. At one time they even had separate prayer books but the ensuing confusion at the end of services caused them to share the same books.

Politics, Prayers & Pigeons

4. Westminster Whitehall Trafalgar

The favorite visual subject of postcards, posters and "Henry get-a-picture" is that taking in the River Thames, Westminster Bridge, the Houses of Parliament with Westminster Abbey in the background. (See back cover.)

When Edward the Confessor decided to move farther up the Thames to establish an abbey outside of The City in 1040, he also built a palace on the riverbank. His successor, William I, took over the new palace and William's son, William Rufus, embellished and enlarged what his father had taken by the sword.

For the next five hundred years Westminster Palace was successively swept by fires and rebuilt until, in 1512, Henry VIII was forced to seek another palace.

From that time on the rebuilt Westminster Palace ceased to be a royal residence and became the Houses of Parliament.

Three hundred years later, more or less, an overheated underground furnace set fire to that Parliament structure, leveling almost all of it. Only Westminster Hall, St Stephen's crypt and cloister built by William Rufus (William II) has survived the centuries of fires.

An architectural competition was won by Charles Barry and

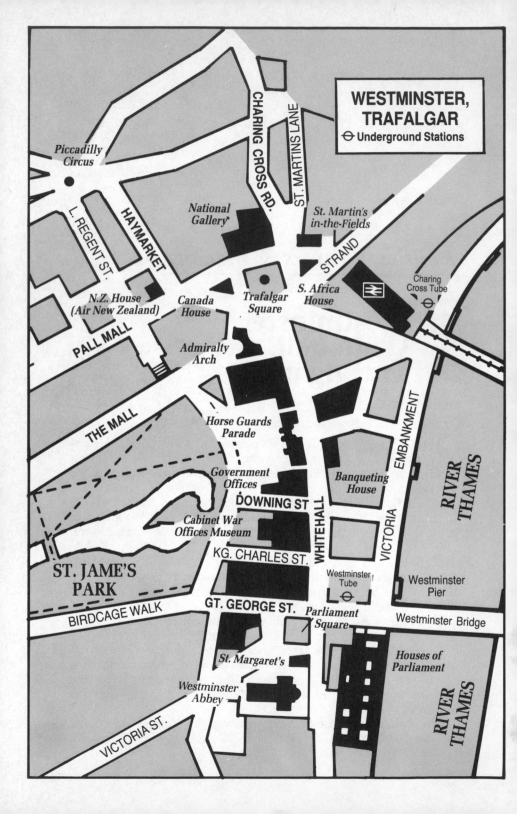

Augustus Pugin who created a single line building with the House of Lords on the south side and the House of Commons on the north side, connecting it to the Westminster Hall.

Towers were built on each end, one to mark the royal entrance, the other a clock tower which also houses the 13-ton bell and its 5-ton electrically wound mechanism. The entire facade by Pugin is classical Gothic with pinnacles and windows relieved by carvings and niches and mediaeval tracery.

The famous Clock Tower, London's most visual trademark at roughly the height of a 31-story building, was completed in 1859. Its nickname, Big Ben, probably stems from Sir Benjamin Hall, then the Commissioner of Works.

If the light above the clock is on, the House of Commons is sitting.

There are two ways you can see the inside of the Houses of Parliament and witness Parliament in session: with an invitation from a Member of Parliament or by queueing at the entrance to St Stephens Porch (opposite Westminster Abbey) when Parliament is in session, usually Monday through Friday.

People who know people in their own governments tend to use their influence for arranging visits to the Strangers' Gallery of one or the other house.

Should you queue, know that because seating is limited there is no guarantee you will be admitted inside the Strangers' Galleries even if you get inside the building. Still, just seeing Westminster Hall, St Stephen's Hall and the Central Lobby is worth the effort.

We are told that chances improve after 6PM, after people with prearranged passes depart. Debates usually last until 10PM or so.

Also know that the Prime Minister takes questions in the House of Commons Tuesdays and Thursdays at 3:15PM, providing the liveliest sessions.

When Parliament is not in session, visits are limited to Saturdays, some days in August and September. To be sure, call.

A Place For Poets And Kings And Queens

I do my usual go-to-the-front-and-just-sit-quietly act every time I return to Westminster Abbey. That is absolutely the best part. Then I carefully choose from the magnificent menu of Westminster gumdrops a couple of chapels or vaults or tombs or memorials I have never visited.

Trying to see everything every time is risking disenchantment.

An indispensable ingredient is your imagination.

You have to picture in your mind the trappings of a royal wedding or coronation.

Can't you just see the royal whomp and pomp of Queen Elizabeth's coronation in 1953 or the wedding of her second son, Andrew, now Duke of York, in 1986? The color and the sound and pageantry of such events must be the grandest theater in the world. Where else in the world is such majesty repeated today?

Just sit there for a moment and step back in time.

Historically life and death have swirled around Westminster Abbey for almost a thousand years.

In 1066, eight days after his abbey was finished, Edward the Confessor died and before the year was out, the first of the Normans, William I, was crowned on Christmas Day.

Since that coronation in 1066, every royal who has been crowned an English monarch has been crowned here.

The completion of the abbey also marked the shift of spiritual power from The City of London and the Cathedral of St. Paul's to the City of Westminster and the cathedral of the west, Westminster.

Political power followed.

Nothing remains of the original structure built by Edward the Confessor. Henry III started over and built most of the present nave and a new chapel to enshrine Edward who was made a saint in 1163.

Two hundred years elapsed before additional work was started. Henry VII, inspired by the grand Gothic examples of Amiens and Reims, completed the present church with its go-to-God vaulting, towering rose windows, delicate flying buttresses.

Just sit there and savor the moment.

A conducted group tour can be arranged at the Information counter, to the right shortly after entering the building. Tours occur frequently.

If you are a loner, you should buy a guide book to add to your pleasure. The book store at the entrance sells several very reasonably priced booklets.

Also at the entrance is the memorial to Winston Churchill, beyond which is perhaps the most famous pavement stone of all, that to the Unknown Warrior, surrounded by Flanders Poppies, a symbol of the bloodiest fields of battle in World War I.

Start at the left hand side and walk down the nave where you must pay a small fee to proceed beyond the choir area and into the "top of the cross."

Here is the soul of the Abbey. The Sanctuary where coronation ceremonies are conducted abuts the Chapel of Edward the Confessor, also known as the Chapel of the Kings because the tombs of five kings and three queens ring the Confessor's shrine.

Here also are the Queen Elizabeth Chapel, the Battle of Britain Chapel, and the Henry VII Chapel, the only attraction in the Abbey awarded three stars by Michelin. For its superb fan-vaulted roof, undoubtedly.

Proceeding at a leisurely pace in a clockwise direction, the left apse at the cross, or transept, of the church is filled with the powerful political names of their day: Gladstone, Disraeli, Palmerston, Pitt.

You pass—and peek in at—the Chapel of Our Lady of the Pew, and then the chapels of St John the Baptist, St Paul, and the Queen Elizabeth Chapel. You know it is popular because the flow of traffic is roped for control and marked "Stay to the left."

Elizabeth I is entombed beneath a white sterile marble effigy, her austere ruff seemingly a neck brace. Below her is the tomb of her half sister, Mary, without monument. A small sarcophagus against the wall contains bones found in the Tower in 1674 and presumed to be the murdered Little Princes, one of whom would have been Edward V had he lived.

At the very back of the nave, behind the three-star Henry VII Chapel, is the Battle of Britain Chapel. Note particularly the memorial window. The insignia of the squadrons who took part in the 1940 battle have been immortalized in vividly colored stained glass. So, too, have the names and nations of the participating pilots and crews, each recorded in a chapel book open for your examination.

Pause a moment in the nave of the Henry VII Chapel, and look at the intricate fan-vaulted roof, a remarkably beautiful achievement, and the banners of the Knights Grand Cross of the Order of the Bath.

Find the memorial to Oliver Cromwell, the Lord Protector of the first commonwealth from 1649 to 1658. Cromwell was tough. He did to the monarchy what Henry VIII did to the monasteries. He stripped it of its art collection and melted down or sold the crown treasure.

Cromwell was buried in the Abbey but, two years after the restoration of the monarchy, he was hauled out of his tomb, hung and beheaded.

Just in back of the Cromwell plaque is the tomb of Henry VII and Elizabeth of York.

Proceed then across the bridge facing the entrance to enter the sanctuary of Edward the Confessor.

St Edward's grand central tomb is part marble, part wood; the lower marble being the original and the upper wood being a replacement. That half was destroyed by looters after Henry VIII dissolved the abbey.

Henry III is buried here, 1272, in a tomb decorated with Italian marble, he who built the original sanctuary and the nave using all of his own money—and anybody else's money he could get—until it all ran out. Also here is Edward I, Longshanks, who brought the Stone of Scone to London in 1297 which rests beneath the ancient Coronation Chair in the front part of the chapel.

I was working for a newspaper in Paris in 1950 when the Stone was the subject of headlines. It had been stolen. The details escaped me and I approached a volunteer attendant, Maurice Herrick, a tanned, pleasant, middle-aged gentleman, and asked for a reminder.

"Yes," he said, "it was stolen during the Christmas holidays in 1950. The Stone was gone for ten weeks and George VI made it known that he wanted it back without fail. Well, word came around that it could be found in Arbroath Abbey, a place in southeast Scotland, not far from Perth.

"The theft had resulted from a forced entry. The Stone weighs some 458 pounds, you now, and was probably dropped during the operation. It was found in two pieces . . . although you couldn't tell it now.

"Legend has it that Jacob rested his head on the Stone in Bethel and saw the archangels descend from heaven on 'Jacob's ladder.' You'll find it in Genesis 28, Verse 18. The legend says that the Stone came to Scotland by the way of Egypt, Spain and Ireland and it rested in Scone Abbey where the kings of Scotland would sit upon it.

"Edward I brought the Stone here and had a solid oak chair made to hold the Stone of Scone underneath it, symbolizing the sovereignty of the king over Scotland."

The coronation chair is not a particularly pretty thing. Tall, square built, a V-shaped top, carved of oak. Solid . . . like the crown. Each leg sits atop a carved griffin. The Stone rests beneath the wood seat.

At the time of a coronation, the chair is moved the short distance to the sanctuary.

"Every king of England has been crowned in this chair since Edward II in 1308 with the exception of two," Mr. Herrick went on. "Edward V who was smothered in the Tower as a small child and Edward VIII who never was crowned, abdicating to marry the American woman." He sniffed a bit at the latter mention.

"The last monarch crowned, of course, was Elizabeth II who was crowned on June 2, 1953."

Oh, yes, to be in the Abbey at the time of a coronation!

After you depart the sanctuary duck around the corner to the Poet's Corner, a veritable Who's Who of the literary giants of the empire-cum-commonwealth.

Because Chaucer and Ben Jonson, among other writers officially associated with the palace and abbey, were buried here, petitions were made on behalf of writers of similar rank to the Dean of Westminster whose sole discretion determines who may be buried and whose memorials may be erected in the abbey. Poet's Corner is one result of those decisions.

(Jonson, destitute, asked the Dean to be buried in the Abbey, but volunteered that he wasn't worth a six foot grave. So they buried him standing up—and misspelled his name.)

So many are remembered if not actually buried here. Samuel Johnson, Browning, Tennyson were interred here. Milton, Wordsworth, Thackeray, Dickens, Thomas Hardy and Rudyard Kipling were not, but are honored.

Some of those with questionable lives had to wait years after their deaths for the honor of a memorial, among them Shakespeare, Keats, Shelley, Byron. You'll also find W H Auden, George Eliot, T S Eliot, Blake, Dylan Thomas, Henry James, Lewis Carroll, D H Lawrence, and a host of others.

Did I miss Addison who said, "In the poetical quarter I found there were poets who had no monuments and monuments which had no poets."

So popular is Poet's Corner that it has its own souvenir stand stocked with the usual postcards and booklets of poetry.

The entrance to the Grand Cloisters—and the industrious center for souvenir brass rubbing—is around the corner from the Poet's Corner.

Brasses originated in mediaeval England as status symbols of the knights and their ladies and priests. An engraved sheet of brass depicting the rank of the deceased decorated the top of the tomb.

As merchants, tradesmen, fishmongers and wool merchants climbed the economic ladder they, too, sought this touch of class in brass. Little did they know what a contribution they were making to the 20th century pleasure of souvenir seekers.

The entire side of the cloister is filled with people, heads down, frowning in concentration, and intensely rubbing, rubbing, rubbing.

Buy a sheet of paper and wax, select a subject (more than 8,000 masters have been found in cathedrals and churches) and rub your own wall hanging. Or buy a pre-rubbed one.

Stamina prevailing, proceed to the Chapter House and the Chapel of the Pyx.

One small fee will get you into both.

The Chapter House was built for the Benedictine Monks as a meeting hall by Henry III who said "As the rose is the flower of flowers so is this house the house of houses." Henry III assembled his first Great Council here in 1257.

The House of Commons met in the room until 1547.

It is a lovely room. You have to don felt slippers to protect the original (circa 1255) tiles.

Octagonal, 60 feet in diameter, the room is lighted through eight stained glass windows, most of which were blown away during the Blitz. The monks sat against the walls in stone seats, under a beautifully vaulted ceiling.

The room was used as a storeplace for royal treasury and after its function as the meeting place for the House of Commons it became an archives, the tiles boarded over and a second floor added.

Thankfully, after Word War II it was restored.

Next to the Chapter House is the Chapel of the Pyx. A pyx is a strongbox. Originally a strongroom built in 1065 to hold royal treasury, the chamber was also used as a room where gold and silver coins were tested to see if they were up to standard.

Thieves removed the masonry in one side wall in 1303 and took the treasury. They were later caught and hanged.

The case at the entrance displays the coronation cloak of gold cloth worn by Charles II in 1661.

Other cases in the room hold a collection set up by the Worshipful Company of Goldsmiths in 1986 including immense patens and chalices and large jugs.

Beyond the last chapel is the Little Cloister, a delightful spot in springs and summers, its Gothic walls bordered with gaily colored flowers nodding rhythmically to the splash fountain at the center of a spring-green lawn.

At the end of the corridor is the Dean's Yard, off limits to visitors, once the center of Abbey life and now part of Westminster School, a prestigious school in England.

Adjacent to Westminster Abbey is St Margaret, the church built by Edward the Confessor to serve local parishioners. It has been rebuilt three times.

When the Protector Somerset was building Somerset House on the Strand, he marked the church for demolition in order to get its stones, but the parishioners beat off his workmen with clubs and bows.

Sir Walter Raleigh is buried under the high altar. A commemorative tablet and the west window to Raleigh were donated in the late 19th century by Americans.

The east window was made for Catherine of Aragon, daughter of Ferdinand and Isabella of Spain, on the occasion of her marriage to Arthur, son of Henry VII. When Arthur died soon after, she became the first of Henry VIII's six wives. Divorced, she the first in the rhyme:

> *"Divorced, beheaded, died,*
> *divorced, beheaded, survived."*

Ironically, the statue of Charles I outside the church stares across the street to the statue of Oliver Cromwell who beheaded him.

The pleasant square of green across from the Westminster Abbey is Parliament Square and is enriched with sculpted figures. Churchill anchors one side, Abraham Lincoln another, a decided improvement over the scene in the 16th century when it was a nest of tenements beset with street hawkers, pickpockets and footpads (muggers).

Whitehall . . . And The Last Royal Head

As you leave Westminster and walk up Whitehall toward Trafalgar Square, the massive buildings on your left belong to government administration departments.

In order, the Treasury and Commonwealth Offices occupy the first building. The Foreign Office headquarters in the building just after King Charles Street. Then comes Downing Street.

You can't go into Downing Street and stand in front of No.10 as once you could but you can see the entrance from Whitehall. Security is tight around the Prime Minister's London residence. (The country home is Chequers.)

Continuing on Whitehall, next is the office of the Old Treasury, then the Horse Guards Parade, and finally the Old Admiralty.

Stop, if only for a moment, at the Horse Guards Parade, a U-shaped building surrounding a small courtyard where, in the winter, the mounting of the new guard takes place.

Walk through the courtyard to the parade field where the ceremony is conducted in summers at 11AM weekdays and 10AM on Sundays. It is one of the most colorful daily events in London.

And it is free.

The romantic metal helmeted horsemen with their plumes and capes and gleaming animals symbolize the glamour and world-apart monarchy of Britain.

There are two regiments in the Household Cavalry. The Blue and Royals wear blue tunics and red plumes. The Life Guards are more photogenic in scarlet tunics and white plumed helmets.

Two mounted sentries are posted on each side of the Horse Guards Parade gate between ten and four, the sentries being changed every hour. Despite the thousands and thousands of photos taken of each sentry and his horse, they never flicker.

The picture taking, especially with children, is one of the warmest scenes in London.

At one time the land from Trafalgar Square to Westminster was palace grounds.

Cardinal Wolsey, the clever and powerful clergyman, besides building Hampton Court upriver, *borrowed* church property to build himself a city residence.

In time, Henry VIII took all of Wolsey's marbles—his church and properties throughout England including Hampton Court and the convenient Whitehall Palace.

Henry enlarged the buildings and annexed adjacent lands to create hunting grounds. The area now devoted to St James's Park was stocked with game.

Henry's son, Edward VI, came to the throne at age ten, too young to care very much about property. Not so his administrator. Protector Somerset confiscated all of the land from the Strand to the Thames and started building a palace befitting a king at what is now the entrance to Waterloo Bridge.

When the young king died six years later, Somerset lost his head and his incomplete palace.

A Colonel Trench proposed a scheme for a colonnade from the Tower of London to Chelsea which would have included the palaces along the river—Somerset, Whitehall, Westminster. It would have been one of the great spectacles of Europe.

The Banqueting House

The Banqueting House was designed by Inigo Jones. It was an "add-on" to Whitehall Palace in 1619 for James I. Jones' penchant for the Roman style, seen in the piazza of Covent Garden, is evident in this splendid two-story building.

James' son, Charles I, made many mistakes, first misguided by the treacherous Duke of Buckingham and, after Buckingham's murder, by his ambitious French wife, Henrietta Maria. Strongly insisting on his Divine Right of Kings, he made an enemy of Parliament, abolishing it for eleven years. Later, he moved from London to Oxford, assembled an army of Cavaliers who lost the war against the Parliamentary Army of Roundheads led by Oliver Cromwell.

Charles was imprisoned for two years but Cromwell knew that a living enemy was a dangerous enemy. A Parliamentary trial found Charles guilty of treason and condemned him to death.

On January 30, 1649 in an unshaken performance of how a Divine King should die, Charles walked from St James's Palace to the Banqueting House and was led out of a second floor window to an erected scaffolding and was executed. Never a particularly admirable man, he died a king.

"Nothing in his life became Charles like the leaving it," it was said with a slight borrowing from Shakespeare.

Cromwell governed the Commonwealth for nine years but his

son, Richard, lacked the strength to hold the country together. Charles II, in French exile, was called home.

Fittingly, the monarchy was restored in the Banqueting House where Charles II received Parliament on the eve of his coronation eleven years after the execution of his father.

Besides serving as a ceremonial court, the Banqueting House was a venue for parties, banquets for the Knights of the Garter, Maundy Thursday Services and the Touching for the King's Evil.

"What," I asked the young blond receptionist, "is Touching for the King's Evil?"

"People who were injured or ill were brought before the king and he 'laid' his hands on them. They were always on the road to recovery to be sure, but they always got well."

Later we learned that the "King's Evil" was scrofula, a common skin affliction of the time.

One of the great Crown treasures is in the ceiling paintings of the Banqueting House. Charles I commissioned them from Peter Paul Rubens (1577-1640) to glorify his father, James I. If you had any doubt about Charles' belief in the Divine Right of Kings, it would be removed by the concept of the paintings.

Above the entrance to the hall James is shown being carried to heaven by the angels.

In the center oval he is now safely in heaven surrounded by happy cherubs, a scene depicting peace and rejoicing at his reign.

In another painting, as seen from the throne, James is shown uniting the kingdom with Scotland on one hand—remember he was also King James VI of Scotland—and England on the other.

After the great Whitehall Palace was destroyed by a fire in 1698, Wren turned the Banqueting House into the Chapel Royal.

Now the building itself stands empty but is a work of art by itself and is open Tuesday to Saturdays, 10AM to 5PM and on Sundays from 2PM. Small charge.

Trafalgar Square: Pigeon Heaven & Tourist Rendezvous

At the top of Whitehall is an action center of London, Trafalgar Square. You could say it is the center of London based on the fact that it is the spot from which all distances on signposts are measured. A plaque marks the exact spot.

It is difficult to reconcile that this hectic, frantic square used to be a country meadow. Now it is a scene where red buses and black taxis resemble red Tom cats chasing black girl cats around the square non-stop—where flocks of tourists stand bewildered with open maps pointing first in one direction and then another—where flocks of pampered pigeons hold pecking parades.

The square is London's prime location for tired tourists to sit. They sprawl along the steps of the National Gallery and St Martin-in-the-Fields.

Jeans clad students with knapsacks line the parapets of the square itself.

Tour buses park in front of the National Gallery hawking city tours.

Where the streets now funnel into different sections of square, the small village of Charing existed. When the cortege of Queen Eleanor stopped here in 1290 en route to her burial in Westminster, a cross was erected as was the custom, and it became forever after Charing Cross.

The village church, St Martin-in-the-Fields, probably dates back to the 13th century but was rebuilt in 1544. Today's church is known for its splendid tower. It bears the royal coat of arms over the pediment because Buckingham Palace stands in the parish.

Go inside at noon. Often there will be music in practice or recital. Summers, free concerts are scheduled at noon. A church becomes holier with music.

Before its evolution into a square, an open area to the northwest of Charing Cross was called the King's Mews. Royal hawks were kept and falconers lodged.

Cromwell's army was barracked in the Mews.

The square was to have been another John Nash design but he died before his plan was executed. Sir Charles Barry completed it as a hub between Bloomsbury and Westminster and an important link between the Strand and Whitehall, or King Street as it was first called.

Focal center of the square is the dominant Nelson Column, another postcard-poster symbol of London, the square being named after the place of the Admiral's naval victory. But there are fountains and four magnificent stone lions and fat pigeons that took begging lessons from their Italian cousins in Venice.

Two center granite fountains tiled in blue give dash to the square when it is floodlit at ten o'clock each night.

The north wall in front of the National Gallery delineates in metal the standard linear measures: inch, foot and yard.

The drinking fountains on either side of the square are gifts from the Metropolitan Drinking Fountain and Cattle Trough Association.

Isn't that marvelous?

The statue of Charles I at the corner has a head.

Canada House and South Africa House flank the square west and east, the Admiralty Arch is in the southwest corner, St Martin-in-the-Fields in the northeast corner. Due north is the most prominent edifice, the National Gallery.

"Why are there always scruffy picketers in front of St Martin's, giving out handbills and harassing people with petitions?" asked the Lady Navigator.

They are not picketers, they are protesting the policies of South Africa. South Africa House, headquarters for the South African government in London, is across the street.

"They shouldn't clutter up the front of the church. It's not the church's fault."

Right. Her next job is nuclear disarmament.

Around the northeast side of the National Gallery, on Charing Cross Road, you'll find the National Portrait Galley and, on the opposite side of Charing Cross, narrow streets that lead to Covent Garden.

To the northwest is Piccadilly via Haymarket leading past New Zealand House, American Express, Burberry's premiere store and the government-sponsored Design Centre where newest commercial ideas are on display. It's a mini-museum of the "best of Britain." Upstairs, some items are for sale.

Of special interest to Kiwis are two communication centers behind New Zealand House in the Royal Opera Arcade. Whitcoull's bookstore posts notices of flat rentals, employment opportunities, autos for sale . . . whatever . . . in its window. Farther up the Arcade, inside walls and outside windows of a news agency are plastered with more of the same. You can also find a weekly New Zealand newspaper there.

If you walk straight through the arcade into the next block, at the corner of Norris Street is the Captain's Cabin, a pub where Kiwis have gathered since New Zealand airmen used it as a rendezvous during the war.

The pub keeps a Captain's Cabin log book. Winston Churchill is one of the people who signed in.

Another Kiwi bit: if you had any association with Marist education in New Zealand, there is a Marist church off Leicester Square on Leicester Place near Lisle Street. The church is Notre Dame, and Mass is said in French. Unusual interior design.

At night when the pigeons, protesters and pedestrians have emptied out of the square and the lights are on the fountains and the buildings, does Trafalgar Square drop its bustling tone and take on an aura of nobility and romantic grandeur?

That's when you mentally hug yourself and say, "Hey. London."

A Jolly Good Show

We have a good friend in London who kept asking, "What can I do for you? How can I help? Please tell me what I can do for you?"

Finally we said, "Get us into Parliament for the Prime Minister's Question Time in the House of Commons."

"*Cor!*" said our friend whose speech is influenced by a lucky marriage to a maid of Lancashire.

It was akin to asking for an invitation to the Queen's Garden Party.

But he did.

On a Tuesday we were at the St Stephen's Porch at 2:10PM, letter in hand verifying an appointment with Mr Neville Trotter, Member of Parliament, Conservative, representative of a constituency of Tynemouth near Newcastle.

After mounting the steps we cleared security, far more thorough than at any airport. The young man in front of us had a Walkman in hand, earphones draped around his neck. "Play it" instructed the security guard. They take no chances.

The security X-ray and body scan stations almost obscure the view to Westminster Hall, survivor of many fires and the last architectural evidence of William Rufus, son of William the Conqueror.

It is a wondrous vast mediaeval cavern where Christmas feasts were held, jousting tournaments staged, where kings, chancellors, dukes and princes were tried, where kings and Churchill have lain in state.

A 600-ton hammerbeam, considered the finest timber roof of all time, was added in the 14th century, and steel reinforcement to its beams in 1920. The former enhances; the latter you cannot see. What you do see are the angels flying from the ends of each beam.

We then entered into St Stephen's Hall, a long, impressive hall whose Gothic arches and vaulted ceiling create the right setting for statues and mosaics on either wall. Opulent and just slightly awesome.

The Central Lobby is even more impressive. Four saints in gold mosaics decorated half of the octagonal walls: St George for England, St Patrick for Ireland, St Andrew for Scotland and St David for Wales. The ceiling, 75 feet overhead, sparkled with gold.

We left our names at the information desk and waited along with fifty or so other people for further instruction. Members of Parliament skittered in and out of the Central Lobby, the lobby through which everyone must pass.

"McDermott" the loudspeaker intoned. We were introduced to Diana, secretary for Mr. Trotter, who positioned us in the center of the lobby while she collected our tickets.

"When the time comes for the Procession to begin, the police will edge you behind the black ring line but you will be in the front row," she counseled. An experienced lady. Invaluable too, we were to hear from her employer.

She returned with the admission tickets for the chamber gallery just as Neville Trotter appeared. A tall, amiable, handsome fellow, slightly rumpled, a trifle harried, he was nonetheless in good humor, and suggested we meet early for tea—immediately after the Prime Minister's Question Time—since tables on the terrace are in high demand. His wife would join us.

And off he galloped leaving Diana to escort us.

It all went to plan. Just before 2:30 the lobby police gently herded visitors behind the black circle line of floor marble.

In the distance we heard the steady sound of people approaching in measured step.

"Hats off, Strangers!" bellowed one policeman. All the policemen in the room removed their hats, the only time they do so, Diana told us.

"They don't even remove them in the presence of the Queen. I think it has to do with the presence of the mace and its symbolism as legal authority."

The five-party Procession entered the room. The leader wore

black knickers and a black waistcoat. The Sergeant-of-Arms bore the mace. The Speaker of the House, white wigged and black robed, was followed by his secretary who carried the train of his robe. The final member of the procession was the chaplain in red robes and white surplice.

Solemnly they entered the lobby. Step by measured step, step, step, abrupt right turn. Step, step, step in gaited rhythm, they marched into the chamber. Very impressive.

Our green-tipped visitors cards gave us second row seats in the Commonwealth Gallery overlooking the chamber where the two principal parties occupy facing benches on opposite sides of the room.

The House of Commons Chamber was destroyed in wartime and rebuilt rather simply. There are only 437 seats for its 635 members, a traditional paucity based on a Churchillian precept that a small room made for better debating.

When you later learn about tiny office spaces, miniscule salaries and skeleton staffing, you wonder how the legislative branch works at all.

The Speaker's Chair is canopied. The long table before him bears two bronze, decorated Despatch Boxes, one in front of the right hand bench where the Prime Minister will sit, the other on the left where the Leader of the Opposition will sit. The Mace decorates the table.

Visitors are given an "Order Paper" containing questions asked by members for oral answers by ministers. Small closed circuit TV monitors mounted on the walls tell you which question is under debate and who is speaking.

The daily question session, already in progress when we were seated, is similar to a prep school debating society but not nearly as polite. Much jeering and jibing, jumping up and down to get the Speaker's attention, hooting and laughing. The laughter usually was derisive. The room was less than half full.

Questions for the Prime Minister start at 3:15PM and end at 3:30, and must be posed in writing, in advance. Opposition party members are loath to give that kind of advantage to government. So everybody plays the game to unwritten rules.

"What are the Prime Minister's official engagements for Tuesday, 21st July?" is the *same* question from *seventeen* different members on the Order Paper. It is always the same, Diana had told us.

Then, once the written question has been answered, the member can get on to asking the harder question at hand.

A few moments before three the benches started to fill.

Neil Kinnock, the Leader of the Opposition, came in and took his place before the Despatch Box.

Then from the right hand side of the Speaker's chair came the smartly dressed lady of fair complexion, strawberry blond hair, and iron will. Prime Minister Margaret Thatcher was relaxed and confidently fresh from her third national election victory.

She had just returned from a trip to the United States and Jamaica. Shortly before that she'd been in Europe giving a school principal's lecture in economics to the heads of the European Economic Conference. Earlier in the year, to Russia, broadening the *glasnost* image of Gorbachev.

Margaret Thatcher was no longer a political figure but the leading Statesperson in Europe.

She handled the questions with complete authority and turned one final attempt to embarrass her into a humorous, positive statement of the virtues of privitization—her favorite theme—and left in triumph. Quite a performance.

At her next appearance the following Thursday, another Opposition member tried to embarrass her, an attempt she brushed off with ease. Craig Brown, our favorite newspaper commentator on the House of Commons, reported in *The Times* that it reminded him of a "Tom and Jerry" cartoon where the large housewife gets rid of little Jerry with one fell sweep of the broom.

As Neville Trotter had said just before we parted for the chambers, "It is the best show in town."

We had tea on the terrace with the paper-packing representative from Tynemouth and his vivacious wife, Tiggy, and talked of their honeymoon in Hawaii and of Parliament and the problems of being a Conservative member in an industrial area.

It wasn't an enviable picture.

What were the plus sides?

With fourteen years experience in the House of Commons and as a chartered accountant, he now served on important committees for defense and transportation. But his moments of greatest satisfaction came from the help he was able to give the individuals of his constituency. He had gotten reduced an excessive customs charge for a man who was being harassed. A great victory was in obtaining unbreakable eye-glasses frames for the frantic, near destitute mother of a mentally handicapped son who broke a pair of glasses daily.

Gracious guy. Great wife.

He took us to the House of Lords to arrange seats in the Member's Gallery, and left in a lope for another meeting. He expected to spend the night at Parliament resting in a sleeping bag underneath his desk.

The House of Lords has been described as "magnificent and gravely gorgeous." It is. The throne and its canopy and steps are all in gold, focal points for this elegant chamber designed by Pugin. The brass railing is removed when the Queen reads the Gracious Speech from the Throne.

The canopy represents the Cloth of Estate, to which the Lords bow on entering the chambers.

The Lord Chancellor who is also Speaker of the House, a Cabinet Minister and Head of the Judiciary does not occupy the throne. His presiding platform is the Woolsack, positioned in front of the throne and stuffed with wool from England, Wales, Scotland, Northern Ireland and the other countries of the Commonwealth.

The Mace, emblem of Her Majesty's authority, rests on the Woolsack.

As in the House of Commons, the House of Lords is divided into two banks of facing benches, the party of the Government on one side, known as the "Spiritual Side," the Opposition party members on the opposite "Temporal Side."

Around the walls are statues of eighteen knights who were present at the signing of the Magna Carta.

It is far more regal than the simple House of Commons. But, in truth, not nearly as entertaining.

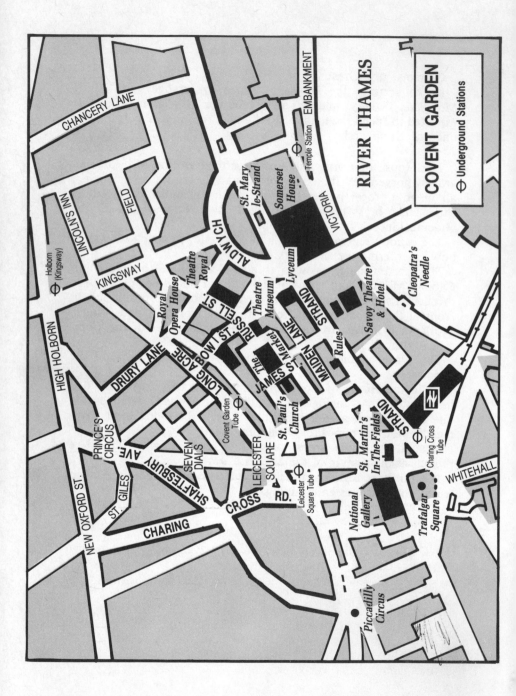

The West End

To give us an idea of what to see and do in London.

5. Covent Garden Wicked Soho Moneyed Mayfair

Each chapter is devoted to a certain part or aspect of London and I close

Piccadilly Circus is the hand of the fan that sweeps from the Strand on the east to Hyde Park in the west, an arc that embraces Covent Garden, Soho and Mayfair. An arc that changes character as fast as a chameleon changes color.

You don't have to be an insider to sense the changes. The set changes. The cast changes. The audience changes.

The three districts abut each other but they are worlds apart, one touched by theatrical grandeur, the other naughtiness and the last with a veneer of moneyed chic.

For 300 years Covent Gardens was the marketplace for fruit and vegetables and flowers in London.

Now Covent Garden, in the heartland of the theater district, is a high energy marketplace for social interaction in a plethora of restaurants, wine bars, and souvenir shops of every quality. Street buskers perform in the portico of St Paul's church made famous as the opening scene of George Bernard Shaw's *Pygmalion* and its later stage and film set for the *My Fair Lady* musical.

Today it is a place to meet and eat, people watch, pick up a new

You can still see street performers today

69

how It Got Its Name.

DATes BACK to xbe 1580's

friend. The young and beautiful make it vibrate.

Not always.

Covent Garden was a convent garden of the Benedictines, part of Westminster Abbey, before Henry VIII divested the Church of its properties. His son, Edward VI, awarded the convent gardens in 1552 to a deserving soldier and diplomat John Russell, who later became the first Earl of Bedford.

The 3rd Earl of Bedford built a mansion house that stretched from the Garden to the Strand.

In the mid-1600's the 4th Earl of Bedford petitioned the throne for a license to erect buildings "fitt for the habitaciouns of *Gentlemen* and men of ability."

Yours for £ 2,000, was the King's reply, providing you have approval for building from the King's Surveyor. Bedford, showing characteristic tendencies of the typical land developer, started construction before the license was granted. Docked another £ 2,000 in penalties.

Getting the message, he then hired Inigo Jones, the King's Surveyor to design his project.

Inigo Jones, who preceded Christopher Wren in London's list of famous architects, left just as indelible an architectural mark on London. Another genius.

Son of a cloth worker, he started as a lowly joiner apprentice but showed such skill and originality that he was sent to Italy to study the masters, particularly the works of Andrea Palladio of Padua.

It was a place of the Rich

His Covent Garden was modeled after an Italian piazza surrounded by three-story terrace houses over colonnaded walkways, coffee houses and shops. A parish church at the west end. The rich and aristocratic rushed in.

Even at the time of the monks, the area was a marketplace. The Bedfords permitted a few stalls to remain. But when the market at the center started to engulf the whole area, Bedford's aristocratic clients moved out.

The houses became brothels and gambling dens; duels were fought in the taverns.

The marketplace continued to grow. Traders in poultry, bird cages, pots and pans and crockery moved in to compete for space with the fruit and vegetable stalls.

In 1830 permission was granted for a special market complex to be built. The three building Central Market complex joined by a glass canopy which you see in place today was designed by

Charles Fowler.

The structure cost £ 70,000 and was described at its opening as a "structure at once perfectly fitted for its various uses; of great architectural beauty and elegance."

The adjacent Floral Hall was opened in 1850.

Had you visited Covent Garden any time before 1974, you would have heard the cries of costermongers and flowersellers and the clatter of heavy wooden trolleys over cobblestones as porters wheeled them through crowded streets and stalls. You would have pushed through streets jammed with trucks and stalls overflowing into neighboring streets. You might have stopped for lunch in one of the many small Italian restaurants or oyster-and-stout bars.

The congestion around Covent Garden—with the burgeoning city crowding in—finally became too much and, in 1921, it was condemned as inadequate space for the need. It took more than 50 years to make the move but finally in November 1974 the 'New' Covent Garden was opened in the Battersea district, south of the river.

Covent Garden survived threats of redevelopment and by 1980 had become the flourishing action center it is today.

The newest development is the renovation of the burned out Floral Hall and an adjacent building by the next-door Royal Opera House as backstage and rehearsal space and a new commercial center with offices, restaurants and shops. Revenues from the latter will go to the opera company.

Naturally, existing Covent Garden merchants protested the idea of additional competition. Petitions and pieces of fur flew everywhere until a compromise was reached.

St Paul's of Covent Garden is the the actors' church.

Back during the initial construction of the piazza residential community the Earl of Bedford, who was running out of money, instructed Inigo Jones to build a church no better than a barn, to which the architect replied "You shall have the best barn in London."

The classical Tuscan portico entrance—the one of Professor Higgins and Eliza Doolittle fame—was never used as an entrance. The clergy refused to sanctify the church because the altar was at the *west* end not at the traditional east end, nearest to Jerusalem.

So, to enter the church you go around to the back, to Bedford Street. There, walk through the small garden—another peaceful haven a few steps from the mobs—note the lamp posts and pick up an explanatory folder at the entrance.

You learn that the church is the only survivor of the original Inigo Jones Covent Garden plan but that it has been through several restorations. Nonetheless, something stirs you to imagine a dramatic offstage whisper . . . "You shall have the best barn in London."

What makes the church famous is the number of actors and artists who are either buried here or whose memorial stones line the walls.

Ellen Terry's ashes are in the southeast corner.

Here are plaques to Sir Noel Coward and Sir Charles Chaplin KBE and Sir Anton Dolin.

Over there is Stanley Holloway, Gracie Fields, Ivor Novello, Boris Karloff.

The final credits roll on and on.

So many famous names.

One guide said that she never takes a group through St Paul's but that someone doesn't exclaim: "Oh, I didn't know he died!"

Underneath many plaques are memorable quotes. Sybil Thorndike's ". . . my head was in the skies and the glory of God was upon me." (*St Joan.*)

A highwayman is also buried in the courtyard.

A local friend said, "Oh, yes.

"There was also an actor who moonlighted as a highwayman. He was always caught but he was so charming that he kept getting pardoned. His best performance, really. Finally, he was mixed up in a murder and they shipped him off to France."

After our visit to the church we returned to the piazza to find a juggler performing to the accompaniment of a companion's accordion under the portico, typical free entertainment fare which has been a Covent Garden tradition for over three hundred years. Samuel Pepys recorded in his diary May 9, 1662 that he enjoyed a "Punch and Judy" show here so much that he came back two weeks later and brought his wife.

Note the Admiral's House in the northwest corner of the piazza, the one alongside the colonnaded building. It is of the type that Inigo Jones designed.

Exiting Covent Garden Piazza to the east, the burned out Floral Hall is on your left. On the right was its replacement, the Floral *market*

Market. When Covent Garden's produce activities were removed to Battersea, the Floral Market space made room for the London Transport Museum (1980) and the new Theatre Museum (1987).

If you are into old trolleys and buses, the transport museum is for you.

If you are a theater buff, you will enjoy the Theatre Museum.

The museum is open until 7PM which means you can fit it in before a first curtain of a theater in the vicinity. The museum goes to dark on Mondays.

The box office at the entrance on Russell Street also serves as a ticket agency for all London shows. The licensed cafeteria seems a civil place.

You descend a ramp leaving distractions upstairs to enjoy the yesteryear of English theater, dance, opera.

Before entering the Main Gallery pop into the room to the right, the Harry R Beard Room, where thousands of theatrical posters, photographs, and playbills have been assembled for personal review in pull-out wall racks. An index accompanies each panel. The earliest graphic dates from 1560.

The Main Gallery collects more substantive memorabilia. A picture of David Garrick in 1741 debuting as Richard III, a prompt script from George Bernard Shaw's *St Joan* and a photograph of Sybil Thorndike in the role.

Noel Coward's monogrammed red silk dressing gown is in a case with a picture of Gertrude Lawrence.

John Lennon's velvet collared Beatle outfit is exhibited.

The Irving Gallery was showing treasures from the costume collection. In one glass enclosure was the once elegant but battered steamer trunk belonging to Alicia Markova, Cunard Steamship Line and posh hotel stickers bandaging some of its travel scars outside, wooden hangers holding gauzy tutus inside.

What's missing in the Theatre Museum? There is a gallery named after Sir John Gielgud but the acknowledgments that one logically expects to find of Sir Lawrence Olivier, Ralph Richardson, Alec Guinness are missing. Is it because they are alive?

Frankly, we were disappointed.

After seeing so much evidence of superior exposition talent in other London museums, we came away unimpressed with this museum's somewhat static, nearly lifeless presentation. In an industry whose job is to "make magic," it misses. Perhaps because it was too new.

But if you love theater, go. You'll find a nugget or two that will make it totally worthwhile.

Unlike its parent, the Victoria & Albert Museum, which is free, the Theatre Museum charges an admission fee of £ 2.50.

London is a bright light in the entertainment world. Around Covent Garden alone there are some thirty theaters where the quality of the performers is unsurpassed and applause for its glittering musical production know-how is building, even on Broadway. (See Chapter 12, "There's No Biz Like Show Biz in London.")

The heritage for excellent theater goes back to the 16th century when, despite the restrictive Puritan ethic, it was a period of tremendous theatrical development. The pens of Shakespeare, Christopher Marlowe, Ben Jonson created a flood of memorable plays.

Most of the theatrical action was outside of The City, either across the river in Southwark or north of the London Wall in Clerkenwell.

It was not until the 17th century and the time of Charles II, who not only enjoyed the plays but adored the actresses, that theater came to Covent Garden.

Two Royal Warrants (permissions to operate) were granted by the king; one to a theater in Drury Lane, the other to the Theatre Royal, Covent Garden. Subsequently called the Phoenix because it burned down so often, that first royal theater today is the Royal Opera House, an architectural gem where the royal box has its own dining room.

You have heard the expression "in the limelight," of course. It was here that they first burned ground lime to illuminate the actors. It was here that the piano was first played in a public theater.

So popular was theater in early London that when an expensive restoration completed in 1809 prompted an attempt to recover costs by boosting ticket prices, a riot ensued. The "Old Prices Riot" lasted 66 days. Theater patrons won. The old prices were restored.

When still another fire destroyed the theater, the present classic portico and pediments were created. Note the frieze which was made of something called Coade Stone, a manmade stone, hard enough to survive an inferno.

The Royal Opera House address is also famous. Bow

Is located in Convenent Gardens.

Street—because the street is shaped like a longbow—was also the location of the first organized police in London.

Until the middle of the 19th century no formal police force existed. Such order as existed was maintained through mandatory community watches in which every ablebodied man participated. Wealthy men hired replacements who were either corrupt or careless. Henry Fielding, the author and also a London magistrate, assembled the Bow Street Runners to try to maintain some order in a district known for prostitutes and "footpads."

Nearby Drury Lane was a notorious bawdy area, yet it became the location of the Theatre Royal, Drury Lane which opened in 1663. It was here that King Charles II met Nell Gwynn, "pretty, witty Nell" who started as a street girl, made her stage debut in 1665 at the Drury Lane theater in Dryden's *Indian Queen* and graduated to the king's bedroom shortly thereafter for a long, successful run.

It established a tradition. In 1779 the Prince of Wales found Mary Robertson on stage. William IV found Mrs. Jordan.

Assassination attempts were made in the theater on the lives of both George II and George III.

Wren replaced the burned shell of a theater in 1674. The Drury Lane theater enjoyed one of its most popular periods starting in 1747, thanks mostly to the talented management of David Garrick. He lived not far away at 27 Southampton Street.

Sheridan was responsible for the theater when he launched his *School for Scandal* production. He was a Member of Parliament and could see from Parliament the fire that destroyed the Drury Lane for the third time.

The present house dates to 1812 and is still one of the largest theaters in London. Many musicals debuted here including *My Fair Lady* which ran up 2,281 performances.

A ghost is said to appear from time to time at matinees, emerging from a place on the left balcony wall, where, in the 19th century, a bricked-in body with a dagger in its ribs was found.

Theater facilities expanded throughout London. At the end of the 19th century, across the street at the Lyceum, the famous Shakespearean actor Henry Irving had a company of 600 actors. It was Irving who introduced the theatrical technique of dimming the house lights and of opening and closing a stage curtain.

Theater moved down to the Strand, once lined with palaces, becoming the Great White Way of London.

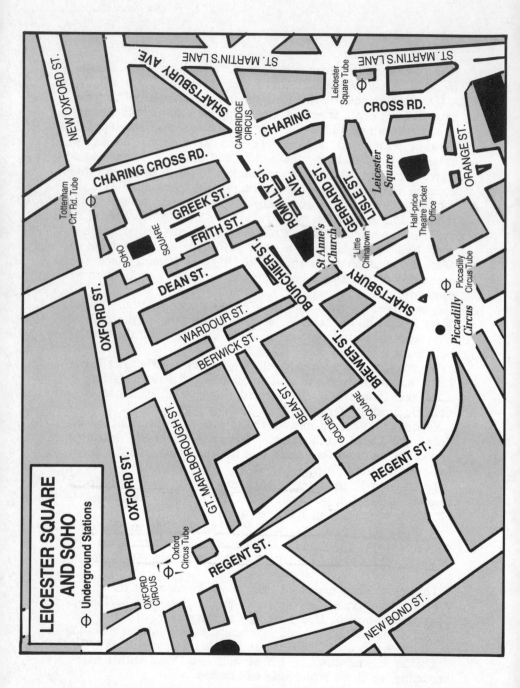

LEICESTER SQUARE AND SOHO
⊕ Underground Stations

NEW OXFORD ST.
SHAFTESBURY AVE.
ST. MARTIN'S LANE
ST. MARTIN'S LANE
Leicester Square Tube
CROSS RD.
CHARING
CAMBRIDGE CIRCUS
CHARING CROSS RD.
Tottenham Crt. Rd. Tube
Leicester Square
ORANGE ST.
GREEK ST.
SOHO SQUARE
FRITH ST.
ROMILLY ST.
AVE.
GERRARD ST.
LISLE ST.
St Anne's Church
"Little Chinatown"
Half-price Theatre Ticket Office
DEAN ST.
BOURCHIER ST.
OXFORD ST.
WARDOUR ST.
SHAFTESBURY
Piccadilly Circus Tube
BERWICK ST.
BREWER ST.
Piccadilly Circus
BEAK ST.
GOLDEN SQUARE
GT. MARLBOROUGH ST.
REGENT ST.
OXFORD ST.
Oxford Circus Tube
OXFORD CIRCUS
REGENT ST.
NEW BOND ST.

The Savoy Theatre was built adjacent to the hotel in 1881 to the designs of Richard D'Oyly Carte for the presentations of Gilbert and Sullivan operas. Here the first electric lights in a theater were employed. It is said that the manager came on stage and smashed a light bulb on the floor to prove that the electrical lighting was safe.

During the reign of Queen Victoria, the Strand glittered with a multitude of music halls. From here "West End" theater, like the vibrantly alive thing it is, spread its wings to flutter off and build nests beyond all boundaries. Today West End theater stretches from the core of The City to Sloane Square, from Oxford Circus to south of the Thames.

But that's a chapter unto itself.

Soho (Blue Plaques and Red Lights)

Soho means sin.

Soho means prostitutes (red lights) and drugs and evil men.

Soho means gambling and theaters and sex shops and all those things.

These are the reasons why, for so many years, so many people have been going to Soho.

However, the future of naughtiness is dim.

In seven years the "sex establishments" have gone from 161 to five.

One day, years off, the Westminster City Council may well be hiring pseudo streetwalkers to keep up the reputation of the neighborhood.

But there was always another face of Soho.

The former respectability of the area is reflected in the proliferation of Blue Plaques on building facades denoting the many famous people who used to reside in Soho.

Originally the area which starts just above Leicester Square and sits between Charing Cross on the east, Regent Street on the west, and Oxford Street as its northernmost boundary was a vast green field used by Henry VIII as hunting grounds. The huntsmen's cry

"SO-HO!" gave the district its name.

In the 17th century the Earl of Leicester was granted permission to build a house with the understanding that he would landscape the property. What he did was build a large house and then enclose three sides of a small patch of green with other houses which, being close to Parliament, were easily sold.

This was the original Leicester Square.

When the property deteriorated the Earl moved away to another grand house.

His palace was taken over by the Prince of Wales who had been tossed out of St James's Palace by his father, George I. The Prince not only lived in Leicester House, he lived like a king, called himself a king, held court, and hosted levees. His father detested him.

Eventually he did become George II and he, in turn, tossed out his son. It was a thing that ran in the Hanover family.

The son, Frederick, moved into the same house in Soho, beginning a new refrain of the same old song. He died before he could take the throne and was succeeded by his son who became George III.

You wouldn't think it today but Leicester Square was known for its royal parties.

Today's Leicester Square is still known for its after-dark energy. Cinemas and discos encircle it but it is better known as the site of the Half Price Theater Ticket kiosk. (The Swiss made standing in line for discounted tickets more tolerable when they installed a huge Swiss clock on the corner of Swiss House. People come to watch the milk maids and farmers and cows ambling around the dial face when the clock strikes at certain hours. (Glockenspiel hours are posted in the window.)

During the time of George III, London was the settlement city for many nationalities, first the French then, in succession, the Spanish, the Swiss, the Germans, the Jews.

Soho was the first district they lived in.

The immigrants were thrown in with the natives, the rich intermingled with the poor, the famous with the infamous, the literati with the whores, prostitutes and pimps.

Because of these roots, Soho's contemporary fame is as the place of Blue Plaques and Red Lights.

At one time one third of the houses were lived in by Jews and one third occupied by brothels.

The seafood restaurant, Manzi's, at the corner of Lisle and Leicester marks the site of a former German immigrants hotel. Karl Marx first lived there with his wife, children and servant until they moved to Dean Street. (I'm told Manzi's seafood is excellent.) *Andwer street*

Edmund Kean, the famous actor, grew up at 7 Lisle Street. He was the runt of the family, constantly abused, and constantly running away. His family put a brass tag around his neck asking people to send him back home.

Parallel to Lisle Street is Gerrard Street.

In the 17th century Gerrard Street was a known literary quarter.

Resident John Dryden's pre-dawn writing habits from four until eight were based on watching people go to work, one of his inspirations for characters.

Survival was another inspiration.

Dryden was adept at changing steps in an uncertain literary dance. He wrote a glowing eulogy about the Puritan Oliver Cromwell which won the great favor of his son, the then Lord Protector, Richard Cromwell. When Richard was deposed by Charles II, Dryden quickly became a Royalist . . . and the monarch's poet laureate. When Charles was replaced by a Catholic king—you got it—Dryden became a Catholic. Then a Protestant took the throne. Enough was too much. Dryden ceased switching loyalties. He also ceased being the poet laureate.

Where the Loon Moon Supermarket on Gerrard Street now stands was once the Turk's Head Tavern, a literary club frequented by Samuel Johnson and his chronicler, James Boswell, and Edward Gibbon, author of *The Decline and Fall of the Roman Empire*.

In another era Gerrard Street became a furniture center and when that succumbed to the marketplace the district disintegrated into a disreputable back alley of Soho.

The Chinese, the last wave of immigrants to Soho, have restored its respectability in the last ten years. Between the red lacquer Chinese gates at either end of the two block long street and beneath the colorful Oriental paper lanterns are window after window of pressed duck and dim sum menus.

Crossing Shaftesbury Avenue, a rich and vibrant theater street, to Dean Street, you come to the cross street of Romilly, named after the Sir George Romilly. The famous jurist succeeded in reducing the penal code death penalties from 97 to just 3: murder, piracy, treason.

A friend said he thought there was a fourth: setting fire to a Royal dockyard.

Today only treason is a cause for the death penalty.

The Romilly Street area was a first haven for French immigrants. George Romilly's grandmother, Etienne Romilly, was from a prominent Huguenot family.

In 1736 historian William Maitland wrote "Many parts of this parish so greatly abound with French that it is an easy Matter for a Stranger to imagine himself in France."

From the corner of Dean and Romilly you can see the remaining tower of St Anne's Church. Look at the top of the steeple. The clock is set on the side of a large beer barrel, or more correctly, a tun.

Once, Soho was part of the St Martin-in-the-Fields parish until population increased beyond its capacity. St Anne's became the Soho's parish church. The main body of the church was destroyed in the war.

Farther up Dean Street, look at the dark crooked building front at No. 88. It dates back to the 18th century.

Nearing Oxford Street is a restaurant Leoni's Quo Vadis at No.26-29. A two-room flat on the top floor comprised the residence of Karl Marx, his wife, Jenny, the servant and five children after they left the German Hotel. They all lived in one room. The second room was reserved as a den for Marx where he wrote *Das Kapital.*

Marx was terribly poor but aided a bit by his wife's inheritance. Much of his support came from Frederick Engels who was a wealthy Manchester industrialist. (Engels also rode to the hounds like a country gentlemen, claiming he was training himself to lead the workers' revolutionary cavalry.) His contributions not only kept the family alive but he was also said to have married Marx's servant girl when she became pregnant with Marx's child.

Later Marx and family moved to Hampstead where he is buried in the Highgate Cemetery under the words "Workers of all lands unite."

You can duck through different narrow alleyways to get to Soho Square if you have a curiosity about the width of streets in the old days.

In the middle of the square is a Tudor hunting lodge. Charming. "How marvelous," you think "that such a bit of history has been preserved." Actually it was built in 1936 to store the gardening tools for the flowers and lawn but it is a pleasant touch. Pseudo Tudor.

It is not without legal heritage.

When all of this land was a hunting park, the tired hunters in need of refreshment would tie up their horses to the ground floor posts and mount stairs to the second floor for a sip of this and a swig of that.

Before the hunting lodge tool shed existed, the square's main feature was a fountain presided over by a statue of Charles II from whose hand water spouted into four basins representing the four rivers of England. It is now positioned at one side of the square, the water pipe still visible in the monarch's clenched fist.

Where Barclay's Bank now stands once was the residence of the Duke of Monmouth, a bastard son of Charles II by Lucy Walters, one of his several mistresses. Monmouth, claiming that the monarch had secretly married his mother, tried to wrest control of the throne but James II defeated, captured and executed the pretender.

Greek Street, one of the streets leading into Soho Square, offers a rainbow of ethnic restaurants: the Gay Hussar—a favorite— Old Budapest, Le Mirage, Greek Prince, La Cucaracha . . . reminders of Soho's multinational heritage.

It was in a shop on Greek Street that Gainsborough found a filthy little boy, scrubbed him clean—several applications of soap were necessary, we are told—and immortalized him as the elegant satin clad *Blue Boy*.

Parallel to Greek Street is Frith Street, known as music street. A famous jazz club, Ronnie Scott's, is sited across the street from the first residence of Mozart who came to London as an eight-year-old child protege.

In 1986 the Westminster Council made a move to upgrade Soho from its swing'n'sin image.

The Peeping Police have successfully reduced the naughty enterprises to near zero. You don't need tea leaves to forecast the future for sin in Soho.

Along with strengthened law enforcement, a plan is afoot to turn some streets into pedestrian malls.

A new feeling of being "safe" aided by cheap rent has tempted a number of fashions designers to open salons where formerly the most fashionable merchandise to be found was a beaded G-string

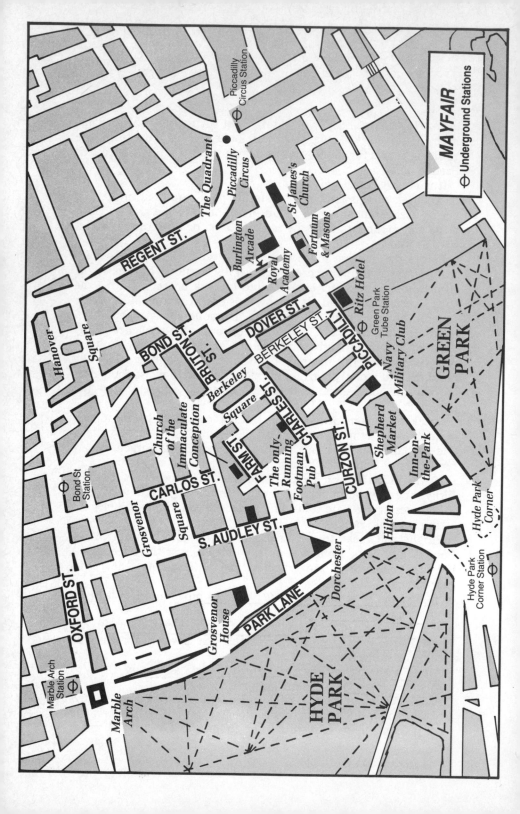

worn by a stripteaser.

Meanwhile back at Lisle Street, if you peek inside the open doorways, you'll still find adverts offering a "French Model" or a "Busty Model, Top Floor."
The world's oldest profession clings to its turf.

Mayfair Chic

Mayfair is money. Big money.
Its reputation for chic is of recent vintage, relatively. Its origins were humble. From mediaeval times until the 18th century it was a gathering place for a spring fair—May Fair—an event that became so popular with pickpockets, prostitutes and drunks that it had to be canceled.
The district is bound by Regent Street, Oxford Street, Piccadilly and Park Lane.
This perimeter of hype and hospitality is a familiar track to most London tourists.
Park Lane, paralleling Hyde Park, is lined with big name hotels: The Grosvenor House, a highly respected English hotel, the Hilton, the Dorchester, now Arabian owned, the Inn on the Park. All are five-star, big tariff establishments.
Oxford Street, the north border, and Regent Street, the east border, are London's most famous shopping streets. Anything you want, at any price.
Its southern border, Piccadilly, runs from Piccadilly Circus to Hyde Park Corner.
In the late 17th century a men's neckware fashion called *picadil* was the invention of a tailor in the Strand named Robert Baker. Baker made a fortune which he invested in what was then rural land where he built a manor house. The house was promptly nicknamed by the wags "Piccadilly Hall." When the country lane to the manor house was turned into a more formal street, officials named it Portuguese Street, but common usage made it Piccadilly.
The southside of Piccadilly between the Circus and Green Park serves up Lilywhite's, London's most complete sports store, then a clutch of "traditional" stores in wonderful 18th century buildings— Swaine Adeney Brigg, Hatchards, Simpson's, and Fortnum and Mason—all pricey, all prestigious. St James's Church comes next then the Ritz Hotel—you really *must* go tea dancing on

Sunday at the Ritz.

On its north side the stops of visitor interest are the Burlington House, the present day home of the Royal Academy of Arts, and the adjacent Burlington Arcade.

Because the Academy levied works of arts from its member artists, it has a valuable, permanent collection of paintings including those self-selected paintings by Britain's most prominent Academicians, Gainsborough, Turner, Reynolds, Constable, etc.

An unusual and most precious item in the Academy's collection is the Carrara marble *Madonna and Child with the Infant St John* by Michelangelo, one of only four important works by the master sculptor outside of Italy.

The Academy frequently sponsors important exhibitions. One of the most popular is the annual Summer Show of new talent where a thousand prejudged works have been accepted. (Prince Charles showed a painting in 1987.)

At the westernmost end of Piccadilly are the Park Lane and Athenaeum hotels and then the Hard Rock Cafe with long lines out in front where everybody goes to eat a hamburger and buy a T-shirt.

Inside these Mayfair borders you'll discover in less than a square mile the heartland of London Chic. An area of quiet elegance matched by smart shops and established respected inns.

At the core of this reserve are the oh-so-expensive town houses built around green squares and along curvy quiet ribbon-like streets.

This is an easy area to stroll on your own or with a guide. We have done both.

Start at the Green Park tube station and walk west to 94 Piccadilly opposite Green Park. This is the former home of Lord Palmerston who was the prime minister still at age 84. In his prime Palmerston was a lady's man and, once, when visiting Queen Victoria at Windsor a scream came from one of the apartments. It came from a Lady In Waiting. Who was in the room? Palmerston. He had a rendezvous with another Lady in Waiting who had changed rooms but neglected to tell him.

On his death bed, when it was suggested that he was facing his last moment, he loudly protested, "Die? It is the last thing I shall do!"

It was. He did.

Now the Palmerston manor is the Naval and Military Club.

Locally it is known as the In and Out Club because the two gates are prominently marked In and Out.

At one time there were two hundred or so gentlemen's clubs in London. There are forty-nine today. It couldn't be that London is running out of gentlemen. I think the gentlemen are running home to 20th century wives.

At the top of White Horse Street is the beginning of Shepherd Market, the village center of Mayfair. It is a small street lined with shops, especially antique shops and pubs and restaurants. It has a certain reputation for strolling girls at night.

Before turning into Shepherd Market, note next to the Black Sheep shop, the antique store of Denisa the Lady Newborough. She was one of the characters of Shepherd Market. A redhead who spoke fourteen languages, made it as a chorus girl, a pilot, she was a lady of almost every talent.

"The only things I've not been is a spy or a whore, although I have had many opportunities," she was once quoted.

In Paris, rumors had it that she had five admirers at the same time, each being unaware of the others.

Her other famous saying was, "I never believed that jewels or motorcars could be considered vulgar because of their size."

She recently died. What a shame.

The restaurant at the corner of Trebeck Street and Shepherd Street is the Tiddy Dol's Eating House, so named in 1741 after a popular gingerbread man, the king of the itinerant merchants, whose street song had "Tiddy Dols, Tiddy Dols" in its lyrics. The restaurant combines eight small houses.

How expensive is property in Mayfair? At the top of Trebeck Street on Curzon Street is Crewe House which sold a few years ago for £37 million. (The owner wanted £50 million.) Saudia Arabia bought it for its embassy.

One block north and parallel to Curzon is Charles Street and the Chesterfield Hotel. Next door is the hotel's landlord, the English Speaking Union. Not a poor club.

Seeing the club unexpectedly while walking in the area—I had forgotten where it was exactly—brought back a flood of memories. I was attending a celebration dance there on "VJ Day" in 1945 when word spread that the royal family was going to appear on the balcony of Buckingham Palace. We left the dance and ran down the Mall, joining thousands of others and the royal family came out in the floodlights and we all cheered and danced in the streets.

It was a moment of great relief and joy, a turning point towards a new life.

Stop at number 40 on Charles street, at an 18th century house with a wrought-iron fenced entrance, and note the flute shaped piece of iron facing down at an angle.

My Mayfair expert guide explained that this was known as a "link extinguisher" used by a "Link Boy" hired to precede your carriage with a lighted torch. After you were safely indoors, he stuck his torch into the iron flute to put it out.

Another custom in those pre-motoring days if you didn't have your own carriage was to call out "Chair-ho" as you left a host's house.

In time this evolved into the English farewell "Cheerio."

A Link Boy is depicted on a pub sign at a corner of Charles Street and Hays Mews. "The Only Running Footman" sign shows the Link Boy carrying his "wand" a hollow cane which contained a concoction of brandy and egg white to ward off the cold.

Charles Street leads into Berkeley (pronounced *Bawk-leigh)* Square, famous in song for nightingales. The sponsors of a 1953 celebration, desiring to return the lyrical sound of nightingales once again to the Square, first thought of importing the birds then rejected the idea in favor on putting amplified tape recordings of the songbirds in the surrounding plane trees.

(Plane trees, a type of sycamore, are common in London squares because they proved in times past capable of withstanding the terrible air pollution which existed prior to the Clean Air Act of 1956.)

On the west side of the square, the house at number 50, is reputed to be the most haunted house in London. Not just one ghost but several. There are ghosts of a three-year-old child murdered by her governess, a girl who threw herself out of a window, an elderly recluse.

In 1870 two sailors without a place to sleep broke into the house. Later that same evening one ran out babbling, found a policeman and reported he had been approached by some strange mass in the house. They returned to find the sailor's companion impaled on the house fencing.

Clive of India lived on this street.

Farther on, the house at number 44, designed by William Kent, is considered to be the most perfect terrace house in London. It certainly is one of the most moneyed. Upstairs is the Clermont Club, a gambling club, where you can drop £ 50,000 in an afternoon. Downstairs is the famous Annabel's, a disco where Prince Edward gave a prenuptial bachelor party which was invaded by "police."

In fact, the "police" were the Princess of Wales and the to-be-Duchess of York disguised in uniforms.

Zig zag on Hill Street (off the west side of the square) a block north to Farm Street, once famous as the residence of Tallulah Bankhead, the throaty American actress who confessed that she "was as pure as the driven slush." May West had a similar line. She said she was born Snow White—but she drifted.

The Manor House on Farm Street was built in 1757 by the Berkeley family. The original Berkeley stake came from an ancestor who, as standard bearer for Henry VIII, was awarded the land. The family held it until 1940 when they were faced with keeping their London property or selling historic Berkeley Castle.

The family sold the land in town and kept the castle.

(A sordid page in the castle's history was the horrible death of Edward II. Edward II was not a nice king. A known homosexual, his throne was taken away from him by his queen's army and his death was supervised by her lover. It is said that his bowels were burnt out with a red hot iron inserted through a metal horn and his agonized shrieks could be heard in the village. No body scars.)

Across the street is the Church of the Immaculate Conception, famous for its music, and popularly known as "Farm Street." Mass is still said in Latin especially for those Catholic visitors who do not understand English.

When the ushers have passed the collection basket, currency has been received from twenty-seven countries.

A few yards from the church is a pub called The Punchbowl, a political pub where Whigs gathered, the punchbowl being their party symbol.

At the corner of Farm Street, which becomes South Street as it intersects Park Lane, and South Audley Street is the famous china and glass store of T. Goode & Co.

On South Audley is the Grosvenor Chapel, frequented by American servicemen during the war. From Park Lane it looks exactly like a New England church.

The street takes its name from Sir Hugh Audley, a major landowner in the 1660's. He built the Manor Ebury in a then remote area which, today, is Belgravia.

His heir, Mary, was engaged at age seven by her mother to a Berkeley, an engagement which was broken. She became the wife, at age twelve, of a Grosvenor.

Thomas G Grosvenor and Mary had three sons and the family developed land in Mayfair in 1730, Belgravia in 1826 and Pimlico in 1850.

The oldest Grosvenor now (he's a young man) is the 6th Duke of Westminster and is considered the wealthiest man in England. He owns some 300 prime acres of London. His income several years ago was estimated to be some £11,000 *per hour*.

South Audley leads into Grosvenor Square dominated by the blocklong United States Embassy. The American government tried to buy the land from the Duke of Westminster who agreed to trade it for the 12,000 acres the family lost to the colonies in Florida. When it was found that part of the 12,000 acres included a section of downtown Miami, the trade was forgotten.

The 35-foot eagle atop the Embassy represents a terrible gaffe. The eagle's head faces the arrows of war instead of the symbols of peace.

A statue of Franklin D Roosevelt stands in the square. The money for the statue was raised by five-shilling donations requiring 200,000 subscriptions. The money was raised in 24 hours.

In May, 1986, Prime Minister Margaret Thatcher unveiled another memorial to the Eagle Squadron, the volunteer fighter pilots who joined the RAF before America entered the war.

John Adams, the second president of the United States, lived at No. 9 Grosvenor Square when he was "minister plenipotentuary" or, effectually, the ambassador to Britain. The house, one of the few original still standing, has been extensively remodeled. He was remembered for his definition of diplomacy: "having the ability to tell a person to go to hell in such a manner that he would look forward to the journey."

The Britannia Hotel and a second Canada House face the square, the latter to ease the burden on the Canada House at Trafalgar Square.

Around the corner from Grosvenor Square on Carlos Place is the luxurious Connaught Hotel with perhaps the best hotel restaurant in London. Terribly expensive.

Across the street is Allen, said to be the best butcher in London (no posted prices) and next to it, John Baily, the best poulters.

John Wayne bought his sausages at Allen's.

If you then cut across the top of Berkeley Square, you reach Bruton Street where, at number 17, once stood the townhouse of the Earl of Strathmore. Here his daughter, the Duchess of York, gave birth to Elizabeth Alexander Mary. When Edward VIII abdicated, her father became George VI and she, in turn, was crowned Elizabeth II.

The townhouse has been replaced by an apartment house but a plaque marks the significance of the location.

Bruton Street leads into New Bond Street, home of Asprey, the jewelers who have expanded around the corner to Grafton Street in a house once occupied by Lord Cornwallis—he who surrendered to George Washington.

Grafton Street melds into Dover Street, and leads to Browns Hotel . . and, morning coffee, afternoon tea or lunch. You should.

A butler for Lord Byron, James Brown, established a house where "a gentleman could feel comfortable." The hotel became internationally famous. Mark Twain, Alexander Bell, Kipling, Theodore Roosevelt, all of the above and hundreds of other statesmen and celebrities have stayed there. Richard Widmark, the actor, said he could never feel that he had been to London unless he had tea at Browns. You still can. Coat and tie and about £ 8. You get more than one cup of tea and platters of sweets and sandwiches.

At the corner of Dover and Piccadilly is a sculpture of a horse and a bald, naked male rider by a popular sculptress, Elizabeth Frink. She called it Horse and Rider. Others call it "London's Kojak." An American suggested that it be called "Lord Godiva."

My walking tour of Marvelous Mayfair ended here.

There are various alternatives.

You are in the shoppers' Garden of Eden, the rich shoppers that is. New Bond Street is a couple of short hops east (women), Savile Row (men), the Burlington Arcade (both).

Or, behind the Arcade a step or two right is another exquisite British Museum outpost, the Museum of Mankind.

Or, there's the Ritz across the street with one of the ritziest bars in town. But don't try to go in jeans. A friend of ours, so clad, was turned away from even entering the lobby.

"And they were *designer* jeans," she wailed.

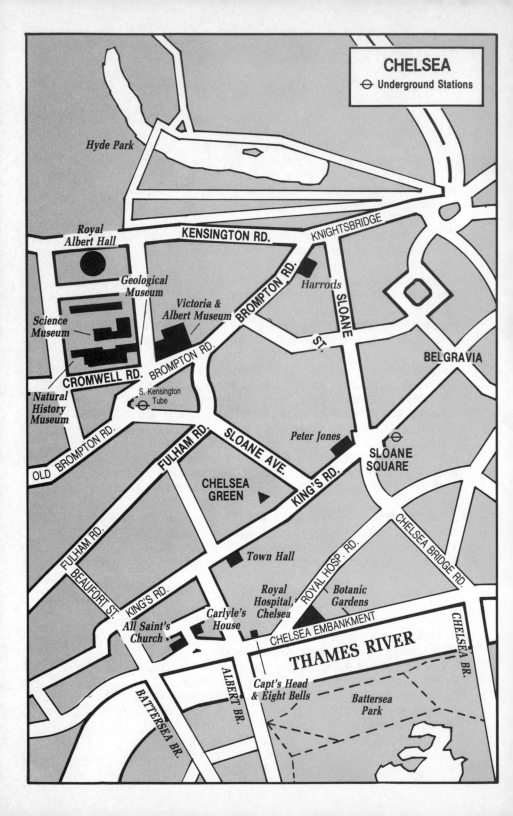

North of the River, South of the Park

6. Chelsea and The Neighborhood

Belgravia, south of Hyde Park Corner, is where newborn Rolls Royce limousines go to nurse.

This quiet corner of titled wealth started back in 1826 when Earl Grosvenor, the owner of the land, obtained a Parliamentary permit to build a square surrounded with terraced houses.

Unfortunately the soil was unstable damp clay. To provide a firmer foundation, landfill was brought from the excavation of St Katherine's Dock. The clay, made into bricks, was used in the buildings.

Twenty-three different mansions were completed around the square, each resting on the pillars of society. The Duke of Bedford at No. 15, the Earl of Essex at No. 9. Queen Victoria rented No. 36 for her mother, the Duchess of Kent, while Kensington Palace was under repair. Earl Grey sipped his tea at No. 30, the Earl of Pembroke slept at No. 6, Earl Beauchamp, no reason to be superstitious, chose No. 13. And so went the illustrious lot.

For good reason this was the theme location of the popular TV series *Upstairs, Downstairs.*

No. 40 is the location site for the filming of *Poor Little Rich Girl* tracing the life of Barbara Hutton, the Woolworth heiress. The house with large ballroom and grand staircase is on the market for £ 3.5 million if you'd like to buy it.

Today the square is occupied mostly by embassies and association offices but the surrounding area of Belgravia is still pretty, rich, residential and dull to walk through.

Farther along the south side of Hyde Park one enters Knightsbridge which is dominated by shops, hotels, and restaurants. Beyond Knighstbridge is Kensington featuring the multiple buildings of "Albertropolis" which houses The Royal Albert Hall, the Victoria and Albert Museum, the Natural History Museum, the Science Museum and the Geological Museum.

Between the river and Kensington is Chelsea with its umbilical cord, the King's Road. The area is wild, crummy, elegant, desirable.

This is the land of the Sloane Ranger, characteristically slim, long-legged, usually blond. She is recognized by the way she swishes her mane haughtily. She and her companions, the Hooray Henrys and Champagne Charlies, are the long established but non-titled daughters and sons of The Established.

To this bowl of social cream has been added a strong dollop of the newly upward mobile professionals, the Yuppies, with their smart cars and dashing clothes, and their married companions, the Dinkies, the double-income-no-kids couples.

Not all of Chelsea's colorful characters necessarily live in the district proper. They have visiting privileges. Especially on Saturdays.

You have to walk King's Road on a Saturday.

The Sloane Ranger set and the Cloned Sloanes will be there doing weekend shopping chores. So will the metal-studded, black-leathered bizarre punks with mohawk haircuts in rainbow colors, along with the young and exuberant with either crimped or washing machine hairdos, shirts down to their knees and skirts up to their navels. Jeans with gapping slashes are big too. Oh, it is lovely.

Action centers around window shopping the mod boutiques, sipping at pubs, rubbing against each other like the friendly dolphins at the Natural Science Museum.

In quaint contrast are the military pensioners from nearby Royal Hospital, Chelsea in their black uniforms—red on holidays—and military caps.

For all its chic raunchiness, Chelsea has the historic players for street drama.

Four centuries ago Chelsea was known as a "Village of Palaces."

Thomas More, the "Man for All Seasons," built a country house on the northern bank of the Thames. So did the Earl of Shrewsbury, the Duke of Norfolk.

From his country house Chancellor More sailed down the Thames to the Tower of London and his execution for refusing to condone Henry VIII's divorce from his first wife.

"I am the King's good servant, but God's first," were More's last words.

Here Henry VIII built a riverside mansion where Queen Elizabeth I spent her childhood under the care of Catherine Parr, the sixth and last wife.

King's Road originally was a farmers' lane, a track over which produce and flowers were transported to the palace.

Officially, its first kingly use was as Charles II's overland route to Hampton Court and George III's favorite route to Kew. Hence, King's Road. It remained a royal private road until 1830.

After the road became public, it was to provide premises for many enterprising merchants and manufacturers including No. 120 occupied by the firm of Thomas Crapper, known for its dependable water closets.

Just off the road facing the river, Charles II, a good king, though not slavish to his duties, built a hospital for war veterans, the Royal Hospital, it is said but not proven, at the suggestion of one of his mistresses, pretty, witty Nell Gwynn. Upright pubs and respectable apartment buildings remember her name in the area if not her basic prone profession.

In the 19th century Chelsea had a Bohemian reputation being the home for the art and literary set. As you weave in and out of the streets between King's Road and the river you'll find charming cottages tucked away in small alleys and quiet streets, terrace houses wearing the distinguished Blue Plaque bearing the name and date of a famous occupant: Oscar Wilde, Henry Fielding, Tobias Smollett, Ellen Terry, Henry James, George Eliot.

If your high school English literature classes included works by Thomas Carlyle, you have to stop in at No. 24 Cheyne Row where the renowned historian, essayist, author lived for nearly fifty years. He died there in 1881.

Since 1985 the house has been a National Trust home, open to visitors as a memorial to the "Bard of Chelsea." The rarity of the

Carlyle house is its authenticity. Inspect the painting by the fireplace in the downstairs parlor, a portrait of the room painted at the time of his occupancy. Then look around you to see the same furnishings still in their same places. His favorite chair by the fire, the piano in the corner, a desk over there . . . everything still as it was. Rare indeed.

The drawing room, the parlor, the dining room, the downstairs kitchen, all are fully furnished with Carlyle tastes. He penned his tomes in an attic workshop converted to keep out street noises. Light lost from double walling the windows was replaced by a skylight, beneath which is his adjustable top desk.

Besides being the birthplace for many famous literary works, the Carlyle home was the gathering place for the famous literati of the time, Wordsworth, Emerson, Dickens, Tennyson, Thackeray.

Chopin came and played the piano in the parlor. The same piano.

Every room had a fireplace which triggered a dim memory. Wasn't one of his manuscripts, not yet published, accidentally burned by a careless maid?

"No," said the keeper of the house.

"It is said that the manuscript was given to John Stuart Mill to read and that *his* maid burned the papers. But it might have been Mill's girlfriend, later his wife, who was terribly jealous of Carlyle."

In the house are many pictures of Carlyle, a handsome man, and a few of his wife, Jane Baille Welsh, a learned lady, who knew Latin at the age of five, who married the stonemason's son.

She thrived on all the company.

He preferred to smoke a pipe in the downstairs kitchen.

They differed. They fought. But their letters, when apart, were full of warmth of feeling for each other. She was a gifted writer.

"Why didn't she write professionally?" we asked.

"He wouldn't let her," we were told.

"No wonder they fought," said the Lady Navigator.

After leaving the house, walk up Cheyne Row to the river where you'll find a great pub, the King's Head and Eight Bells. Buy a pint, cross the street to the swath of green facing the river and you'll find a statue of Thomas Carlyle.

As you enjoy the view of the river—ignore the traffic whizzing by—think on earlier patrons of the pub. Originally it offered separate bars for officers—the King's Head—and for crew—the Eight Bells.

Nell Gwynn once lived behind the pub. She was a favorite among the officers before she captured the king's eye.

James McNeil Whistler, the famous American painter, lived around the corner on Tite Street. He frequented the pub and his famous nocturnes of the Thames were painted here on the river-bank.

The Chelsea Old Church (All Saints), less than two blocks upriver, has an even longer lineage. Originally a Norman church, it was rebuilt in 1528 by Sir Thomas More as his private chapel.

Chelsea Old Church is a pleasant place to visit. When it is open, there is usually a lady of the parish on duty to answer questions and show people around. Mrs. Jean Evisan made my visit that much more absorbing.

The church was blown apart in the war but its pieces painstak-ingly reassembled, including two carved columns attributed to Holbein. There is a tomb in the church which was intended for More, but it is empty.

What happened to the corpse is not known but Margaret, his favorite daughter, took her father's head to her husband's estate in Canterbury where it was interred in a local church.

Outside, at the spot where he sat waiting to be taken to the Tower and where he last saw his family, is the seated statue of Thomas More. The figure bears the chain of the chancellor in his lap. The signature below it is said to be a reproduction of More's own.

Between the pub and the church at Nos. 19-26 was the Chelsea Palace built as a riverside resting place for Henry VIII. Its seventeen chambers were served by three kitchens, three cellars and three drawing rooms. Water was piped in from Kensington.

The house was demolished in 1753. An off-street plaque marks the spot.

In the fence corner of the Chelsea Old Church churchyard next to the sidewalk is an urn-shaped memorial to Dr. Hans Sloane whose collection of books, minerals and art was the cornerstone of the British Museum.

Come look at another of his notable efforts.

Backtrack downstream from the pub and the Carlyle statue to the junction of Cheyne Walk and Royal Hospital Road. Behind that sturdy wall is the Physic Garden (sometimes called the Botanic Gardens), a most remarkable place.

Do you know that the South Sea cotton in your shirt could well have originated in this garden?

And the tea that you drink?

And the quinine in your gin/vodka and tonic?

And the rubber on your car tires or tyres?

Founded in 1673 by the Worshipful Society of Apothecaries of London on land leased in perpetuity from Dr. Sloane, the scientific gardens have led botanical research for over 300 years.

The gardens are open to the public from late April to late October. We were the first people through the gates that Sunday in mid-April . . . and froze. England had had a bitter winter and there wasn't a leaf on a tree.

"Come back in a month," said Mrs. Morris, a volunteer in the garden.

We noted the Rock Garden, built in 1772, one of the first rock gardens created in England. It was built of stone brought from Iceland and, later, from sections of the Tower of London which was being partially demolished at the time.

Entrance is from Swan Walk, the connecting street between Embankment and Royal Hospital Road. A small admission fee.

Continuing downriver, opposite the Chelsea Bridge is the Royal Hospital. Some 400 army pensioners occupy the Wren-designed buildings in spacious grounds facing the river.

Open from 10 to noon, and from 2 to 4PM, the Chapel and Great Hall are interesting stops. A statue of benefactor Charles II by Grinling Gibbons faces the Chapel and Great Hall, classic rooms in classical buildings.

On the entrance wall to the grounds a plaque tells of two bombings of the Northeast wing. A 500-pound German bomb first destroyed it on February 16, 1918. Loss of five lives. The hospital was again hit 37 years later by a German V2. Loss of five lives. The plaque memorializes the reopening of the building in 1961.

"Do you see the insult?"

One of the passing pensioners asked in a friendly gesture. We reread the plaque and couldn't find any affront.

"You see, Harold Wilson was the prime minister and he had politicked to change the hospital into a school of some kind. So the plaque acknowledges the presence of the Prime Minister but, pointedly, leaves off his name."

The rod-straight pensioner shared more background.

"We think that the Germans kept bombing the hospital because they thought it was Buckingham Palace. Big building near the bend in the river. Bombs away. Pigeons seem to have the same idea."

A small museum across from the entrance to the Great Hall and Chapel features medals and uniforms and old pictures. Strong emphasis on Waterloo and Wellington. The regimental colors of a New York regiment captured on the Canadian border during the war of 1812. Three small pictures of Nell Gwynn. Under one picture is a caption saying that it was known that she was a generous woman but there was no way she was responsible for the Royal Hospital.

The idea for the hospital was modeled after the Hotel des Invalides in Paris and was suggested to Charles II in 1681 by Sir James Fox.

Maybe it was a pillow-suggested vote of confidence that made it happen. "Hey, Charlie, that's not a bad idea."

How would the museum know about that?

Adjacent to the grounds are the Ranelagh Gardens, site of the social and colorful Chelsea Flower Show, a late May event of the Royal Botanical Society which has been held here since 1913. (See Chapter 15. Highlight Events.)

The belly-button of Chelsea is Sloane Square where there is a tube station, Royal Court Theatre, Royal Court Hotel, the Peter Jones department store, banks, boutiques and bistros, and a W H Smith bookstore.

A stroll in any direction from the Square yields pubs and restaurants, shops and parks that dot the district.

King's Road is to the west with the punks, pensioners, Sloane Rangers, pubs and boutiques.

The road north is Sloane Street leading to Knightsbridge and Harrods. East takes you into residential Belgravia, south to Pimlico which is bisected by Ebury Street, a quiet street a block from nerve-racking Victoria Station. The once residential-only street now is given to bed-and-breakfast or small hotel operations.

The main attraction of Ebury Street is the line of outstanding restaurants, French, Italian and Chinese.

Every street takes you to some sort of excitement.

That's Chelsea.

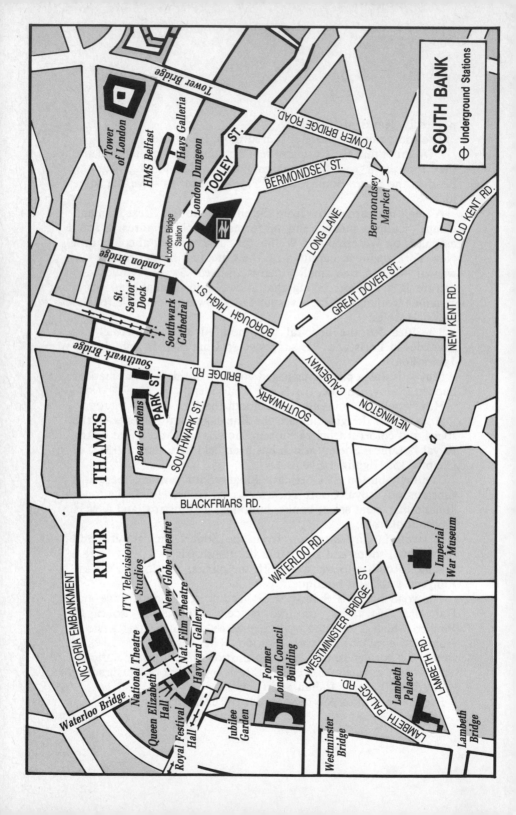

The Coming Area

7. South Bank

What until very recently were decrepit wharves and warehouses is rapidly becoming a bright spot along the London riverscape.

A revitalized South Bank is in the making.

Starting at the Tower Bridge, walk the riverbank with us to Westminster Bridge and hand pick your feast from a smorgasbord of goodies.

1. Inspect a British naval vessel.
2. Experience the newest shopping attraction in London.
3. Shudder and shriek at the horrors of a recreated dungeon.
4. Listen to the sound of music in a church where Shakespeare's brother is buried.
5. See where Shakespeare's Globe Theatre used to be.
6. See where the recreated Globe Theatre will be.
7. Have a pint in an historic pub.
8. Learn about 17th century theater in a museum, formerly a bear-and-bull baiting pit.
9. Stroll on the wide esplanade of the Queen's Walk.
10. Take in a play at the National Theatre.
11. Take in a film at the National Film Theatre.
12. Visit an art gallery or current exhibition or listen to the London Symphony at the Royal Festival Hall.
13. Shop for a used book at a riverbank open market.
14. Catch a nap in a park.

The first stop on the list is *HMS Belfast* moored on the south bank of the Thames. Open seven days a week from 11AM, the majestic old cruiser saw battle during World War II. Seven decks are open to the public and it is a great place to take kids and let them work off youthful steam as they get an idea of life at sea.

A few yards away from the gangplank is the very new Hays Galleria, an architectural triumph and a nucleus for attracting shoppers and diners to the South Bank. The five-story building is U-shaped, the open side facing the river. Under its high arched glass roof is a spacious piazza surrounded by smart boutiques, souvenir shops, restaurants and cafes.

The best of the Hays Galleria—and you mustn't miss it—is the hilariously funny, joyful fountain in the middle of the piazza.

It is a satirical naval vessel (*HMS Bombast?*) with water spouting out of various parts, sidewheels turning, metal paddles occasionally rowing, a whirling globe mounted overhead, and a rotating searchlight(?) radar(?) on the mast. In the rear of the ship are two cockhatted admirals.

The comic fountain has to be the work of Jean Tinguely or a fellow brother genius/madman who is just as creative.

Carts laden with goodies to eat and souvenirs to buy encircle the fountain.

We were in the square before its official opening in September 1987 and asked a security guard who had created the fountain.

He hurumphed: "It wasn't an Englishman I can tell yer!"

He was wrong. We returned a month later to find the fountain named "The Navigators" and the name of the architect/sculptor: David Kemp. Watch the people as they approach the fountain, break into smiles, laugh and point to this and that delight and share the fantasy.

The Hays backs into Tooley Street and almost the front door of the London Dungeon.

Beware. This is not for the faint of heart. This is for screamers. Teen-agers love it and throng around the entrance. I don't need it. The object of the dungeon exhibits is to make you gasp with horror . . . gleefully.

A series of tableaux exploit the cruelest of torture. Racks, hot irons—that sort of thing—in addition to witchcraft and fiendish punishments. If that doesn't touch you, how about some early surgery?

The London Dungeon is open daily. There's a charge of course. They would have to pay me.

Across London Bridge Road, tucked down behind the entrance to the bridge and under the railway embankment is the surviving Southwark Cathedral, one of London's most famous churches. Formally, it is the Cathedral Church of St Saviour and St Mary Overie (a mangled contraction of "over the water"). I came onto the church at noon in time to hear the sweetness of a girl's choir singing before the high altar. Later I learned that during each lunchtime there is a musical event to refresh the workers in the area. Organ recitals or instrumental music or choirs. Lovely.

The church has several interesting features including a carved alabaster figure of Shakespeare (Edmund, his brother is buried in the church). There is a chapel dedicated to John Harvard, founder of Harvard University, who was born in the parish.

Around the corner from the cathedral is Pickford's Wharf and St Saviour's Dock where a top sail schooner, the *Kathleen & Mary,* is moored. The 98-foot-long ship is open for inspection.

The dock dates back to the 16th century and was "a free landing place for parishioners who were entitled to land goods free of toll."

Adjacent is the Old Thameside Inn where I had a warm pint of bitter and a roast *gristle* sandwich also, I think, from the 16th century.

If you continue along the river, you'll be on Clink Street—"going to the Clink"—which used to lead to the Clink Prison. The Clink, one of five Southwark prisons, was for those "who break the peace in the brothelhouses."

You then come to the Anchor Inn with a new upmarket outside pavilion overlooking the river. The Anchor is an 18th century pub with old oak beams and concealed caves for hiding fugitives who had escaped from Clink Prison. Look for the collection of Elizabethan memorabilia in the bar found during renovations.

Continuing along the river, cross over the Southwark Bridge, walk down a grubby riverbank road to Bear Street. Note around the corner from the Thames riverbank the space created in the wall for ferrymen of yore to rest. The seat has a hole in the bottom so they could discreetly relieve themselves.

Turn south on Bear Street to the Bear Gardens Museum, formerly the Hope Playhouse from 1614 to 1656.

A long, long time ago, before its theatrical career, the site had been a bear-and-bull-baiting ring. Animals were matched against vicious hunting dogs. Elizabeth I brought visiting French and

Spanish ambassadors to the ring, it is recorded. Pepys reported that he "saw some good sport of the bulls tossing the dogs, one into the very boxes."

At the entry to the museum you learn about the earlier characteristics of this area called Bankside.

An extension of the entertainment district, its specialities were "stewhouses" (bathhouses). "Stews" of Shakespeare's time were the prostitutes who occupied premises owned by the Bishop of Winchester. The women were known as Winchester Geese.

The most celebrated Elizabethan brothel belonged to Dame Britannica Holland whose prices for pleasure rose as high as £ 5, a fortune.

The best part of the museum for us was the light it sheds on the origin and progression of theater. Street players—minstrels—were its genesis. They performed from elaborate carts.

The first known theatrical structure, called simply The Theatre, was built in Shoreditch, later disassembled and rebuilt as The Globe in Bankside. Its competition were the Curtain Theatre, then the Rose, named after a brothel and closed by the plague, and the Swan, also named after a brothel.

The Globe burned down when its thatch roof was set on fire by two cannons fired during a performance of King Henry VIII. Our knowledge today of the Shakespearean plays could possibly be due to the alertness of a thinking man who saved the unpublished Shakespeare manuscripts from the basement of the burning theater.

By the time The Globe was rebuilt with the help of a royal grant —and with a tile roof—Shakespeare had retired to his family at Stratford-on-Avon.

On Park Street behind Bear Gardens a commemorative plaque bearing a Shakespeare bas-relief claims this the site of the old Globe.

Behind the Founder's Arm pub is the Bankside Gallery, home to two royal artistic societies: the Royal Society of Etchers & Engravers and the Royal Society of Painters In Watercolors. Most of the year there is an exhibition of members' works. Twice annually Bankside presents an open juried show. Talent is strong; prices fair.

Queen Elizabeth II broke ground for the recreation of The Globe Theatre in July, 1987 on a riverfront site less than two hundred yards away from the original Globe. It will be an authentic full-scale replica of the open-air enclosed Shakespearean stage, complete with courtyard and balconies. Additionally, an indoor theater, shop, pub/restaurant and cinema will be included. It is a major step in the new Southbank progress and owes its existence to the energies of American actor-director Sam Wanamaker.

Bankside leads toward the Blackfriars Bridge where you can walk on Upper Ground Street until you reach the imposing studios of ITV. Here you can cut back to the river and Queen's Walk, the broad, decorative esplanade along the riverfront extending from the ITV building to Westminster Bridge.

Note along the walk the elaborate iron work in the dolphin-wrapped lamp posts dated 1980 E(II)R.

The pleasant walk is handsomely paved. Frequent benches entice you to sit and enjoy the vista across and up the river.

At the beginning of Queen's Walk you stand before the National Theatre. Upon its three stages you see the finest theater that England has to offer. The National Theatre Company stages a wide variety of plays in repertory including superior Shakespearean productions in the NT's Olivier, Lyttelton and Cottesloe theaters.

Free foyer entertainment precedes most performances. Tours of the building, including backstage and workshops, are available.

Part of this complex of visual arts is the National Film Theatre. It was conceived as part of the Festival of Britain and later moved into permanent quarters here. Over 50,000 members support the Film Theatre, its latest in cinematic techniques, and its annual London Film Festival.

The Film Theatre's indoor-outdoor cafe fronts the river. Live entertainment is standard outdoor fare in the summertime.

By the river are open stalls where you can browse through secondhand books and prints.

Beyond Waterloo Bridge is the site of the Royal Festival Hall, the Queen Elizabeth Hall and the Hayward Gallery. The rejuvenation of the South Bank started in 1951 when a beat and battered nation showed its pride with a grand anti-austerity fair called the Festival of Britain, one hundred years after the Great Exhibition in Hyde Park.

Situated on a war-derelict site, one of the major buildings for the Festival was the Royal Festival Hall.

Ten years after the Festival a second phase of buildings for artistic presentations was added next door, the Queen Elizabeth Hall and the Hayward Gallery.

A decade later the third phase was completed, the National Theatre and the National Film Theatre.

The entire complex is now known as the South Bank Arts Centre.

The Royal Festival Hall, built to seat 3,000 people, is used for symphonies, ballets, even films.

I went there one Sunday and found people spread around upper level foyers enjoying picnics. I didn't have the nerve to ask if they always came to the theater to picnic but later we realized that eating and drinking is an essential ingredient of English summer occasions.

Picnic baskets and Pimm's, strawberries and cream, champagne and canapes make it happen.

The Queen Elizabeth Hall is sited by the river next to the Waterloo Bridge, the Hayward Gallery behind it. The Hall's main auditorium has a seating capacity of 1,100 and is used for smaller concerts with an adjacent Purcell Room available for chamber music and intimate soloist concerts.

The Hayward Gallery shows major works of artists in changing exhibits arranged by the Arts Council.

Between the Royal Festival hall and Westminster Bridge is Jubilee Park, a nice open green just perfect for a riverside picnic or a quiet nap in the sun. The last time we were there it was swarming with musical group contenders in a radio sponsored contest. Jumping. Throbbing. No place for a siesta.

The huge empty building facing the river just east of Westminster Bridge housed the Greater London Council until the organization was dissolved. The building is now for sale with an asking price of £ 350 million.

If projection holds, the future will see more and more visitors to London finding their way to the South Bank area. And as their numbers grow, even the hulking white elephant of the former Greater London Council building will find a new, functional use.

(If you do nothing else, take the tube to the London Bridge station and go see our favorite fountain "The Navigators" at the Hays Galleria. It is such a pleasure.)

8. The Mighty Thames

Without the Thames there wouldn't be a London.

When the third and last ice cap retreated, the draining water left a channel from the middle of England to the southeast exit at the spreading Thames Estuary.

The water's exit was an entrance for the first hunters and fishermen who had sailed from the rivers of the Rhine to this very distant river mouth.

To them the river provided water to drink and fish to eat. Exploring upriver, the initial invaders found plentiful game to hunt and land fertile to farm. The river provided the means of importing domesticated animals and seed corn and for the easiest transportation within the country.

In times of invasion, the river presented an important barrier, difficult for unfriendly tribes to cross. When Caesar crossed the waters, he called the river *Tamesis* although the root of the name is obscure.

After the Romans conquered all of England, meaning both sides

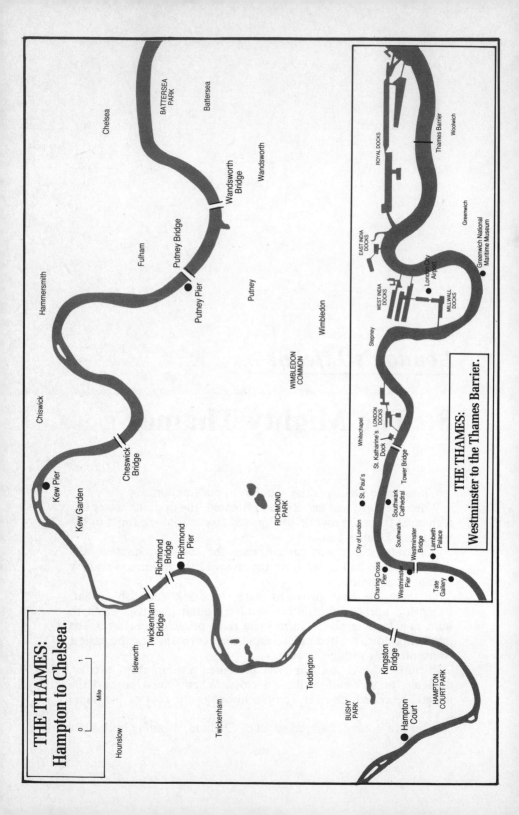

**THE THAMES:
Hampton to Chelsea.**

0   1
Mile

Hounslow

Isleworth

Twickenham

Teddington

BUSHY PARK

Hampton Court

HAMPTON COURT PARK

Kingston Bridge

Twickenham Bridge

Richmond Bridge

Richmond Pier

RICHMOND PARK

Kew Pier

Kew Garden

Cheswick Bridge

Chiswick

Hammersmith

Fulham

Putney Pier

Putney Bridge

Wandsworth Bridge

Wandsworth

Putney

Wimbledon

WIMBLEDON COMMON

Chelsea

BATTERSEA PARK

Battersea

**THE THAMES:
Westminster to the Thames Barrier.**

Charing Cross Pier

City of London

St. Paul's

Whitechapel

Southwark

Southwark Cathedral

Westminster Pier

Westminster Bridge

Lambeth Palace

Tate Gallery

St. Katharine's Dock

LONDON DOCKS

Tower Bridge

Stepney

WEST INDIA DOCKS

EAST INDIA DOCKS

London City Airport

MILLWALL DOCKS

ROYAL DOCKS

Thames Barrier

Woolwich

Greenwich

Greenwich National Maritime Museum

of the river, the Thames became the most important artery for trade and commerce.

As England grew in population and power, it found much of its prosperity thanks to its fleets, commercial and military, centered around the Thames from which explorers sailed to find new commercial possibilities, and from where the Royal Navy sailed to protect the colonies and the trade routes.

The London docks became the heart of the country. Imported raw goods flowed in and manufactured articles flowed out.

London on the Thames became the greatest city in the world.

There is a dark side to the River Thames. Floods.

The history of London flooding was first documented in the Anglo-Saxon Chronicle of 1099. But flooding has been repeated again and again over the years. Westminster Hall has been made successively a rowing pond in 1237, a place entered only on horses in 1242, a fish pond in 1579, a watery grave for 14 people in 1924. The 1953 flood cost 300 lives.

An increasing volume of ocean water from melting polar ice caps, the sinking of the south coast of England by a foot a century and the vulnerability of London's clay bed foundation, all are elements that add up to potential disaster.

If a flood hit London today, drowning its underground subway system, its infrastructure of electrical, gas and sewerage systems would go. The chaos and the cost of rebuilding are incalculable.

Solution to this problem was a £500 million project consisting of a series of steel gates as high as a five-story building at Woolwich which can pivot at 90-degree angles to dam the waters of the Thames during a dangerous tidal period.

A remarkable engineering achievement.

The brochure calls it "The Eighth Wonder of the World."

You can visit the Thames Barrier by train, bus or boat.

There is a bright side of the River Thames. You can explore and enjoy the river.

You can take launches to Greenwich and on to the Thames Barrier.

You can go upstream to Kew Gardens and farther along to Hampton Court.

You can hire individual river boats and poke along the Thames and the many canals that connect the river with the rest of the country.

Greenwich

If you only get out of Central London once, make it Greenwich where every new day begins with Greenwich Mean Time.

You can go by train, by bus or swim down river.

By boat, even though it could be a depressing tub—but a tub with a bar—you have the advantages of seeing London, and taking pictures from less cluttered and different angles. Boats leave from Westminster and the Charing Cross piers frequently. The Embankment tube stop is directly across from Charing Cross Pier.

You get a fine perspective of the scope of the South Bank Arts Centre, that compound incorporating the Royal Festival Hall, the National Theatre, Queen Elizabeth Hall, Hayward Gallery, and the National Film Theatre.

Directly across from the Arts Centre, you see the majesty of Somerset House and Unilever House . . . beyond, the Temple Bar which separates the City of Westminster from the City of London. All entries to the City of London are marked by statues of lions.

There is a splendid if brief view of St Paul's between two buildings, but you have to be fast with your camera to trap it on film.

The guide from the bridge may point out the house directly across the river from St Paul's where Christopher Wren lived while the cathedral was being built.

Shortly thereafter you'll catch a clean view of the Southwark Cathedral on the South bank if your eye is quick enough.

You won't miss the towering magnificence of Hays Galleria.

The Tower of London is considerate of photographers. They have clearly labeled the Traitors' Gate for the convenience of cameramen.

From the river you get a glimpse of riverside pubs you'd enjoy, the Samuel Pepys, the Anchor at Bankside, the Mayfair, the Prospect of Whitby.

The trip takes an hour including a stop at the Tower of London.

A hat is passed at this time for the crew in appreciation for a garbled public speaker announcing the sights you pass, most of which is incomprehensible.

Mercifully there are no other sightseeing messages between the Tower of London and Greenwich.

The menu for visiting Greenwich includes:
1. Visiting the famous clipper ship, the *Cutty Sark,* in drydock at riverside.
2. Going to the National Maritime Museum.
3. Climbing the hill to the Old Royal Observatory.
4. Visiting the Royal Naval College.
5. Taking a boat a half an hour down river to the Thames Barrier.

In a full day, if you go and return by boat, you can squeeze in three courses of the menu with relative ease. All, if you taste and run.

An alternative is to return to London by train or bus at a later hour, giving you more time in Greenwich.

We opt first for the *Cutty Sark.* The admission ticket also allowed us to inspect the nearby *Gipsy Moth IV,* the 53-foot ketch in which the late Sir Francis Chichester, a very senior citizen, thrilled the sporting world by circumnavigating the world alone in 1966-67.

The story of the graceful *Cutty Sark* and her times and trade are told in text and pictures in panels on the entry deck.

She was built in Dumbarton of teak and Oregon pine in 1869 for "Whitehat" John Willis. Her lines were sleek and graceful, built for speed because she was to sail the China tea trade routes on which there was fierce competition. To be the first to reach the London market with the new season's tea meant big bonuses for everyone. Most especially, it meant prestige.

Her best single day run, with 14 acres of sail set, was 363 miles.

She carried a crew of 28 men and officers whose rations were a cask of beef and a cask of port every two weeks.

The Scottish name comes from a charming legend used by Robert Burns in *Tam O'Shanter.*

Tam sees a clutch of witches dancing and calls Nannie, one of the witches, "Cutty Sark" for the short (*cutty*) shift or chemise (*sark*) she was wearing. She chases after Tam but he crosses a bridge before she can catch him. Witches, you know, cannot cross water, but she manages to grasp his horse's tail and pulls it out.

The ship's womanly figurehead, Nannie, is mounted nearby appearing as when the ship was in port, a horse's tail in her hand.

The opening of the Suez Canal ended the era of proud sailing ships. *Cutty Sark* carried her last cargo of tea in 1877 as steamships took over. She became a wool freighter between Australia and England and then was sold to a Portuguese owner who sailed her as *El Pequina Camisola* for 27 years.

She reverted to the English flag in 1922 and transferred to dry dock in Greenwich in 1955.

Have you ever secretly wanted to own a ship's handsomely carved figurehead?

In the lower hold is a marvelous collection. We counted over fifty. The oldest, The Golden Cherubs, vintage 1660, is attributed to the noted English carver, Grinling Gibbons.

Walking through town, then east in front of the Dreadnought Seaman's Hospital brings you to the National Maritime Museum.

Most captivating.

The graceful Georgian buildings set in Greenwich Park are so lovely. In the middle of the complex is the Queen's House, an elegant Palladian villa built to the design of Inigo Jones in the 16th century that conveyed a sense of style never known before in England. On either side, like impressive jewelry settings, are the West and East wings of the Maritime Museum.

The mezzanine floor of the west wing traces the historical story of the British navy from the time of Captain Cook's legendary three voyages in the Pacific through the death of Nelson at Trafalgar.

Heady stuff.

Having written eight books on the Pacific and belonging to the "Cook Groupies" we hastened to the James Cook rooms where our appetites were appeased with several original items.

Three were paintings, two of which any decent Cook Groupie has seen often: *Poedooa,* Weber's sensual painting of a 19-year-old Tahitian princess of Raiatea and Dance's portrait of the famous navigator. Both are included in every book about Cook. But these are the *originals.*

A recently discovered painting acquired by the museum is by William Hodges. It is interesting because Hodges sailed with Cook on his second voyage and had a chance to know the master well. It is less studied than the Dance portrait and, in its way, shows more of Cook's character.

Cook was famous first as a surveyor. His initial expedition to Tahiti was to measure the transit of Venus before the sun. In the

Cook rooms is a model of a canvas astronomical tent used by Cook's crew for that purpose along with the astronomical clock that accompanied Cook on his three voyages. It still keeps time. There, too, is the Georgian reflecting telescope and a portable three-and-and-a-half-foot transit astronomical quadrant used to measure the transit of Venus.

The original observatory was built of wood but on subsequent voyages Cook carried a collapsible tent held up by a wooden tripod. The whole affair collapsed into a box slightly longer than six feet.

Tasman, who discovered New Zealand, navigated and surveyed by log and dead reckoning. On Cook's first voyage his position was determined by lunar distance and the National Almanac. On his second and third voyages he used marine chronometers. Navigators today depend on radio time signals.

A mezzanine exhibit details the naval involvement with the convict colonization of Australia. The human inventory carried by one of the six ships in the First Fleet to Australia is recorded in the ship's record on exhibit. Typical of its entries is:

"Mary Ellis, age: 37. Occupation: housewife. Crime: stealing a mug. Prior convictions: none. Sentence: 7 years."

The British naval involvement in the war with America and in the French Revolution are detailed in other rooms but the best exhibits, for us, are devoted to the greatest hero of the British Navy, Horatio Nelson.

Here one finds a picture of Emma, the famous Lady Hamilton, painted by George Romney, who was, what the London newspapers would call today, a fun-loving girl.

Emma, a beauty, was a central character is a soap opera that had her in a torrid romance with the Admiral, bearing his firstborn while she and Lord Hamilton and Nelson remained close friends. When Nelson was killed, she was ignored and eventually died in poverty in Paris.

Here is a setting of furniture from Merton in Surrey where they all shared a manor house. Look for the combination knife and fork that Nelson invented for his use after losing an arm in battle.

The recounting of the Battle of Trafalgar on the 21st of October 1805 is detailed. Nelson abandoned the established procedure and with two parallel squadrons attacked at an angle. In the middle of the battle he was shot by a French sniper from the *Redoubtable* and only lived long enough to hear that his fleet was victorious.

His body laid in state at Greenwich where 30,000 people passed to pay respects. The dead hero was then taken to the Admiralty in London prior to internment in St Paul's. His cortege was so long that the head of the solemn parade was in St Paul's before the last of the mourners had left the Admiralty.

Paintings, uniforms, and other memorabilia of Nelson—too time absorbing to examine in detail if you plan other stops—are on display.

Downstairs is more, much more, including the history of the America's Cup challenges. You'll enjoy comparing the yachts of yesterday with those of today. For example, America's 1886 entry, the *Galatea,* shows an extravagantly luxurious below-deck main cabin with tiger skin rugs, fireplace, and Victorian furniture. What a contrast to today's gaunt, stripped bare racing machines that cost many times more than the *Galatea.*

For really incredible boats, track down the *Ferriby Boat,* a reproduction of the 43-foot long oak plank boat designed to carry passengers and cargo on rivers in the Bronze Age, *circa 1500* BC.

Or the more recent *Graveney,* a 10th century model found in Kent in 1970.

Compare these ancient vessels with the gleaming barges of Prince Frederick's gold and scarlet barge and Queen Mary's ship in the Barge House.

Unfortunately, the Queen's House which separates the East and West Wings was closed for restoration. The house is known for its Entrance Hall, the Tulip Staircase and the Queen's Bedroom which also features the museum's best paintings.

The East Wing was also closed in preparation for an exhibition on the Armada. To mount a serious Marine Museum exhibit takes more than a year.

Note: time runs out. There are not enough figures on the clock face to allow for lunch in the village and still make it up the hill to the Observatory—a *must*—so pack a picnic if the day is nice to spread on Greenwich Park behind the museum. Or take your chances on the Dolphin Coffee Shop within the museum where the service is equal to the food. It's better than starving, but barely.

To appreciate the Old Royal Observatory, enter the 17th century time warp to return to an age when captains of ships could only approximate their location.

The result was a high percentage of shipwrecks with a loss of precious cargo, a disaster for the men of Lloyd's of London, and in the case of military ships, an equal affront to the gold braid at Admiralty House.

The thought passed across many minds: if there were a way to tell exactly how far the ship was away from home, longitudinally, its location could be mapped. That ability didn't exist except by comparison. After the ship's run was logged each day, the National Almanac was consulted to determine where the ship was in relationship to the sun at that time of year.

But if it could be determined at what rate the sun turned—then an unknown—and establish an agreed-upon place from which to measure time . . . if all maritime captains had a clock set at precisely the same time . . . well, then, with the aid of the sun and stars the position of the ship could be fixed.

That's what it was all about.

In 1675 astronomer John Flamsteed talked George II into establishing the first observatory. Christopher Wren designed a modest structure—very modest—and Flamsteed became England's first Royal Astronomer. He was paid £100 a year and had to buy most of his own equipment. (When he died, his widow confiscated it!)

(Don't miss the Octagon Room in the Flamsteed House, one of the few Wren *interiors* still existing.)

Continued shipping disasters due to erroneous navigation prompted the Longitude Act of 1714. The act established a £20,000 prize—a great fortune at the time—for the first person who could prove by a voyage from Britain to the West Indies that he had devised a navigational system successful enough to plot on a map the arrival of the ship within 30 geographical miles.

After two unacceptable tries, John Harrison, in 1764, finished a voyage with a plotted error of only 9.8 miles.

He wasn't paid off until 1773 when he was 80.

In the Old Royal Observatory you find the history, the people, the instruments used to establish what we now take for granted, Greenwich Mean Time. Original quadrants, telescopes, astrolabes, clocks of Mudge and Le Roay, chronometers.

Different countries tended to use different bases for measuring time. It was not until 1884 in Washington D.C. that the major shipping countries agreed to establish Greenwich Universal Time, an agreement easily reached because 72% of international ship tonnage was already using GMT.

Today, you learn, that atomic clocks coordinated with GMT, are the basis for world time.

Of course you must shoot each other's picture astride the meridian with a foot in each hemisphere.

Taking my Lady Navigator to the Royal Observatory was a day of bewilderment for her. As there are people who are color blind and those who are tone deaf, she is clock blind. She had no sense of time—absolutely none.

Although she has an uncanny sense of direction and can find an obscure Fijian village on Viti Levu or a lost castle in Ireland with only her nose and an 18th century map, her best appreciation of time is to know for sure what day it is.

"Do you understand any of this?" she was asked in a whisper.

"Not a clue," she whispered back.

Did she enjoy it?

"I feel better knowing that it exists," she said.

And you will, too.

The Docks

The reach of the Thames between The City of London wharves and Greenwich grew in activity as the country grew.

The Romans built riverside docks. The Anglo-Saxons used the sheltered entrance to the Fleet River.

Later The City built quays for licensed operators. One quay for wool. Another for hides. Billingsgate for fish. Seventeen in all.

Ships would anchor in the river and lighters would remove cargo to the quays. Robberies were rife leading to river police and execution docks where river criminals were hung until they had been washed over by three tides providing a feast for the birds. The deteriorating bodies hanging there were supposed to be a deterrent to other criminals.

A famous historic pub is the Prospect of Whitby where the notorious "Bloody" Judge Jeffreys would sit and enjoy the executions he had ordered.

Upstream from the Prospect is another Thames-side pub, The Town of Ramsgate, taken from the name of a ship. Prior to that it was known as the Red Cow because, it was said, the barmaid had flaming red hair.

It was a staging area for 18th century prisoners before they were placed aboard unnavigable ship hulks in the river because the prisons were overflowing. Later the prisoners, chained in the cellars, were shipped from the pub to Australia.

Here "Hanging Judge" Jeffreys, now outside the law, was caught trying to escape. He was dressed like a common sailor but as he slipped out of the tavern and bumped into another sailor he said "Pardon me" as a gentleman would, but like a sailor wouldn't.

The social error led to his identification and his brutalization by a mob. He was rescued and locked in the Tower of London where he died.

The monopoly of The City quays was finally broken in 1802 when the West India Company built enclosed docks with adjacent warehousing east of the Tower Bridge, outside The City's jurisdiction, and hired a private police force to guard them. Similar docks were added as late as 1920 by which time London was the largest port in the world.

After World War II the London docks died.

Inadequate facilities, slow modernization, dock strikes, containerization, larger ships that could not wait for high tides, foreign competition, and the modernized facilities at Tilbury . . . all contributed to the demise.

London shipping fell to a world ranking of 622nd.

Where warehouses and abandoned wharves stood, a new city is now emerging. A different city based on today's industries—communications, finance, marketing—providing housing, new office complexes, recreational facilities.

Since 1981, expensive new riverside apartments have been converted from gutted warehouses. Over 300 new businesses have moved in, infusing a £2.5 billion investment from the private sector.

What was an industrial cemetery has become a vibrant place of regeneration.

The area, now called Docklands, is under the control of the London Docklands Development Corporation (LDDC). Its 5,000 acres is equivalent to the land between the Tower Bridge and Chelsea.

Shopping centers, floating restaurants, pubs, riverside walkways and parks are planned.

Tobacco Dock is to be the new Covent Garden of the East End with shops and cafes.

West India Dock is planned as a festival marketplace similar to Boston's Quincy Market or South Street Seaport in New York. Three historic buildings and several old ships are to be part of the new development.

Canary Wharf, a future financial center, is the largest single commercial development in the world. It will have hotels, the tallest office building between New York and Hong Kong, and family housing ranging from affordable one bedroom flats to luxury penthouses.

A preview of the future exists in the ten-acre St Katherine's Dock built in 1820 and rebuilt in the 1980's. Across the road from the Tower of London, the new yacht harbor is the focal point for office buildings, including the World Trade Centre, the Tower Hotel, cutesy shops, likable pubs and decent restaurants.

A reminder of the old St Katherine's docks remains in the 30-foot high stone protective wall at the eastern boundary. The law mandated its height, the material used (either stone or brick) and a six-foot moat separating the warehouses from the wall. No one was allowed into the dock area without authority and trespassers were easy targets for private policemen; men armed with spiked clubs, cutlasses and pistols; men famous for their brutality.

Beyond St Katherine's Dock were the London Docks in Wapping, now fast becoming the center of London's daily newspapers, taking the place of Fleet Street.

The mighty Murdoch publishing empire was first to move its London headquarters from Fleet Street to Wapping, a move that led to a nasty, long lasting conflict, scored with violence. The headquarters, still wrapped with razor wire fencing and Big Brother television cameras, is known as Fort Wapping.

Other daily newspapers, however, are following the same move.

Communications to the burgeoning Docklands area is by rail, air, water, and road.

In the autumn of 1987 the first totally automated light rail system in the UK became operational, connecting Docklands directly to Central City, the Underground system, and British Rail Services.

Riverbuses, jet-powered catamarans, were also scheduled to be introduced to cut ferry time in half and compete with the heavy road traffic.

London City Airport, just six miles from the heart of the financial district, opened to accommodate STOL (short-take-off-and-landing) aircraft. Anticipating considerable business traffic to European cities, an initial 170 flights per day were scheduled.

Upriver

Another bright day in summer we tried to take a launch to Hampton Court from Westminster Pier.

The queue was long and by the time I reached the window the first trip was sold out. Hampton Court, which we had visited the preceding November, is a three-and-a-half hour boat trip from London.

We settled for the first boat to Kew. Two hours away.

You see so much from the river. Get such a different perspective.

The first view is of the Houses of Parliament.

"The awnings you see alongside the palace are where the Members of Parliament have tea. The members of the Tory Party go to the green awnings and the members of the Labour Party go to the red awnings. The members of the Alliance Party go to a telephone booth."

(When we later had tea on the terrace with MP Neville Trotter, he said the members of the House of Commons used the facilities under the green awning and the members of the House of Lords were protected by the red awnings.)

On the left is St Thomas's Hospital where Florence Nightingale returned after the Crimean War to teach nursing. Her students were known as "Nightingales" and still are. In the 15th century Richard Whittingdon established a ward with eight beds for "young women who had done amiss" but in 1561 unmarried pregnant women were refused entry because the hospital, according to the governors, was erected for the relief of "honest persons and not of harlottes" (sic).

In 1700 one of the house rules forbade more than one person in one bed. Sticky governors!

It now contains almost 1,000 beds.

The crenellated building a bit farther on is Lambeth Palace, home for the Archbishop of Canterbury. After it, the little church of St Mary-at-Lambeth where Captain William Bligh of the *Bounty* is buried.

The little house where Tony Armstrong-Jones wooed a princess is pointed out, as is Dolphin Square, entered in the Guinness Book of Records as the largest apartment complex in Europe.

From the river you can see the statues on the supports on the Vauxhall Bridge which are not visible elsewhere.

You pass, on the south bank, the hulking Battersea Power Station, no longer operative and now being planned as a theme park.

Beyond the Chelsea Bridge on your left in Battersea Park; watch for a tall Oriental pagoda. The 110-foot monument is the London Peace Pagoda built in 70 days in 1985 by a Japanese order of Buddhists, and is one of 70 such pagados the order has erected around the world.

Its four niches contain gilded figures of Buddha. The roof tiles were handmade in Japan.

A bit farther on is the former gas works, now a major residential development known as Chelsea Harbour.

The launch was not new. A forward bulkhead plaque was awarded for its participation in Operation Dynamo, the evacuation of the troops from Dunkirk. The vessel belonged to the "Little Ship Association" and flew the association's flag.

One advantage of being on the river is that there are no licensing laws. The draught bitter from the ship's bar was excellent. And it was Sunday. The section of river between Putney and Mortlake is crew country. We passed markers for the annual crew race between Oxford and Cambridge, and dozens of shells, skiffs, sculls, crews of four, of eight.

By the time we reached Kew the river was so low the ship scraped the riverbed. The captain said it was an unusual tide and that by three o'clock the river would rise 22 feet.

The tide makes a great difference in getting to and from Hampton Court. To travel there and back makes too long a day. A better idea is to take a morning train from Waterloo Station to Hampton Court, visit the palace then take an afternoon boat back to London on an outgoing tide. Or vice versa, if the weather is nice in the morning. You don't take a gloriously sunny day for granted in London.

Kew is a pleasant town. It being a summer Sunday, there was a cricket match in progress on the village green. We had a pub lunch and watched the bowling and then explored nearby Kew Gardens, a huge park of 300 acres especially attractive to plant lovers. There are hot houses that are over a hundred years old. Modern rock gardens beautifully done. A small lake with ducks and geese being over-fed from crusts of leftover sandwiches.

Officially its title is the Royal Botanic Gardens and its purpose, as a scientific institution, is the proper identification of plants from around the world. It acts as a depot for receiving and distributing plants to and from other botanical gardens in Britain.

Three major hothouses are centered in the garden. The most famous is the Palm House built in 1844 but presently being reconstructed. The other is the Temperate House.

An immense structure of curved and ornamental glass retaining the heat of the sun where, on a summer's day, poking through the thick green growth makes you feel as if you are lost in Darkest Africa.

Where *is* Dr Livingstone?

You can get above it all by climbing a staircase to an overhead walkway which traverses the hothouse. Gives you a good overview of the greenery.

The third structure is a new (1987) £5 million hothouse inaugurated by the Princess of Wales and named for her.

Kew Palace is almost a curiosity. That's because it was never intended to be a palace.

There had been several splendid palaces in Kew including one known as White Lodge which George III acquired. Attracted by the revival of Gothic architecture, he commissioned a vast castellated palace to replace White Lodge and the family moved into temporary quarters at the Old Dutch House, built in 1631 as a country home by a London merchant.

Unfortunately the king became ill and died before his new Gothic palace was finished. His unfinished White Lodge was demolished in 1827.

Queen Charlotte continued to use the small Old Dutch House, so it remained "Kew Palace." You can tour the rooms for a small fee.

An hour upriver is Hampton Court.

How unpretentious Kew Palace is compared to Hampton Court Palace with its hundreds of rooms and vast acreage.

Why didn't George III move into this impressive palace?

At Hampton Court you learn that George III disliked the place intensely because, as a child, his grandfather, displaying the

Hanoverian heritage of hatred for the male progeny, had boxed his ears at Hampton Court.

Hampton Court started as Thomas Wolsey's home. The son of an Ipswich butcher, young Wolsey rose swiftly in the politics of church and state to become a Cardinal of the church and Lord Chancellor of England. He was wealthier than the king himself.

Extravagance was part of his nature. He built the palace of Whitehall in London and purchased the property at Hampton Court from the Order of St John of Jerusalem to build a country palace. There were guest rooms to accommodate 250 served by a staff of 500.

When he stumbled in popularity with Henry VIII, he offered his palace to the king, hoping to regain favor. He not only lost Hampton Court, but he lost his church as well.

Henry enjoyed his new Hampton Court toy and added royal luxury on top of church luxury. He built galleries, wings, the Great Hall, libraries, courtyards. He enlarged the gardens, added orchards, a tennis court still used today, transforming the estate into the most luxurious palace in Europe.

Succeeding monarchs used the country palace and hunting grounds for extravagant entertaining. Elizabeth staged theatrical productions in the Great Hall and stag hunts in the adjoining park.

Oliver Cromwell first put the property up for sale and then decided to occupy it himself.

Charles II restored the damage done by Cromwell's Puritans but it was William and his Mary who remodeled the palace in a classical French renaissance style.

All of the famous British names in architecture and interior design are represented at Hampton Court: the designs of architects Christopher Wren, Inigo Jones, the wood carving of Grinling Gibbons, ironworks by Jean Tijou, landscaping by "Capability" Brown.

George II was the last monarch to use the palace.

Queen Victoria opened the gates to the public at which time the administration of the property was transferred from the Crown to the Government. It is now under the office of the Department of Environment which supervises maintenance and restoration of the buildings and the care of the gardens.

Many of the rooms are occupied by former royal retainers in

what is known as "Grace and Favour" lodgings. One of these elderly people accidentally set fire to her rooms in 1986. The fire spread to the State Apartments with sickening devastation.

Progress is being made toward restoration but it will take time.

Our visit on a cold but bright November day was an ideal time in spite of the fire's damages. The palace was virtually ours . . . devoid of visitors. The soft wintry sun heightened the texture of wall coverings, gently enlivened famous paintings and coolly played pin-the-shadow on barren trees in courtyards.

I remember being impressed with the first courtyard, the Clock Court which displays Elizabeth's badges, Henry VIII's coat-of-arms and those of Wolsey, once removed but restored. The famous Astronomical Clock over the entrance to the courtyard—Anne Boleyn's Gateway—was made for Henry in 1540 and is in fine working order. It shows the hour, the month, date, signs of the zodiac, year and the phase of the moon.

Your walk through the King's Rooms is in the progression you would follow if you had a royal audience. Up the King's Staircase with ironwork by Tijou to the King's Guard Chamber, the First Presence Chamber, the Second Presence Chamber, the Audience Chamber, the King's Drawing room.

You may tour more than forty rooms but you can't absorb it all.

Among our highlights are:

In the Cartoon Gallery a painting dating to Henry VIII: *Field of the Cloth of Gold.*

In the Communications Gallery, the famous display of *Windsor Beauties,* friends of the overly friendly Charles II.

Wolsey's Closet is historically absorbing because it contains the Cardinal's original furnishings.

The Great Hall needs a roaring fire and a table burdened with suckling pig and joints of beef and Yorkshire pudding and flagons of wine, and hundreds of roisterers feasting at a banquet. (It's pneumonia cold in November.)

From the lobby you get an overview of the Great Fountain Garden, an inheritance of William III and Queen Mary who were responsible for Kensington Gardens.

Two curiosities: at the edge of the Thames is the Great Vine planted by Capability Brown in 1768. It now has a girth of almost 80 inches and produces an annual crop of grapes of 500 to 600 bunches.

Next to the Lion Gate, at the north entrance to the property, is the well known Maze, originally planted by William III as part of a nine acre "Wilderness."

Still Other Ways To Enjoy The River

The Thames for all its economic importance and historical value is a favorite place in today's London for riverside relaxation, specifically at the maritime pubs which stretch from the Bell and Crown just downstream from Kew Bridge to the Gate House at Woolwich, built in 1610 where Nelson stayed on more than one occasion.

Twickenham upriver is a particularly rewarding area for riverside life, quite removed from the heavy traffic areas.

The White Swan, the Dove, the Old Ship are but three of the many more than satisfactory pubs in the area.

Add the City Barge, Bull's Head and the famous London Apprentice, suggested a Twickenham resident.

While cruising the river during periods of low tide you will probably see people exploring the shores with metal detection devices or others digging pits. They are "mudlarking" or searching for treasures from times far past. Occasionally they succeed.

Our expert said that most don't go deep enough . . . and, that it is necessary to get nine feet down between the changes of the tide.

The Avalanche

---

9. Famous Galleries and Must Museums

It is a question not of how many days do you have in London, but how many lives do you have to give to visiting all of the city's galleries and museums.

Visual richness beyond measure in galleries.

Monumental historical objects to savor in museums.

In the Michelin Guide to London we counted 19 prominent galleries and 55 museums.

The challenge is to cherry-pick the best in the best, avoiding museum burn-out, aching bunions, and the stunned, glazed-eyed fatigue which comes from trying to see and appreciate too much, too fast.

Build into each visit a deliberate change of pace. Combine a museum or gallery with a theater matinee. Or a pub lunch and a pint of bitter. Or a nearby park—with benches. (It feels so good to sit down.)

A logical place to start, if only because of its central location, is The National Gallery facing Trafalgar Square, an institution recognized worldwide both as a guardian of an outstanding collection of European paintings and as a backdrop to the often photographed Nelson's Column.

In its larder are Italian, Dutch and Flemish, Spanish, French and British classics dating from the 13th to the early 20th centuries.

The origin of the NG is traced to a City banker whose mansion on Pall Mall was a repository for the masterworks of Titian, Rubens and Rembrandt among the many European artists he collected.

Parliament bought the 38-picture collection in 1824 and showed them at the Pall Mall estate. In the first seven months 24,000 people saw the government's £ 57,000 investment.

Today there are 2,050 paintings in inventory, virtually all of them always on display, a unique feature in the museum world.

Equally unique is the NG's relative wealth. It is fat-cat rich having recently been fortified with £ 50 million from the Getty fortunes for purchasing and £ 30 million from the Sainsbury Foundation for building. Such funding may be traced to the appointment of Jacob Rothschild, said to be a financial genius, as chairman in 1985.

The 3,000,000 visitors a year attest to the gallery's popularity.

As an historical footnote, the original collection included Titian's *Venus and Adonis,* Rubens' *Rape of the Sabines,* Rembrandt's *Woman Taken in Adultery,* Hogarth's series *Marriage a la Mode,* among others. A noble beginning.

My personal favorite European artist is Caravaggio and the Gallery has his *Supper at Emmaus* which I visit every time I am in London. Recently the gallery added his erotic and somewhat disturbing *Boy Being Bitten by a Viper.*

Pick your own favorite . . . from the 15th century *St George and the Dragon* by the Florentine, Uccello, to the 19th century *Water Lilies* by the French impressionist Monet.

The Gallery publishes and sells in its shop "A Quick Visit to the National Gallery" featuring sixteen of the more famous paintings.

One painting is drawing a flood of new visitors because of the publicity given to a Christie's auction sale in 1987.

One of a series of paintings called *Sunflowers* by Van Gogh, the Impressionist, was sold at auction for £ 24 million. The new owner, perhaps appropriately, was Japanese because, originally, there had been seven sunflowers in the series but the seventh was burned in a fire in Tokyo.

Four others are located in Amsterdam, Munich, Philadelphia and Berne.

The sixth existing painting is in the National Gallery.

Turn to the right immediately upon entering the building and in Room 44 is *Sunflowers*. The only difference between the Japanese and the NG versions is background color. The Japanese-bought Van Gogh is greenish-blue, its English cousin is yellowish.

Stand apart from the swarm of visitors. You can almost hear the viewers asking themselves, "Is that worth £ 24 million?"

In the same room are two other Van Gogh's, *Pipe On A Chair* and *Tall Grass and Butterflies* which you might find more attractive.

Monet, Manet, Renoir, Pissarro, Seurat, Degas, Cezanne, Toulouse-Lautrec are among the many familiar French names featured in the extensive 19th and 20th centuries French collection.

On the left side of the entrance is the sizable collection representing six centuries of Italian painting.

When the National Gallery opened in its present building in 1838 behind the classical Corinthian columns, it was a neoclassical building in harmony with its similarly porticoed neighbors. The right building in the right neighborhood.

A recent movement to create a new wing for improved display of the Renaissance Collection met with predictable controversy in London. (Anything *new* leads to an immediate controversy in London.) In this instance, the suggested plans for the new wing were scathed by no less a person than HRH The Prince of Wales. Prince Charles, a trustee, looked at the model and decried it to be a series of "carbuncles."

The suggested scheme was sunk without a bubble.

The proposed—and accepted—model of the forthcoming "Sainsbury Wing" is displayed in a separate room off the far left of the entrance.

If you are familiar with England, you know that the Sainsbury name is synonymous with grocery stores as in super- or near-super markets. (A mirthful but informative book, *The Sloane Ranger,* describes them as *"Rairly Soopah"* and *"Nairly Soopah."*)

The new model, if you believe the PR puff piece, exudes an "informal monumentality" which goes along with the "friendly grandeur" of the National Gallery.

No carbuncles.

The new wing will be sited at the northwest corner of Trafalgar Square and visually attached to the left side of the Gallery.

Behind its stone facade, the addition will feature a glass wall enclosing a lively public area which, in turn, will surround the quiet space of the gallery.

The architectural commission was won by a Philadelphia firm headed by a professor of architecture, Robert Venturi.

Facts: There are 46 galleries plus supplementary galleries on the Lower Floor.

Admission is free. Open weekdays 10AM to 6PM, Sundays 2-6PM. Closed most national holidays.

Periodic special exhibits feature selections of paintings from the Gallery Collection assembled either by subject or artist (such as a retrospective). It is worthwhile to check the newspapers or stop at the Information Desk to find out what is current.

Tube Stop: Charing Cross.

Break Suggestions: Feed a pigeon in Trafalgar Square.

Go to Rules, an historically old English restaurant, for lunch. (Maiden Lane en route to Covent Garden)

Walk over to St James's Square, sit on a bench and take your shoes off.

The National Portrait Gallery . . . How Dull Is It?

Around the corner from the National Gallery is the National Portrait Gallery.

It sounds dull.

Give it a chance . . . but save it for last.

The reason is that during your visit to London you will be constantly confronted with the names of the central figures involved in the drama. By the end of your London visit The National Portrait Gallery gives you great satisfaction of putting faces together with the playbill. In chronological order.

Take the elevator to the top floor and walk down floor by floor to pass through the pages of English history, king by king, queen by queen, and the many supporting cast members in the drama.

Here is the famous painting of the bull-shouldered, threatening Henry VIII by Holbein.

Here is Mary and her dominating, spinster sister, Elizabeth I, who used the proposal of marriage as a device, not a conclusion.

Here is a letter condemning to death her favorite, the Duke of Essex. He made the mistake of trying to touch her scepter.

Here is George III and the story of the loss of the American colonies.

Each room has an historical theme supported by maps and engravings to provide a narrative framework, even weapons to heighten the drama.

One section tells the story of mediaeval portraiture which took the form of effigies on tombs.

The royal family, pre-war and post-war, comes at the end.

In between there are captivating glimpses. A white marble statue shows Queen Victoria shamelessly fawning on her beloved Prince Albert and marks a sizable Victorian display on the first floor which includes such notables as Matthew Arnold, Thomas Carlyle, John Stuart Mill, Dickens, Tennyson.

There is an eerie painting of the Bronte sisters, Charlotte, Emily, and Anne. The painting looks as if it had been found in an attic but the faces are hauntingly alive . . . and done by their brother, Branwell.

As a student of the Pacific I was disappointed that the painting of Captain Cook was so unimportant but pleased with that of his moneyed botanist, Joseph Banks.

Facts: The National Portrait Gallery, established in 1856, has been in its present location since 1896.

The collection contains about 9,000 items with more being purchased or contributed each year.

Photography plays an increasingly important role in the collection.

A major Gallery Shop on the ground floor has a separate entrance and is very busy, a testimony to the gallery's popularity.

Hours are 10AM to 5PM Monday to Friday, 10 to 6PM Saturday, 2 to 6PM Sunday. Closed major holidays. Admission is free.

Location: Trafalgar Square.

Tube Station: Charing Cross.

Break suggestion: Time your visit to take in a noontime concert across the street at St Martin-in-the-Fields.

The Tate & The Clore

While much of the 1987 art news was centered around the

National Gallery's expansion plans and the purchase of Van Gogh's *Sunflowers* by the Japanese, a small torrent of media attention focused on the opening of the Clore Gallery adjoining the Tate Gallery.

Was the architecture of the Clore controversial?

Of course. The critics jumped on the subtly modern exterior facade with knife-wielding delight.

Was the interior controversial?

Naturally. The colors of the oatmeal walls, opined one writer, dampened Turner's vaporous white and yellows, stealing the drama and the contrast that Turner loved in his paintings.

The tone in the British press was "I didn't come to see the Turners. I came to sneer at the building."

Balderdash.

The new gallery is a delight . . . a fitting monument for one of England's most memorable and prolific painters.

Born the son of a barber in 1775, Joseph Mallord William Turner first exhibited his work at age fifteen at the prestigious Royal Academy. For the following sixty-one years he continued to grow in technique and in popularity, exhibiting frequently at the Royal Academy and in his own gallery.

When Turner died, he willed the pictures remaining in his studio to the country, *provided* the country housed them in a separate building called "Turner's Gallery."

The will was contested by the family. Eventually a compromise was reached giving 300 original finished and unfinished paintings and 300 sketchbooks containing over 20,000 drawings and watercolors to the people of the nation.

The "people" took the treasures but it took them more than a hundred years to fulfill their part of the bargain.

Lady Navigator: "It was supposed to be called Turner's Gallery. Why isn't it?"

"Because the money came from the Clore Foundation."

"Who was Clore?"

"Shoes."

"Why didn't they call it the Shoe Gallery?"

"Lady!"

The Clore Gallery adjoins the Tate from a sunken terrace on the right. Enter the new gallery here and rent a tape machine to guide you through the rooms to those paintings the curator considers to be most important. Worthwhile.

But first, if you are a real Turner devotee or student, watch the video programs in the downstairs auditorium for another layer of understanding.

Seven of the Turner masterpieces came from the National Gallery. Whether they go back or not seems to be uncertain.

Another several paintings which have been in custodianship to the Tate since 1984 were shown during the opening months. Normally these hang in Petworth House in Sussex, once the home of the 3rd Earl of Egremont, an early Turner patron. The Clore hopes to show them from time to time during winters when Petworth House, now a National Trust house, is closed.

But back to the mother ship, the Tate, which you enter either from connecting Clore corridors or through its classic columned porticoed front entrance. Frankly, we prefer the familiarity of the front entrance.

The Tate owes its name to a sugar baron who in 1891 not only offered his own vast collection of modern art to the government but also £ 80,000 for a building if the government donated the land.

Six years later the Tate opened, originally chartered to show "modern" British art, which meant anything after 1790 and before 1860. Since then acquisition policies seem to have changed to one of buying modern paintings before the artist's brush has dried. Both British and foreign artists.

The marriage has never been an easy one.

The result is a peculiar mixture of the romantic staid British art preceding 1860 contrasted with the comparatively shallow, hard-to-relate-to modern art.

Hence, in the central hall you will see Henry Moore sculptures that are difficult to explain to Mother, but also Rodin's *The Kiss* which needs no explanation at all.

William Hogarth's self portrait with his dog Punch, George Stubbs, Joshua Reynolds, William Blake's *Divine Comedy,* John Martin's *Coronation of Queen Victoria,* dozens of John Constables are part of the English collection.

Impressionism (Gallery 33) is represented by Cezanne, Sisley, Pissarro, Van Gogh, Gauguin, and in those delightful bronze dancers sculpted by Degas.

Among modern artists—the cubist, futurist, surrealist, abstractist, pop or minimal art followers—you'll find the likes of Picasso, Jackson Pollock, Andy Warhol. You have to see Warhol's *Marilyn Diptych.* Looks like Marilyn Monroe's face in fast forward.

Since its opening with eight galleries, five major additions have been made, the first one only two years after the 1897 opening. Still, for all of its total 61 galleries, only 20% of its 13,000 works are on display.

To make more of its 20th century paintings available to public viewing, the Tate Gallery Liverpool opens in summer 1988 in converted warehouse buildings. Not London. Liverpool. The Tate is spreading its wealth.

Facts: Free admission. Open daily 10AM to 5:30PM, Sunday afternoons 2PM to 5:30PM. Closed on national holidays.

Location: On the River Thames near the Vauxhall Bridge in Pimlico.

Tube Station: Pimlico Station. Follow directional signs; it is about a ten-minute walk.

Break Suggestion: An oasis for wine connoisseurs is the booking-required, waitress-service Tate Restaurant in the basement. (Opposite is an "I'll-eat-anything-I'm-starving" cafeteria.) Ring 834-6754 for restaurant reservations and take cash. *No credit cards are accepted.*

The food is overpriced (get an omelette which is reasonable) but the fantastic wine list is underpriced.

A bottle of Chutes La Tour-du-Pin Figeac (Grand Cru) '71 is a mere £16.

Or toss the key out of the window and order your table a bottle of '63 Fonseca Port (allow 20 minutes for decanting). Cost: £38.50.

What a great way to enjoy an art gallery.

Courtauld Institute Galleries

Our shopping list of London galleries to revisit, in order, are the National Gallery, the Tate with its little shoe-shod brother, the Clore, the National Portrait Gallery and, now, the Courtauld.

We'd been many times to the first three. Never to the fourth.

Map in hand we went off in the general direction of the University of London from the Russell Square tube station and, finally, after weaving in and out of various school buildings, there was Woburn Square and the galleries.

A big drawing card for going was the popular Impressionists' works collected by Samuel Courtauld. Many of the paintings were friends from printed pages whom we had never met . . . the offspring of Manet, Degas, Bonnard, Gauguin, Van Gogh,

Cezanne . . . many of our favorite artists.

On arrival we learned that the heart of the collection was on tour to America. Back in nine months.

One of the reasons for the tour was to solicit funds to help shift the collection in 1988 to a new exhibition space in Somerset House, near Waterloo Bridge, between the Strand and the river. The new home will give a beautiful collection a more adequate and centralized location. (I had read in a guidebook that the move was to have happened in 1986.)

The price tag placed on the move is £ 5 million, probably one of the reasons why it hadn't yet occurred.

Nevertheless, even without the full palette of masterpieces, there is much to recommend the gallery: its Primitives, Renaissance paintings, Italian classics.

In one room alone (Gallery III) there were 32 paintings by Peter Paul Rubens, part of the Princess Gate collection given to the nation by Count Antoine Seilern.

Other works in the same collection include drawings by Michelangelo and works by Breughel, Leonardo, Tiepolo, Durer, Rembrandt, Kokoschka, Bellini, and Tintoretto.

Also, seek out the four paintings by Rubens' most celebrated pupil, van Dyck.

Not on the road were singular works by Edouard Manet, Degas, Cezanne, Utrillo and the famous self-portrait of Van Gogh in 1889 with a damaged ear. If one of his *Sunflower* series sold for £ 24 million, one wonders what would this more famous painting bring?

What is certainly a stop-and-gasp object is not a painting but Lord Charlemont's Medal Cabinet, a huge 12-foot tall by 14-foot wide "hobby chest" made of mahogany, sandalwood and box-wood.

Built by Sir William Chamber, it has small drawers for coins and large cases for trophies. Over several cabinet sections are gold inscriptions in Latin to label:

Coins of the Roman Families.

Coins, Gold & Silver, of the Roman Emperors.

Coins of Greek Kings and Worthies.

Marvelous.

The cabinet is destined to go to Somerset House, an asset to the Fine Rooms which Chambers also designed.

Facts: The gallery exhibits the major art bequests to London University in an intimate setting enhanced by lovely furniture, carpets, sculpture and china.

Open daily from 10AM to 5PM. Sundays from 2PM to 5PM. Closed on major holidays. Admission charge.

Location: In the Courtauld-Warburg Building on the west side of Woburn Square.

Tube Stop: Russell Station.

Notable Neighbors: Down a block on Tavistock Place is the Percival David Foundation of Chinese Art, one of the world's most famous collections of 14th- to 18th-century Chinese porcelains. Also in the neighborhood is the British Museum.

Break Suggestions: Watch the birds—feathered birds and town-gowned birds—in nearby pleasantly quiet Russell Square, the heart of the Bloomsbury district.

Or visit a friend, the Friend at Hand pub on Herbrand Street, just up from the President Hotel off the northeast corner of Russell Square.

"Friendly as it sounds," reports colleague and travel editor of the Miami Herald, Jay Clarke.

The MUST Museums

Let us repeat the delicious problem.

The British Museum and its brethren are too rich.

The once-in-a-lifetime visitor may feel compelled to *do* the museums, to try to see and absorb everything. Patently impossible.

With so much to see, a wiser gameplan for fuller appreciation is to pick two or three targets at the museum of choice, enjoy them thoroughly, and leave. Come back another day, or several days, *but leave.*

Any *one* room can take a lifetime of study. Why try to *do* an entire museum in five hours?

Fortunately, individuals have different tastes.

Here are our personal favorite museums and what we return to see, trying always to add at least one new museum to broaden our appreciation.

British Museum tops the list. If you haven't seen the Elgin Marbles and the Rosetta Stone you haven't been in London. The Lady Navigator loves the little jade Egyptian cat on the ground floor.

Victoria and Albert, hereafter referred to in the jargon of the locals as the V&A, is a virtual classroom of the arts. We always go back to admire the Minton tiles in the old Refreshment Rooms. New to our list is the Toshiba exhibit.

The Science Museum for its exciting Space Age Exhibit, the aeronautical display on the third floor, and the Wellcome medical history exhibits on the 4th and 5th floors.

The Geological Museum lets you experience the Anchorage, Alaska earthquake. You hear the rumble of earth and feel the tremors underfoot as you witness the results of an awesome earthy convulsion.

The Natural History Museum has two fantastic exhibits, "Discovering the Mammal" and "Human Biology." Both beautifully done.

The Cabinet War Rooms, behind Whitehall, is a "don't miss" if you have any interest in World War II or Churchill. The Meeting Room, the Telephone Room where Churchill used to talk to Roosevelt, the Map Room and Churchill's Quarters are highlights.

Now for details:

The British Museum

The catalyst for the British Museum was Sir Hans Sloane, (Sloane Square, Sloane Street, Sloane Avenue, the first Sloane Ranger, the founder of the Physic Garden in Chelsea) who in 1753 left his extensive collection to his country. Britain already had an embarrassment of riches—the Royal Library donated by George II, the mediaeval manuscripts of Sir Robert Cotton.

A lottery raised the money to purchase an old mansion as the first home of the British Museum.

Opened in 1769, it soon became everybody's attic. Fossils, manuscripts, stuffed animals, dried plants, paintings were piled into hallways and staircases. No labels. And, like today, no charge for admission.

During the next two hundred years, donations piled on more donations while Parliament-funded purchases gave the British Museum the finest historical objects to be found in the world: original coins, manuscripts, sculptures, bronzes, terracottas, minerals, and music collections. Treasures poured in: Egyptian antiquities, Roman antiquities, Prehistoric antiquities, Romano-British antiquities, Oriental antiquities. Colossal stuff.

Eventually the collections were spun off into separate museums. Natural History Museum, the Museum of Mankind, the Geological Museum, the Science Museum.

Today the British Museum in Bloomsbury is devoted to time-eating exhibits of the world's treasures.

Two of the most famous are the Rosetta Stone in the Egyptian Sculpture Gallery (Room 25) and, from the Parthenon in Athens, the Elgin Marbles (the gin is pronounced as in begin not as gin in a martini) in the Duveen Gallery (Room 8). Old friends.

We also make returned visits to the Grenville Library (Room 29) to peer upon some of the great collections of literature, manuscripts and documents such as the Magna Carta. Did you remember that a Papal Bull made the king renounce the original Magna Carta—and only later was it implemented?

On our last visit we picked up the nugget story of John Donne, the famous poet. Donne married Anne, the daughter of a lord, but without permission. The furious father had Donne sacked and thrown into prison (later reduced to house arrest) prompting the poet to write:

"John Donne—Anne Donne—undone."

Having walked the walled Londinium and having been back again and again to the Museum of London to absorb more about the occupation by Romans and Anglo-Saxons, a priority was to see what the British Museum had in its early London collection.

The Romano-British collection is nicely introduced by a major piece of Roman mosaic. The pavement has a Christian motif signaling its creation at a time when the Roman Empire had largely adopted Christianity.

Before going into Room 40, examine the case next to the entrance showing rare samples of goldsmithing in the Bronze Age.

While we tend to think of humans of the 1300-1500BC era as being knuckle-dragging barbarians, examples of their craftsmanship such as the Mold Cape quickly dispel that impression. The Mold Cape is an elaborate gold shoulder covering, delicately embossed. Other jewelry—rings, necklaces, earrings, armlets—show a fine talent for working alluvial gold—plentifully found in England at the time—into charming ornaments.

Room 40 is a treasure trove of objects used during the 400-year Roman occupation of Britain.

The statuettes in the first case on the left often were part of a religious tradition. One was found in the Thames. Note the dynamic 10″ high archer. Beautifully crafted.

Glassware, including the then new technique of glass blowing, served its owners as status symbol, as did silverware. Lead and tin was combined to create pewter, a cheap imitation of silver.

The Romans had a rudimentary idea of medicine based on the use of herbs. They were trained to treat military wounds and capable of intricate surgery. They understood hygiene, evidenced by the Roman baths and latrines and sewage systems.

One exhibit case is devoted to tablets found at Vindolanda in the north. These thin slices of wood accepted ink writing as opposed to the usual wax tablets incised with a stylus. The tablets were devoted to military matters.

Was writing a rare talent among the Romans?

No. Apparently not.

The tablets revealed the handwriting of eighty different scribes.

How early did the English woolen industry start?

Roman militarymen coveted a garment called *birrus britannicaus,* a sort of water repellent woolen cloak. (One is reminded of the New Zealand Swandri bush shirt.)

Traces of the Roman treasury in Britain have been discovered in comparatively recent times. The Thetford Treasure found in Norfolk in 1979 consisted of 4th century gold and silver. Of the 33 silver spoons found, all but three bore the same inscription.

Probably buried during the revolt of Queen Boudica (60AD) were 860 silver coins excavated near the temple of Mercury in Gloucestershire. Tiny coins.

Who did they belong to? The Queen herself?

You tend to dream scenarios as you gaze at these objects of curiosity.

Another find was the Water Newton Treasure in 1974, a coin hoard consisting of 30 gold *solidi,* dated 350AD and attributed to Constantine I and his sons, together with two folded pieces of silver bullion. A year later a treasure of Christian silver was uncovered.

The finest discovery of Roman wealth was the Mildenhall Treasure found in Suffolk in 1940. It is considered to be the finest set of 4th century silverware to be found in the Roman-British Empire and characteristic of the 360AD period. The major piece is a serving platter almost two feet in diameter and elaborately etched with relief figures of Pan, dancers and musicians at a festive occasion.

Upstairs, in Room 42, is a small exhibit devoted to the Roman army. One can understand the fear that these professional, well equipped soldiers inspired in their relatively crude enemies.

The Roman foot soldier was armed with javelin, sword and dagger . . . protected by bronze helmet, iron mail, and strips of metal made into an apron to shield his delicate parts.

He was flanked with cavalry, usually recruits from conquered tribes.

The Roman army was tightly organized into proud legions. A legion consisted of 5,000 men divided into cohorts, centuries and centurians.

Their cities and military units were connected by solidly built Roman roads. Five roads led into and out of London, unlike any other city in England.

Room 41 casts a shred more light on the Dark Age of the Anglo-Saxon.

The most dramatic exhibit in the room is the Sutton Hoo Burial treasure, a burial ship of an East Anglian king of the early 7th century, perhaps King Raewald (624-235AD).

King Raewald went to the next world in comfort and style. He was placed inside a ship provisioned with foods and dining implements—drinking horns, cups, bottles—a lyre for musical entertainment, beautiful decorative objects in etched silver, and ceremonial jewelry. Ready to assume his rightful place in the next world.

Burial mounds were well known in the area, but no serious excavation took place until 1939 when the dramatic contents were discovered.

Who owned the treasure? The State or the property owner? A judgment decreed that the historically and monetarily precious objects belonged to the owner of the property who then graciously gave the "find" to the British Museum.

Relatively new (1985) are the basement Wolfson Galleries devoted to classical sculptures. Showcased is the Charles Trownley collection of Roman sculpture purchased in Rome in the late 18th century.

Also, if you've ever walked the cobblestone and marble streets of the once great Roman-Greek city of Ephesus on the Turkish coast, you'll want to see the aerial photos of its skeleton.

Whichever direction you go—the Sutton Hoo, the Elgin Marbles, the Magna Carta or the sculptures in Wolfson Galleries being typical—there are nuggets of the past around every corner.

Facts: Admission is free. Open Mondays to Saturdays, 10 to 5 PM, Sundays 2:30 to 6PM. Ground floor level cafe is not very good but very convenient. Seventy galleries covering Egyptian, Western-Asiatic, Greek-Roman, Oriental, Prehistoric and Mediaeval and Late Antiquities.

Location: Bloomsbury, adjacent to the University of London.

Tube stop: Holborn.

Break Suggestions: Same as for the Courtauld Galleries. Or duck into one of the rare old book and print shops in the neighborhood or a Westaway & Westaway woolen/cashmere shop facing the museum entrance on Great Russell Street for goodies and gifties.

ALBERTROPOLIS

South of Hyde Park in Kensington is a cluster of buildings which is a cultural depot of London. It owes its existence to a Saxe-Coburg prince whose princely father was once rated "an unmitigated disaster" and whose mother was banished for adultery.

The son was Prince Albert who became the prince consort of Queen Victoria. He was a polished, intellectual gentleman who did the thinking for his forever dependent queen.

In 1847 Prince Albert established the Society of Arts and elected himself president.

Adopting an idea proposed by Henry Cole, assistant keeper of the Public Record Office and a remarkable achiever for a person of undistinguished office, Albert pushed through the Great Exhibition of 1851 staged in a "crystal palace" in the middle of Hyde Park.

A glittering, marvelous, monumental work, the building was 1,848 feet long, 408 feet wide and 103 feet high. Quickly constructed by the use of prefabricated framing, it used 30,000 panes of glass.

The Crystal Palace was large enough to encompass the elms on the 18 acres it covered. One resultant problem was that the sparrows remaining in the trees showed a consistent lack of respect for the 14,000 exhibitors.

Queen Victoria asked the Duke of Wellington how to get rid of the birds.

Replied the Duke: "Try sparrowhawks, Ma'am."

The Exhibition ran from May 1 to October 11, 1851 and drew 45,000 visitors a day on average. The one shilling entrance fee (five shillings, twenty-five pence on Saturdays) produced receipts of £ 522,000 and a profit close to £ 200,000.

The money was used to buy 87 acres in South Kensington just south of Hyde Park for the creation of a center for learning and exhibitions. Today part of those 87 acres incorporates The Royal Albert Hall, the Imperial College of Science and Technology, the Science Museum, the Geological Museum, the Natural History Museum and, across Exhibition Road, the Victoria and Albert Museum.

Welcome to Albertropolis.

The Victoria & Albert Museum

Many of the objects from the hugely successful Great Exhibition formed the base for the Victoria & Albert.

Today it is a vast center of design and art.

Think of it not in the context of a museum or an art gallery but as a school of design affording you millions—yes, literally *millions*—of examples of international craftsmanship, from ancient to modern, in every field of man's endeavor.

The V&A exhibits represent a large slice of civilization as designed by mankind. Its largesse of objects traces the evolution of fashion in textiles, in apparel and tapestries, in glass and china, in silver and gold, in jewels, in tiles and terracotta, in musical instruments, in furniture, in prints and drawings, in paintings and photographs. (The museum only has 300,000 photographs in its photographic archives.)

Then you have to stop and consider. The V&A has seven miles

of corridors, 600 rooms.

Awesome.

What interests you and how many miles do you want to walk?

Know in advance that the V&A has been going through a swing of new additions which has caused the temporary closure of some exhibits. Before heading off to see a specific collection, get a free map, inquire at the information desk where it is and if you can get to it. Also check on the special temporary exhibits, then plot your visit.

The Henry Cole Wing was added in the early 1980's where, among its paintings and prints and drawings, you'll find a roomful of works by landscapist John Constable.

A new gallery underwritten by Toshiba focuses on Japanese design. We gasp at the stunning kimonos. We lust after any one of the 500 netsukes on display.

The Boilerhouse, so called because it occupies the old boilerhouse yard, features changing exhibitions dedicated to modern industrial design.

In 1987, the mother museum launched the Theatre Museum at Covent Garden and completed a new Italian-style courtyard, the Parelli Yard, on premise.

Picking your target destinations may be made easier by knowing that the treasures are laid out in two sequences: as Primary Galleries where a wide variety of objects are grouped together to give the sense—the feeling—of a period of a civilization; and as Subject Galleries to show the development of a single artform, such as ceramics, or of a specific factory making that object. Another reason for seeking the counsel of the information desk personnel.

As noted previously, our favorites are the former refreshment rooms at the very back of the ground floor. The Morris Room, the Gamble Room and the Poynter Room, named for the artisans who created their magnificent stained glass windows, ceramic tiled walls and panels, were saved from demolition a few years ago. These Victorian rooms are so enchanting you are grateful there are no people munching and chattering to clutter them up.

Go to the far room first, the Poynter Room, often called the Dutch Kitchen for its brass and iron grill and its Delft-styled tiles.

The blue tiled walls celebrate the months of the year. Four-by-six-foot romantic toga-clad figures decorate the upper half of the room, below which are smaller mythical figures, seascapes and trees and flowers.

All of the tiles were painted by female students from two local art schools.

Set into the side wall is the huge 7- by 10-feet grill for cooking, dated 1868 and signed by Sir Edward Poynter. The £165 appliance-cum-art-object was used daily until the outbreak of war in 1939.

The Gamble Room is a delightfully frothy concoction of yellow and white tiles and five huge stained-glass windows proclaiming:

Hunger is the best sauce.

A good cup make all young.

Good wine teaches good Latin.

The frieze in this large room, difficult to read because it bends around corners, is just as delicious. Spelled out in huge capital letters on white tile is this message:

THERE IS NOTHING BETTER FOR A MAN
THAT HE SHOULD MAKE HIS SOUL
ENJOY FOOD IN HIS LABOURS.

Four columns soar to a gilded ceiling from the middle of the room. I think this room had to be the inspiration of the Food Halls in Harrods.

Next door, the somber room of the three, the Morris Room has walls of sage green. Panels designate six months of the year and six stained glass windows bear motifs of the other six months.

The white ceiling carries a rich yellow enameled tin.

Near the entrance to the eating rooms, in Room 12, stop and admire the twelve round blue and white glazed terracotta tiles, one for each month, created to decorate the Florence office of Piero de' Medici in 1450-56.

Note the circular borders indicating the relative amount of daylight for each particular month, light blue for daylight, dark blue for nighttime. At the top of each roundel is the sun in its appropriate position in the House of the Zodiac and, on the opposite side, is the position of the crescent moon.

The center figure in the roundel depicts the appropriate agricultural occupation for the month: plowing, sowing, planting, reaping, picking, pruning, chopping.

Special photo exhibits out of the museum's huge collection are common. We saw one: "Towards A Bigger Picture." Just too good to miss.

Such an entrapment is so typical of the temptations you face in the V&A. It's the salted peanut syndrome. How do you stop?

For instance, do you want to see seven of the ten original Raphael cartoons (the working drawings) depicting the Acts of the Apostles? Go to Room 48. These initial concepts were for Sistine Chapel tapestries. One of the finished tapestries hangs opposite its cartoon.

Want to see the world's most comprehensive collection of John Constable paintings? Go to Room 621 in the Henry Cole Wing. The 19th century landscape paintings, watercolors and sketches were the gift of his last surviving daughter. (Many of the study drawings capture the essence of his art better than the more formal finished oils, depicting native landscape in a naturalistic manner.)

Want to see a 40-foot square 17th century marble Dutch *Roodloft,* the screen between choir and congregation? Go to Room 50. The massive edifice was pulled out of a Dutch cathedral in the 19th century because "it interfered with the congregation's view" of the high altar.

How about reviewing the history of European apparel fashion for the past 300 years. Go to Room 40.

Or Continental Art? Hie thee to rooms 1 through 9.

But remember, there are 600 rooms to pick from . . . with subjects equally as extensive.

Another cherry is the wood paneled National Art Library overlooking the courtyard. You can find, most probably, every written word on any decorative or applied arts subject.

Rich.

Little wonder that it has been written that the V&A is the most complex museum in Britain to run.

Under-funded, under-managed, over-unionized, it became independent of the Department of Education in 1984. The trustees who took on the operation found a creaking piece of machinery with great assets but no funds. Since then, it has marched ahead boldly under the chairmanship of Lord Carrington, described as one of the G&G set—*Great and Good.*

The new exhibits and the new developments are indicative of the new spirit that pervades the formerly crusty museum.

A welcome note was added in the summer of 1987 when a new director was appointed. A *woman.* Front page news. Elizabeth Esteve-Cole, 48, a member of the staff, will be guiding the museum in the future.

Its progress will be interesting to follow.

The Lady Navigator thinks the new shop in the V&A is one of the best for quality crafts in London. Reorganized by one of the trustees, the shop plans to create replicas of many of the museum's prize objects and also buys from other museums around the world. One of the first museum repros will be alphabet tiles from the Morris, Gamble and Poynter rooms.

Facts: Open from 10AM to 5:50PM week days; from 2:30PM on Sundays. Closed on Fridays but being reviewed. No admission charged but receptionists at entry desks, resembling ticket takers, are there to encourage donations. (They need the money.)

Tube Stop: South Kensington. (The good news is that there is a rain-free pedestrian subway from the tube station all the way to the V&A and other museums in the Albertropolis.)

Break Suggestions: The New Restaurant which has the most pleasant ambiance of all the London museum snack shops. Its high ceilings and interesting archways compensate somewhat for the quality of the food which remains the same as the other museums.

Lots of interesting eateries en route to the South Kensington tube. Thai restaurant named Tui at the corner of Harrington and Thurloe. Next door is an Italian restaurant which is cheek-to-cheek with an Indian restaurant.

Or walk up to Hyde Park and go rowing on the Serpentine.

Or up Brompton Road to Harrods to view their world famous Food Halls.

The Science Museum

The most popular museum in Albertropolis undoubtedly is the whoop-and-holler Science Museum.

It was not designed to be a collection of industrial technological displays to be admired in reverent silence.

Oh, no. Anything but.

The tone of the museum is quickly set by the first room to the right of entrance, a Hands-On Technology Experience where swarming children DO THINGS. They push pedals, pump water, direct water flows, form a water-bubble sheet, take a tiptoe test, run a robot—one of many—all with good humored pushing and shoving and excited exuberance.

(In order to avoid the shouting of students of all sizes—and get a chance at the machines personally—go to the museum when it opens at 10AM or after 4:30PM when you might have the place to yourself for an-hour-and-a-half. It closes at six.)

The second recommended exercise is upstairs in the Synopsis Room where the seven-acre museum is compressed into the story of the development of technology and the rise of science.

Pick out what you want to see.

On my first trip I became enmeshed in the Space Exhibit, then moved up three floors to the aviation exhibit. Three hours disappeared in a blink.

I made a return trip to see the Puffing Billy, the oldest surviving locomotive in the world (1813) and the Caerphilly Castle, the awesome Caerphilly Castle—the Great Western Railway engine of 1923. I admired the 1909 Rolls Royce "Silver Ghost" and the astronomical table clock dated 1630, Sir Issac Newton's 1668 reflecting telescope, and Falcon's loom driven by punch cards—in 1728, can you believe.

And so it is with the Science Museum as with the others. So much missed. So much to look forward to.

What I learned in the Space Exhibit was that the invention and use of rockets dated back to the 16th century when the armies of India carried thousands of rockets into battle.

In the Mahratta Wars, late 18th century, the Indians used rockets with metal casing, much better than the cardboard rockets used in Europe, allowing greater concentration of gunpowder which resulted in heavier warheads and longer thrusts.

But the use of rockets couldn't match the accuracy of new rifled, breech-loading artillery.

However, the potential of rocket power was not lost on the imagination of Jules Verne and H G Wells who envisaged, and wrote about, space travel propelled by rockets. Their writings, in turn, inspired a Russian school teacher, Konstantin Tsiolkovsky (1857-1935) to write a theory on space travel powered by liquid oxygen and liquid hydrogen.

On March 16, 1926 Robert H Goddard in the United States launched the first successful liquid fueled rocket, technology which was repeated in the Saturn V's first trip to the moon.

A short film describes the first days of modern rocketry.

Another exhibit, very important in London history, reviews the development of the V1 and V2 rockets of the Germans. "V" for Vengeance.

It was a frightening time when 1,100 V2 bombs, unstoppable because of their 3,600-MPH speed, landed in England, each carrying a one-ton warhead. (To keep things in historical perspective the exhibit reminds the viewer that, at the same time, Allied bombers were dropping 3,000 tons of bombs *a day* on Germany.)

On exhibit is the actual Apollo-10, the first space machine to circle the moon in May 1969. The scorched scars from its reentry into the earth's atmosphere are still visible. Only the simulated figures inside the capsule are not real.

Also there is a lifesized model of the Apollo-11 which, traveling at 40,0000 kilometers per hour, reached the moon in three days and one day later, when its capsule descended to the moon's surface, Neil Armstrong made that thrilling historical announcement:

"The Eagle has landed."

The model depicts Armstrong and Aldrin outside the Eagle with their equipment. Continuous-play videos recall the television coverage of the event. Marvelously staged.

Take the escalator upstairs to review aviation history. One small diorama shows the Montgolfier brothers launching mankind on its aerial voyage near Lyon in 1783 when their hot-air balloon stayed aloft for a 25-minute flight and landed five miles away. A miracle.

Another miniature scene recreates a second flight from the Tuileries Garden in Paris using a silk bag and "inflammable air" (hydrogen gas made by putting iron filings into sulfuric acid) resulting in a two-hour flight that covered 27 miles. A later solo flight ascended to a height of 9,000 feet.

Not far away is the actual 1974 hot-air balloon used to set the altitude record of 45,836 feet by a British team. The balloon was called Daffodil II and was launched from central India.

Shown are model airplanes devised by John Stringfellow in 1848 and a model tri-plane exhibited in 1868 and work from Sir George Cayley, father of British aviation who proposed aerial carriages in 1843 with navigable balloons, the original dirigible.

A 1-to-7 scale model is shown of the Henson's Proposed Aeroplane, circa 1843, a steam-powered airplane with the boiler in the body. The creation of William Samuel Henson and Stringfellow, the sizable craft used two propellers but weighed only 25 pounds. Shown with the model are illustrations submitted in patents of the first carriage.

Overhead, suspended from the ceiling, are historic airplanes or life-size models. One model is an exact copy of the original Wright brothers' power-flight flyer. The original machine was the property of the Science Museum but was given to the Smithsonian Institute after World War II as a goodwill gesture.

Here, from a lofted footbridge, the visitor can see the glider models of Pilcher and Lilienthal, pioneers who tried to emulate birds but died during experimental flights.

Here is a Vickers Vimy which made the first nonstop crossing of the Atlantic in 1919 and also the *Jason,* a Gypsy Moth flown by Amy Johnson in a solo flight from England to Australia in 1930.

Here are the famous British fighters of the Battle of Britain: the Hurricane and the Spitfire.

Here is the first rocket propelled fighter, the Messerschmitt ME163 which debuted in 1944 near war's end. It had only 10 minutes of fuel, discarded its landing wheels on take-off, flew to 30,000 feet in two-and-a-half minutes and landed successfully on skids or—as frequently happened—blew up.

The sleekest of all, however, is the Supermarine S6B, a piece of aerodynamic sculpture, which won the Schneider Cup for seaplanes in 1931 with a speed of 340.08 MPH. Later it was to break 400 MPH. It is a sweet aircraft.

(The Schneider Cup was launched at Monaco in 1913. The first winner reached an astounding 45.75 MPH.)

I return again and again to the Science Museum which I rank as one of the great museums of the world. Grateful I was, on one return, to discover the Wellcome History of Medicine occupying the top floors. Unlike anything else I know.

Where else would you see a steel codpiece? Or see a polychrome tile from the bathroom of Pope Urban VIII showing the circumcision of Christ—where the surgeon is wearing spectacles? Or learn that a Mesopotamian surgeon was awarded five shekels if he saved a nobleman's eye, or life. And, if he failed, his hand was cut off.

Doctor, would that improve your surgery technique?

Now what do you want to learn about science? Roadmaking, shipping, electrical machines, steam machines, railways, iron and steel, photography, medicine, ceramics, printing, textiles, undersea exploration, leisure and pleasure, buildings, astronomy, clockmaking, old crafts, modern industries?

It is all here.
Pick your subject. Set your watch. Go.

Facts: A division of the British Museum, admission is free.
Open daily 10 to 6PM. Sundays 2:30.
Location: Exhibition Road between Cromwell Road and Kensington Road. (Part of Albertropolis.)
Tube station: South Kensington.
Break Suggestions: Go to tea or lunch in the New Restaurant in the V&A. Pick up Christmas presents in the Science or Geological Museum shops or at the excellent V&A shop.
Also see suggestions under the Victoria & Albert Museum.

Natural History Museum

"Natural History Museum?
"Yuck in spades," said the young lady.
"Things pickled and stuffed. Pinned to the wall. Not for me."
Too bad. The young lady missed the Natural History Museum in London, another branch of the British Museum, with several of the most outstanding, exciting, absorbing exhibits we have ever seen anywhere.
The nucleus of this vast horde of historical and educational national treasure was part of the purchase by Parliament in 1753 of the Hans Sloane eclectic collection that stimulated the formation of the British Museum. In 1860, the additions to the natural history section had been so vast that a separate museum was started in South Kensington and completed in 1880.
Facing Cromwell Road, it was built in a Romanesque cathedral style architecture.
A visiting friend of ours spent half an hour just studying and admiring the detail of the front of the building. "You must tell your readers to look at the carvings on the pillars and the buff-and-blue terracotta pediment above the entrance.
"No two columns are alike. The facade is incredible!"
The second initial object of awe in the museum is the central hall.
It is huge. Baronial in its splendor of floral designs, pillars and balconies and stairs which are decorated with terracotta moldings of animals and plants.
You could now leave having justified the modest admission

charge. (You can get in free after 4:30PM.)

But there is more.

Go to the new exhibit called "Claws."

A couple of years ago Bill Walker went digging in a sand pit in the suburbs of Surrey. Fossil hunting. He was awarded the most sensational find in a hundred years: a claw of an animal not known to have existed in England.

At one time the lands of Surrey were swamplands and, now, it is known that among the other animals living there 124 million years ago was a carnivorous dinosaur.

A team of scientists took over the dig where rock encased the rest of "Claws" remains.

The team brought back twenty tons of rock, patiently chipped away fragments of rock until enough of the animal's skeleton was revealed to reconstruct its entire body.

They were even able to deduce the animal's last supper—fish—devoured with jaws similar to those of a crocodile.

The exhibit includes facts and visuals about the Claws discovery and recreates missing parts of its skeleton. An explanatory video on dinosaurs is excellent.

Claws, for all of its timeliness and fascination, was listed as a temporary exhibit, such is the caliber of the museum. (It has 50 million items on inventory, only a fraction of which is on display at any given time).

Claws deserves to be in place as a permanent exhibition.

In 1972 the Trustees moved to combat the "pickled and stuffed" attitude most people harbor about natural history museums. Their aim was to create entertaining and involving presentations to more easily explain mankind and the world around us.

The first of these new exhibits was "Human Biology—An Exhibition Of Ourselves."

Sound dull?

It is the liveliest, most visual, easiest to understand education about the body you will ever see. Not just see, but experience because, here again, the hands-on technique is fully employed.

For example, you stand inside a womb and hear a mother's heartbeat.

The aim of the Trustees couldn't have more on target than with this permanent exhibit.

The second effort towards enlivening the museum is "Discovering Mammals" situated adjacent to the human biology exhibit.

How does a dolphin go grocery shopping?

Why is a horse's leg different from that of an elephant?

How do whales make love?

The answers to many such questions are found in this huge hall, once known for its gigantic blue whale, but now filled with fun-to-find-out lessons of breathing creatures—past and present—on sea and land.

Through video displays, tapes, recorded sounds, through participatory exercises you learn how whales are able to stay so long underwater, how they mate by singing love songs, show off by splashing and caressing each other. Sounds like King's Road on Saturday night.

You learn how dolphins track their prey through sonar. Then you try it yourself on a computerized video display unit using the same techniques of widening and sweeping your target area with an up-or-down button under your left hand while directing the area of search with a joy stick in your right hand.

(*Get away, kid. —This machine is mine!*)

We find it a fascinating possibility that a dolphin, once its sonar locks onto a fish, can intensify its sound so much that the victim is stunned . . . immobilized . . . dinner.

The exhibit is full of such goodies.

Watch rare scenes of hippos and sea cows underwater.

Travel over deserts and into the hearts of woodlands and hear the sounds of the forest.

The whole exhibit is spectacular.

We went to the Natural History Museum with a feeling of reluctant obligation . . . in the name of research.

Now, it goes into our list of the top ten things to be seen in London.

Facts: Like its parent, the British Museum, the Natural History Museum is open every day, 10AM to 6PM, Sundays 2:30PM to 6PM. Note: there is a small admission fee until 4:30PM, thereafter it is free.

Location: Cromwell between Exhibition Road and Queen's Gate.

Tube Station: South Kensington.

Break Suggestion: You are not too far from Old Brompton Road and the New York Cafe which has been there for 60 years.

Rocks And More Rocks . . .
The Geological Museum

Sandwiched between the Science Museum and the Natural History Museum is the Geological Museum. The entrance is on Exhibition Road.

If you are enamored of gemstones, the center area of the ground floor is devoted to a world famous collection of gemstones. During my first visit I looked at hundreds of rocks. They stared back at me. We didn't have much to say to each other.

I then asked the Lady Navigator to go on her own and give me a better feel of what a "world famous" collection of gemstones meant to her.

She spent four hours at the museum and never got beyond the rocks.

A slight exaggeration, but only slight.

She pronounced the gemstone collection the finest she had ever seen.

"I had never seen tiny insects entrapped inside opals. Wouldn't you love to wear a sparkly fossil?

"I never knew there was a *white* jade or that all jade has a toughness surpassing that of steel.

"And did you know that jade was used in China in the 14th century, *before Christ*?

"Tourmalines—which I've always thought to be green—can be any color in the rainbow. It is the chameleon of the gemstone world.

"And beryl—sounds so, well, un-chic—is really my birthstone, aquamarine, or an emerald. Shows you can't judge a gem by its tacky name.

"The shop has some of the finest pieces of geodes in attractive settings at the fairest prices I've ever encountered."

Okay. Okay. But what about the moon rock, I asked?

"Moon rock. Is there one there? Didn't have time to see that. I'll go back."

Did you get into the 'Story of the Earth' exhibit, I asked.

"Tried, but it was under repair. I'll go back."

She didn't have to. She did what she enjoyed most. Looked at rocks.

What I found to be well done was The Story of the Earth,

showing how the earth—and other earths—evolve. (That's where the piece of moon rock brought back by the American space explorers is on exhibit, Lady Navigator.)

In another exhibit the make-up of the crust of the earth and the involving plate tectonics are explained graphically.

The source of various minerals, what they look like, how they are used in our modern world, is both entertaining—those hands-on buttons and levers and lights a'flashing again—and highly educational.

Best of all, for children of all ages, is the exhibit devoted to the major earthquake in Anchorage, Alaska where the viewer sees "before" and "after" pictures, hears the rumble of an actual earth convulsion, and feels the earth's movement during a modest sized shake created by a platform that shifts and bucks at the same time. The realistic enactment of nature is slightly terrifying. It makes you grateful that you have never had the sickening experience of a major upheaval, especially if you have been through several minor earthquakes.

It is the only *feets-on* exhibit we know of.

Much more at the Museum of the Institute of Geological Sciences which is an important research center as well as repository for a huge and impressive collection of rocks, minerals and fossils.

Facts: Open daily 10AM to 6PM, Sundays 2:30 to 6PM. Small admission.

Location: Exhibition Road between Cromwell Road and Kensington Road.

Tube station: South Kensington

Break Suggestions: Same as other Albertropolis museums or go rest your feet in the front garden of the Natural History Museum on Cromwell Road and look at the carved entrance. It is serenely beautiful.

A Memorial Museum— Churchill's Cabinet War Rooms

It doesn't seem that long ago.

August 15, 1945.

The news had been floating in London all day. The second

devastating atom bomb had been dropped on Japan and the Emperor had sued for peace.

At midnight a joint announcement was made in Washington D.C. and London. The war with Japan was over. The Allied Forces had done it: Victory over Japan . . . VJ Day.

At one end of the Mall the Royal Family appeared on the balcony to wave at the crowd.

The crowd was ecstatic, roaring with happy hysteria, including this Denver-born artillery captain on leave from the 3rd Army in Europe.

At the other end of the Mall in the bowels of a governmental office complex on King Charles Street, the staff of a small subterranean city toasted this night as the last operational day of the Cabinet War Rooms. By that time—VJ Day 1945—the rooms under the New Building facing St James's Park had been expanded to three acres accommodating 500 people.

Besides offices, the amenities included emergency beds, a shooting gallery, messes, canteen and hospital.

Winston Churchill had suggested the creation of such offices for the Cabinet in 1936. Three rooms were opened in the summer of 1938 as the threat of war with Germany grew stronger.

Fortunately, in the post-war period most of the important rooms were left intact. Then, in 1981, the rooms were opened to the public. All rooms were faithfully restored to their wartime functions. Only minor alterations were made to accommodate the flow of visitor traffic.

The result is a recall of an era hectic, frightening, demanding, but, somehow, fulfilling.

The war with Germany started in 1939. By June of 1940 the continent of Europe had been overrun. England stood alone.

Winston Churchill was in command of the government on September 7, 1940 when the Luftwaffe bombed London. The German aerial war began with fighters and bombers and, in 1944, shifted to a jet-propelled, pilotless, flying bomb, the V1. A deadlier V2 followed, a rocket powered flying missile. Flying at a speed of 3,600 MPH it was impossible to shoot down. A time of terror. Forty thousand civilians lost their lives in the attacks and another 61,000 were injured.

No one above ground was safe.

London went underground.

Subway stations became overnight, sleep-on-concrete hotels for thousands of Londoners.

A thousand bombs were to fall within one hundred yards of the New Building but it never received a direct hit.

You are given an excellent brochure with a strip map leading you through 20 stations.

Four rooms are the most important: the Cabinet Room where the War Cabinet and Defense Committee met; the Telephone Room where Churchill talked with President Roosevelt, the Map Room which was the operational nerve center, and Churchill's private quarters. He seldom slept there.

The first room on your visit, the Cabinet Room, is viewed through a glass panel which permits you to see it all from the corridor.

Neville Chamberlain's War Cabinet met here only once but Winston Churchill's Cabinet convened over a hundred times during four years of the war.

Besides being Prime Minister, Churchill, in character, kept the portfolio of Minister of Defense and convened his Defense Committee here as well.

The room is nearly filled by a large table surrounded by folding chairs. Papers and pens are at each place. The center chair, a large polished wooden affair in front of a world map, was Churchill's. The clock on the wall is set for five. All the clocks in the complex are fixed at the same hour.

At War Cabinet meetings Clement Atlee as the Deputy Prime Minister sat to Churchill's immediate left.

A large slot in the middle of the table accommodated the chiefs of staff of the armed services—Army, RAF, and the Navy—during meetings of the Defense Committee. They sat facing the Prime Minister in what must have been considered hot seats. What a growling grilling Churchill must have given them. One can almost hear him.

To the left above the door are two small electric bulbs. One is painted red denoting an air raid in progress when lit. Another is green to signal All Clear.

The transatlantic Telephone Room where Churchill communicated with Roosevelt and, subsequently, Truman after Roosevelt's death, is small. Its distinguishing accessory is a clock on the wall with double hands to designate London and Washington times simultaneously.

Communications, although scrambled at one end and unscrambled at the other, were never secure until "Sigsaly" was developed by the Bell Telephone Company in 1943. But Sigsaly, a sophisticated scrambler, presented another problem. Its machinery was too large to fit into the Cabinet War Rooms. It was stored in the basement of the Selfridges department store on Oxford Street and connected by cable.

A more delicate problem was one of protocol—ergo, ego. Churchill did not want to pick up the telephone until Roosevelt was on the line. Roosevelt had the same quirk. It was a tippy-toe time for the staffs of both chief commanders.

The Map Room (Room 65) at Stop 16 was a third highlight. Manned around the clock during the war, it served as the intelligence center: collecting, sorting and sifting, mapping and summarizing daily action concerning all war fronts and then distributing the information. Its heart lay in the dozen colored phones sitting atop the bridge dividing the long table. The line of telephones, known as "the beauty chorus," linked the Map Room with each of the armed service chiefs and other operational centers.

An ivory telephone at the desk of the Duty Officer—the head of the table—was a direct link to No. 10 Downing Street.

The Map Room's daily and weekly summary news bulletins always went to Buckingham Palace where the king remained in residence throughout the war, refusing all suggestions of leaving London.

Next to the Map Room is the Prime Minister's Room, his emergency office and sleeping quarters. Actually he slept here only three times. Churchill and Mrs. Churchill lived in private apartments on the ground floor of the New Building in another operational headquarters.

On one occasion when she left London overnight, she instructed Churchill's aide to make sure that he went to bed in his underground room. Churchill obeyed. His aide returned to find Churchill in his dressing gown preparing a sheaf of papers and preparing to leave.

"I came downstairs and went to bed as promised. Now I'm going upstairs to sleep."

Churchillian memorabilia is displayed in a cabinet in the adjoining room. His chromium plated helmet is there. So is a chamber pot. (One reason, the descriptive card explained, for Churchill's reluctance to stay in the basement was its limited lavatory facilities.)

For many veterans of the European war and residents of England during those uncertain times, the Cabinet War Rooms will flood the mind with memories, memories mostly pleasant now. The ugliness and the horror and the moments of terror have slipped back into subconscious shadows. Time, the great healer.

Facts: The Cabinet War Rooms museum is a part of the Imperial War Museum which also operates the cruiser *HMS Belfast* as a museum in additional war archives and exhibitions at its headquarters on Lambeth Road.

Cabinet War Rooms are open 10AM to 5:50PM. Closed Mondays, and major holidays and on some State occasions. Admission charge. Portable tape machines are for rent. Worthwhile.

You can buy a postcard and other remembrance gifts in the Souvenir Shop (Room 68).

Location: Clive Steps, King Charles Street which comes off Whitehall.

Tube Station: Westminster.

Break Suggestion: Take a stroll in St James's park fronting the Cabinet War Rooms.

Places Of Peace
Places Of Pomp

10. Parks and Palaces

One of the nicer features of London is greenery
Places where birds sing.
Breathing space.

At almost at every corner in London there is a village green or a public garden or a tree filled square where you can recede from the rush and smell the flowers.

Dominating the central map of London are five major continuous open spaces: St James's Park, Green Park, Buckingham Palace Gardens—for the Royal Family only—Hyde Park, and Kensington Gardens. Hundreds of additional acres in the public domain include Regent's Park on the north and Battersea Park, south of the Thames, and Holland Park in West London.

I remember one autumn morning walking in Green Park, next to the Ritz Hotel on Piccadilly, stretching my legs before starting a ten-hour flight from Heathrow at noon, kicking at red autumn leaves and thinking how lucky I was to have a peaceful place to savor a last hour in London. I can still smell the pungent leaves.

Another time, in the height of a summer season, I left the

155

jammed packed crowds of Piccadilly at the door of St James's Church, one of the prettiest Wren churches in the city, walked down Duke of York Street, stopped to smile at the ancient Wheeler's restaurant at the corner of Apple Tree Yard, and strolled into St James's Square.

There I sat in a square block of greenery on an old wooden bench all by myself. Not another soul around.

It's like that throughout London.

We lived most of one spring-summer period one street removed from the constant whiz and fizz of King's Road.

But a hundred yards away from our flat was Chelsea Green, a tiny swatch of peace with four benches in its grassy crosswalk and tree branch homes for the fat hungry pigeons. Its lunchtime occupants came from the small neighborhood shops around its triangular perimeter. Between the commercial anchors—the pub on one corner, a restaurant at another and the inevitable estate dealer—the green grocer, the pie man, the butcher and fishmonger provided the daily needs of the community.

It could have been a far removed country village.

Every morning we awoke at dawn to the sound of birds.

What's the sound of London? It is not the fog horns of San Francisco or the wail of sirens of New York or the 24-hour muted roar of freeway traffic in Los Angeles. It's the sound of birds at dawn.

"And the distinctive sound of four-cylinder diesel taxis and buses," said a friend.

"And jackhammers," added another.

Okay, but first of all, birds at dawn.

Buckingham Palace Gardens, of course, are private but seen by thousands during the summer royal garden parties. The others, designated as royal parks, are public and usually spotted with deck chairs rented for a few pence and bandstands where military bands play stimulating music during summers.

The establishment of St James's Park, the first of the Royal Parks, is a legacy of Henry VIII who drained a marshy bog where leper women in St James's Hospital kept their hogs. His original use for the area was tilting tournaments, jousting with lances and horses, later adding a bowling alley and a nursery for his deer.

Eventually he converted the area into a vast hunting ground which extended from Whitehall Palace as far north as Hampstead Heath.

James I formalized a garden and established a zoo for wild animals—including two crocodiles—plus an aviary.

The great Versailles landscape architect, Andre Le Notre, was hired by Charles II to expand and redo the park. Fruit trees were planted, deer from several countries were imported, and several small ponds were rearranged to form a long strip of water known as the Canal. It was along the Canal that Charles II walked with his mistresses and dogs, feeding the ducks, even taking an occasional swim.

The south side aviary became Birdcage Walk.

The acreage of what is now Green Park was added.

Duck Island was built for William III who enjoyed watching the wild birds.

The park suffered some indignities for a time. It became a haunt of prostitutes and, although the gates were locked at night, permission was granted for 6,500 keys.

In the 19th century John Nash redesigned the park and changed the Canal into its present day graceful shape, added refuge islands for ducks and geese and replaced the surrounding stone wall with iron fencing.

Today St James's Park is one of the most elegant, most beautiful parks in London.

Feeding the ducks, as did Charles II, is still a favorite pastime for the lunchtime crowd. If you think the St James's Park ducks waddle is over emphasized, it is because the fat creatures gorge daily on leftover sandwiches.

Summers, canvas lawn chairs are arranged around the lakes and ponds and in groupings for visual enjoyment. Sit in one that pleases you. A man comes around to collect a few pence. Take in the sun. Relax.

It is forbidden to play radios or bring dogs into the park, two regulations which add to St James's enjoyment.

The history of Hyde Park, "the lungs of London," also began as part of Henry VIII's royal hunting grounds. He walled the grounds to prevent his deer from escaping and to discourage poachers.

Later in its history, the park was sold to an individual who charged admission but the sale was rescinded and the park returned to government ownership. It was alternately used as a race course, an ammunition dump, a royal riding trail. The latter connected Kensington Palace with St James's Palace and was regally called *route du roi,* meaning route of the king in French. In best British tradition, the name was, in time, corrupted to "Rotten Row" by which the remaining horse trail in Hyde Park is still known.

The notorious Tyburn gallows stood where Marble Arch now stands.

Duels were fought in the park, military executions took place in the northeast corner against the wall, and footpads—muggers—stalked the park for victims. One such was Horace Walpole, the diarist and son of the Prime Minister, who lost a watch and eight guineas.

In 1730 a lake was added under the guidance of Queen Caroline, a keen landscape gardener. The lake, that graceful body of water that starts in Kensington Gardens as the Long Waters and a series of fountains, broadens out as the Serpentine in Hyde Park. Queen Caroline floated two royal yachts on the lake.

Today the gentle, curving lake serves as a focal point for lakeside picnics and strolling, and for the occasional boater.

Today the 340-acre park is an important playing field for pick-up soccer games, cricket practice, frisbee throwing, even loose softball games.

Today it is equally important to picnickers and pram pushers, dog walkers and squirrel watchers, joggers and horseback riders, and soapbox lecturers at Speaker's Corner, London's symbol of free speech.

Hudson Bird Sanctuary is part of the park—some 90 species of birds have been identified—and there is a nice restaurant-cafe-bar complex near the Serpentine Bridge which separates Hyde Park from Kensington Gardens.

Just to the west of the bridge is The Serpentine Gallery, a frequent venue of art shows.

Hyde Park flows into Kensington Gardens without interruption.

The Gardens were originally designed as part of Kensington Palace and comprised some 20 formal acres. Today there are 275 acres with many stroll-worthy walks amid a forest of trees radiating alongside wide paths off of Round Pond. London seems miles away when you are wandering the spacious grounds of Kensington Gardens.

Minor statues dot the grounds but on the south side is a major statue monument, the Albert Memorial.

A 175-foot monstrosity, it consists of a gothic canopy, spires and mosaics and enamels and polished stones and diddlydos. Under the canopy is a 14 foot seated figure of Prince Albert, facing the Royal Albert Hall and holding a catalogue of the Great Exhibition. Below him are no less than a 169 life-sized figures in a white marble frieze.

It is so Victorian awful that it is borderline wonderful.

The mishmash of mosaics, spires, pinnacles and allegorical statues unfortunately combines all the worst features of the confused stolidness of Victorian era artistic taste. Little wonder that it took 20 years to build.

Albert deserved better.

Today it is blocked off to save pedestrians being hit on the head by falling stone because it is falling apart.

The canopy has been leaking and the iron rods holding the monument together are rusting away. The statues are roped in place.

A movement is underway to get funds to undertake a major repair operation. A difficult decision.

Regent's Park, a mile north of Hyde Park, merits a visit for several reasons. A major reason would be to visit the London Zoo and see the panda and one of the best of elephant houses. Alas, my favorite polar bears, too delicate for their surroundings, have been removed.

Another charming reason is the Regent's Canal which curves through the north end of the park. There are docks in the zoo from where you can take a narrowboat cruise from Camden Lock to Little Venice whose banks are lined with Georgian houses.

Still another reason, summertimes, is the Open Air Theatre sharing the center of the park inside the Inner Circle with Queen Mary's Gardens.

Included in Regent's Park is a massive boating lake, a Broad Walk, playing fields and a sports pavilion, a tea house, and of course the zoo at the northernmost end. The US ambassador lives in Winfield House on the northwest side of the park in a neo-Georgian house designed for the 3rd Marquess of Hertford who, it was rumored, used it as a harem.

Henry VIII was in on the inception of Regent's Park as well. In one of his land-grab schemes, he traded Marylebone Fields for other confiscated church property farther afield to enlarge his hunting reserve.

Ownership weaved and bobbed for the next two hundred years from Crown to individual, back to Crown again. Its trees were cut for lumber, its soil tilled, but the circular shape laid out for Henry VIII's hunting grounds remained.

It was this shape that inspired John Nash to propose a plan which won for him the 19th century royal commission to re-develop the area as a profit oriented garden suburb. His plan was exquisite.

Townhouse terraces of palatial proportions ringed the outer circle. Villas on the inner circle were to be concealed behind heavy shrubbery to maintain an open park environment. A curved lake at the southwest corner and an arm of a canal at the northern boundary were central to the park plan as was a summer pavilion for the Prince of Wales, approached by a long straight avenue (the Broad Walk).

The Prince Regent's involvement undoubtedly was the come-on for terrace buyers. As Nash's patron, the Prince Regent supported him over seven difficult years, hence the name: Regent's Park.

Nash's plan was never totally completed, and part of it was demolished during the second war, but terraces to his style still rim the southern part of the circle and they are a classroom text book, for architectural students.

They are well worth seeing. Idea: go by tube to the Baker Street station, grab a taxi and ask the driver to drive the Outer Circle road of the park passing the terraces, then drop you at the zoo.

The London Zoo is a principal visitor attraction in London.

Popular from inception in 1827, the Zoo's animals were oohed and aahed at by 30,000 visitors in the first seven months.

Giraffes, lions, snakes, elephants, penguins and the giant panda joined the menagerie over the years.

Simulated natural environment facilities and pavilions have been continually added since the war: an aviary, an elephant and rhino pavilion, new lion terraces, etc. But no polar bears.

If you come to London with children, you must go to the London Zoo. If you come to London without children, go anyway. You'll love it.

South of Regent's Park, on Marylebone Road adjacent to the Baker Street tube station, is Madame Tussaud's waxworks which, for some reason we have never understood, remains one of the to-do things in London. It is the National Portrait Gallery and

Hollywood in three dimensions. Long lines. The Planetarium is next door.

One block west of the tube is Baker Street, the fictitious address of that Sherlock Holmes whose adventures have thrilled Arthur Conan Doyle readers for more than one hundred years.

The Fringe Parks

South of the Thames is Battersea Park, once known as a place for shooting pigeons, and each other. Wellington and the Earl of Winchilsea staged a famous duel here after Winchilsea accused the Duke of being a traitor. At the order of "fire," Winchilsea kept his firearm at his side and the Duke, therefore refusing a free target, shot wide. Winchilsea then fired into the air and apologized. A very civilized duel.

Almost 200 acres are planted with grass and flowers and shrubs today with a boating lake, tennis courts, deer park and playing fields and a children's zoo.

As a visitor, you may never see the park unless you stay in the area, take a river boat trip, attend the big family annual Easter festival or witness the start of the Veteran Car Run to Brighton which starts here every November.

The Easter affair brings out thousands—rain, hail or sun—to see a major parade with themed floats, vintage cars, and clowns of course. There are hot-air balloons, skydiving demonstrations, rock bands and all the other fuss that goes along with a big traditional community effort.

If you cruise upriver to Kew or Hampton Court, you'll get a good view of the 110-foot tall London Peace Pagoda on the bank.

A few blocks west of Kensington Gardens is Holland House and Park, a sanctum of tranquillity in kinetic Kensington. Three formal gardens surround Holland House, the Rose Garden, the Iris Garden and the Dutch Garden, the latter is floodlit during the summer until midnight.

The ironic note is that Holland House was famous in its time for lavish banquets, balls, salons and the parade of prominent names that passed its portals.

Today what is left of the war-damaged house is occupied by a youth hostel (George VI Memorial Hostel). A public restaurant is in the former Garden Ballroom. Summertime open-air plays, concerts, operas, are performed at the Court Theatre on the front terrace of the ruined house.

Its rehabilitation is the work of the former London County Council which bought the property in 1952, restored the gardens and part of the house.

Note: Four Royal Parks have daily band concerts from late May to late August: St James's, Regent's Park, Hyde Park and Greenwich Park, the latter reviewed in Chapter 8, The Thames.

Puppet shows are performed in Kensington Gardens, Regent's Park and at Greenwich twice a day during the spring-summer season.

Get details and schedules from a London Information Office.

Palaces, Big And Small

The evolution of London palaces reads:

The Palace of Westminster (Edward the Confessor to Henry VIII), destroyed by fire.

Whitehall (Henry VIII), destroyed by fire in 1695 set by a careless laundrywoman.

St James's (Henry VIII to the present).

Kensington Palace (William III to Queen Victoria to the present).

Buckingham Palace (Queen Victoria to the present).

Out of chronological order but first on our list is Kensington Palace because it is the only palace of the three remaining in London that you can easily visit.

A visit to Kensington Palace, the birthplace of Queen Victoria, and a stroll through the vast park that is Kensington Gardens is one of the more satisfactory non-hectic historical visits you'll make in London.

One of the reasons for the satisfaction is that there are relatively few visitors.

The reason for Kensington Palace was royal asthma.

In 1609 William III (1609-1702) became disenchanted with Whitehall and St James's because the riverside atmosphere interfered with his asthmatic ability to breathe.

He moved out of London to a distant manor house called

Nottinghams, purchased for £18,900, free of the River Thames' wet air and the city's pollution. Christopher Wren was commissioned to redesign the building when it then became known as Kensington House.

A diarist of the day referred to it as "a patch'd building . . . " "very noble, tho not greate . . . the gardens about it very delicious."

"Not greate" tho it may have been, it *was* the royal palace. And, as can be imagined, where the king lived was where everyone wanted to be.

William and his queen, Mary II, lived here until their deaths.

Queen Anne, who used Kensington for a summer hangout, built the Orangery, the building north of the palace with a superb view of the grounds. She died of overeating.

George I, "an honest blockhead" as a lady of the court called him, who preferred to spend his time in his native Hanover, enlarged the buildings. His son, George II, 1727-1760, was the last monarch to make Kensington the principal royal palace. He died in his water closet.

(The front-runners of the Hanover House who ruled England for almost two hundred years were a funny lot. George II used to go into rages and kick his wig around the room. George III, the ruler at the time of the American Revolution, lived the last of his life in a strait jacket. George IV's death gave his brother, William IV, the throne for seven years. He had a pineapple shaped head and was also given to uncontrollable ranting and raving.)

The Duchess of Kent, wife of the deceased Duke of Kent, fourth son of King George IV, found herself the mother of little Victoria, the closest heir to the British throne. A formidable lady, the Duchess moved into seventeen rooms in Kensington Palace, precisely against William's orders. The sovereign was enraged. At a birthday party, a black wig covering his odd-shaped head and cosmetics his face, he railed out at the Duchess promising he would live until Victoria was eighteen to prevent the Duchess from becoming her regent.

His one ambition was realized. He died on cue.

At 18, the legal heir, the petite Victoria became queen and moved out of Kensington Palace into Buckingham Palace.

Today, Kensington Palace is home to two branches of the royal family: the Prince of Wales and his lovely Princess Di, and Princess Margaret.

It is doubtful you will encounter any of the royals, but the State Apartments which were opened to the public by Queen Victoria on her 70th birthday merit the effort for themselves. Enter from the back of the palace near the sunken garden and Orangery.

Your bonus is the Court Dress Collection depicting 200 years of London Society.

You learn that Court Dress has always been precisely dictated. (And may be the reason dress standards are still set for many of the London "social" events.)

Acceptance at the court was paramount to a sanction to carry on one's way of life, be it political, professional, royal, military . . . whatever.

"Nobody can carry on the King's business if he is not supported at Court," Robert Walpole, Prime Minister for George I, wrote.

Court acceptance was very democratic. All occupations were recognized; all except, as the dress code booklet stated, "at trade known as retail the line is drawn."

Being supported at court meant being properly gowned. ("Retail" had the last laugh.)

No one had to guess at the rules of dress. They were carefully detailed, published and distributed to all to be presented at court. And they were rigorously maintained.

Once, in 1765, Queen Charlotte even dictated that all court gowns were to be made of Spitalfields silk, an effort to support a home industry. ("Retail" may have been below the line of court acceptance, but it had a very strong friend in court.)

The last edition of a dress code booklet was in 1937, coinciding with the last year of debutante presentations at court.

Up until that time, to be presented at court to a debutante was equivalent to "an introduction into the world."

We expressed surprise to a guard that all of the court dresses looked so new.

"Court dresses were worn only once."

"Why?" American curiosity got the better of the Lady Navigator.

"Because a person was introduced at court only once."

The Lady Navigator, undaunted: "What a waste. What happened to the the hundreds of other gowns that are not in this collection?"

Guard on duty: "Most were passed along to the servants to modify or make over. It would have been socially unacceptable to be seen in the same gown twice.''

The final showcase in the elaborate exhibition of silks and satins, ruffles and furbelows, knee breeches and velvet coats is of the lovely Lady Diana on that magical day in 1981 when she became the perfect Princess Di.

While you are on the ground floor walk through the Red Saloon, the room where the new young queen, Victoria, met with her council June 20, 1837 to plan for her ascendancy to the throne.

Next door are the apartments of the Duke and Duchess of Kent, Victoria's parents. (Her father was extremely handsome if you can trust the painting in the room. Victoria, it seems, took after her mother.)

The North Drawing Room was where Victoria was born in 1819.

The upstairs apartments are approached on the Queen's Staircase, built in 1691 as part of the Wren improvements. You enter the Queen's apartments via a long richly decorated gallery with Vauxhall mirrors above the fireplace.

The room next door is the Closet, site of the explosive meeting terminating the friendship between a heretofore subservient Queen Anne and her overbearing, contemptuous confidant, Sarah. The queen stripped her of all her honors and privileges and sent her into virtual exile.

Sarah and her husband, the Duke of Marlborough who had won every battle in which he was engaged, were powers in the Empire, using a gullible and pliant Anne as the spokesperson. After the quarrel, the couple was allowed to retire with their riches to Blenheim Palace.

The Queen's Dining Room has an elaborate marble chimney piece but it is the Drawing Room that perked our historical senses. The restored war-damaged ceiling bearing the initials W & M reminded us that both William & Mary University and Williamsburg, first capital of Virginia, were named for the sovereigns.

The last two Queens Chambers are the Privy Chamber and then the Presence Chamber. The ceiling of the first was decorated by William Kent who was known for his elaborate, romantic ceiling paintings. The light and gay ceiling of the Presence Chamber is the earliest example of arabesque decoration in England.

The King's Grand Staircase separates the King's Apartments from the Queen's.

The King's Gallery is a finely proportioned room by Wren intended to showcase paintings from the Royal collection. It does. A group of 17th century paintings. (The museum blahs begin to overwhelm you about here.)

The Victorian Rooms were redecorated by Queen Mary, wife of King George V, but the rooms are filled with memorabilia of Queen Victoria. Note the bright Victorian wallpaper.

An ugly, monstrous clock dominates the King's Dining room but from the windows you can see the landscaping scheme of the Round Pond with its avenues radiating in different directions. Little boys sailing model boats and running foot races have replaced the once great formal gardens.

The last room is the Cupola Room, done for George I in 1718, and is the grandest of the apartment rooms with blue and gold vaulted ceiling and an immense marble fireplace. Queen Victoria was baptized in this room.

Save time to visit the small sunken garden which heralds the coming of Spring each year with bursts of daffodils and tulips on terraces then gets replanted with seasonal plants the rest of the year.

St James's Palace

One of the prettier sights and short walks in London is from the Admiralty Arch at Trafalgar Square along The Mall, past St James's Palace to Buckingham Palace.

The Mall was created at the same time Le Notre redid the adjacent St James's Park. Covered with crushed cockleshells it was designed as a playing alley half a mile long for *paille maille,* a game played with a mallet and a polished ball.

Later it became a promenade for fashionable ladies by day, other "ladies" at night. As Pope wrote:

"Some feel no flames but at Court or Ball
And others hunt white aprons in The Mall"

In 1911 the present 115-foot widened avenue was opened from the Arch to the Queen Victoria Memorial in front of Buckingham Palace.

(At the Admiralty Arch end is a statue to our hero, Captain James Cook.)

St James's Palace was built by Henry VIII in the confiscated St James's Hospital. The entrance to the four courts was through the gatehouse entrance which is the only part of the old palace still standing.

The crenellated, red brick Tudor buildings always looked to me slightly sinister.

Queen Mary, Elizabeth I, James I, Queen Anne, George I, II, and III all resided here, the principal palace after the destruction of Whitchall. Charles I spent his last night here before being marched across St James's Park to his execution at the Banqueting House.

Bordering The Mall are Carlton House, Marlborough House, Clarence House and Lancaster House, all royal residences once. The Queen Mother today resides in Clarence House.

Ambassadors are still appointed to the Court of St James.

None of the State Apartments are open for public viewing.

Only the Chapel Royal is open for Sunday services, and only from the first Sunday in October to Good Friday.

Buckingham Palace

It's a coin toss. Whether a session of Parliament or the Changing of the Guard is the best free show in town depends, perhaps, on the issues of Parliamentary debate or if the Prime Minister is taking questions that day.

The Changing of the Guard is more reliable and easier to witness.

In any event, it is a primary focus for any London visit, partially because it happens outside the residence of the royal family, Buckingham Palace.

James I planted the land at the west end of St James's Park as a mulberry garden. It was later given by Queen Anne to the newly created Duke of Buckingham (John Sheffield) in 1703 for a manor (Buckingham House).

George III bought the house for his bride in 1762.

When George IV inherited the throne he set about creating a grander, more imposing palace than his royal residence, Carlton House, in St James's Palace. He chose Buckingham House where his brothers and sisters had been born.

The building estimate of £252,690 was slightly underbid. The total tab exceeded £ 700,000, and that didn't include the Marble Arch at the entrance.

John Nash, the architect, was sacked.

His replacement enclosed the courtyard by adding the front wing facing The Mall and moved the Marble Arch to Hyde Park Corner.

George IV died before the palace was finished and his brother, William IV, never occupied the palace.

Royalty has occupied Buckingham Palace only since the last century. Yesterday in British time.

The Palace become a royal residence when the teen-age queen, Victoria, moved from Kensington, her birth place.

It was a mess. Windows didn't open, doors didn't close, drains leaked, bells didn't ring. But Queen Victoria grew to love it.

Since the war the palace has been through another renovation and redecoration.

Although the palace contains some 600 rooms Queen Elizabeth and the Duke of Edinburgh occupy only a dozen rooms overlooking Green Park.

Within the palace, however, are rooms of outstanding grandeur.

Towering elegantly draped windows, reflecting mirrors, sparkling chandeliers, grand staircases are incorporated into the decorative scheme of the State Apartments, the legacy of George IV who was quite carried away with the whole project.

The Ball Room is as wide as a football field and over twice as long. It is the setting for state banquets and investitures at which time the royal couple occupy thrones beneath a gold fringed canopy at one end of the room.

Familiar to those 9,000 lucky people who annually pass through it on their way to the summer garden parties is the Bow Room.

Buckingham's State Apartments are not open to the public. Even if you are never invited to a state banquet or a garden party, you can still enjoy royalty from the fringes.

First, of course, is the daily Changing the Guard in the summer and alternate days in the winter.

Royal protection rests with five regiments of guards: the Grenadiers, the Coldstreams, the Scots, the Irish, and the Welsh which, chronologically, go from 1656 (Grenadiers) to 1915 (Welsh). Each regiment is garbed in scarlet tunic (perfect for photographers), great bearskin hats, and dark blue trousers.

Different plumes and buttons distinguish one regiment from the other.

"You are seeing the best part of the Changing the Guard," our double-decked bus tour guide said as a squad of soldiers marched toward the entrance to the Palace.

"And see that little man taking pictures and money from the passing tourists? He keeps the money and the tourists never see a picture."

The Changing of Guard is a noble event. The military sound of a regimental band. The precision of evenly matched marching toy soldiers. It is all so ritualistic. So colorful. The type of pageantry we all come to London to enjoy.

Summer crowds are legion.

Unless you arrive at the entrance very early and line up along the fence facing the palace, you won't be able to see into the courtyard.

The regimental band and the guard approach the palace from the southeastly Spur Row coming from the Wellington Barracks down Birdcage Walk. If you place yourself on the Queen Victoria Memorial facing south, the band and guard will march straight into your camera and then wheel to their left into the palace. Good shot.

The retiring guard will retreat on the same route.

Many tour guides, I've noted, take their groups down to the corner of Birdcage Walk and Spur Row and see more of the bands and guards coming and going.

> **Note 1:** the schedule for the Changing of Guard is at 11:30AM daily during the peak spring/summer months but is changed to alternate days from September to March.
>
> **Note 2:** Signs everywhere in crowded places and at crowded events warn the visitor to guard the wallet and purse. We have never known a victim of London pickpockets but such constant warnings would indicate the plucking of visitors' pockets to be a local industry.

Two closer looks at Buckingham Palace are available for small fees.

The Queen's Gallery on Buckingham Palace Road is actually part of the Palace complex. A couple of exhibitions a year are mounted. It may be paintings from the royal collection, or as happened during our last trip to London, a photographic show.

The major exhibit in 1988 will be "The Queen's Best Paintings," the last exhibit to be mounted by Sir Oliver Miller, the

Keeper of the Queen's Pictures, who will be retiring.

The second Buckingham experience occurs on Wednesday and Thursday afternoons from 2 to 4PM when The Royal Mews are open to the public.

The buildings around the shaded courtyard are occupied by a saddlery, the stables and the royal coaches. On a nice day the Gold State Coach, which has been used for every coronation parade since 1820, is brought out into the sunlight for the benefit of picture takers.

One wing holds a marvelous collection of carriages. Wagonettes, a pony phaeton, a single horse sleigh, a governess's cart, a single brougham . . . any one of which you'd like to take home with you.

In the saddlery section, there are cases filled with working harnesses, saddles and bridles. You can see the presentation Western saddle given to the Prince of Wales in Alberta, Canada in 1927 and Princess Elizabeth's first saddle.

For most people the object of the visit is the Carriage House where the elegant and historical carriages are kept. Here is the Ascot Landau with basketweave sides used by the royal family at the Royal Ascot Races.

Here is Queen Victoria's last carriage. Over there is a Balmoral carriage.

"It looks like a large bassinet," said the lady behind me.

Queen Alexander's State Coach with the ornate carriage lamps is particularly elegant as is the Irish State Coach used by the Queen traditionally for the opening of Parliament.

Here is Queen Victoria's last carriage.

Horses we have known would love the stables. Painted cool cream and light green, their bricked floors are immaculately clean. Each stall is covered with crisp straw; all 32 bearing the name and age of its equine occupant.

Note: the Mews is popular and you can expect to stand in line in the summer time. Go early. The crush just to see the carriage in which the Queen rides is another indication that the royal family belongs to the world and sets England and London apart. Without the royal family, England would be just another overnight baggage-sticker stop on the European tour.

Found And Treasured

11. Shoppers' London

London is a dilemma.

Whether 'tis nobler to spend your day at the theater, at a museum, or toddling around old St Paul's or Westminster Abbey is the question.

The tapestry of London is so rich. The choices so wide. The hours never stretch far enough.

The shopoholic faces no such frustration.

She (he?) goes for the jugular. Heads straight for Harrods, Liberty, Fortnum & Mason . . . those heralded, traditional English emporiums that know no clone.

Shops 'til she drops.

Even on Sunday, despite England's long tradition of "Keeping The Sabbath," she can spend a bundle at Antique Fairs scattered in hotels throughout the city or at Petticoat Lane, a cockney/Jewish street market of 17th century Huguenot origin.

Sooner or later she will find the extraordinary values at Marks & Spencer, Peter Jones and John Lewis.

Sooner or later, if she has children or grandchildren, she will find Hamley's for toys and Mothercare for everything a Mum needs—except time.

And sooner, not later, she will poke around the smart boutiques and prowl the department stores for clothes and shoes she cannot find back home.

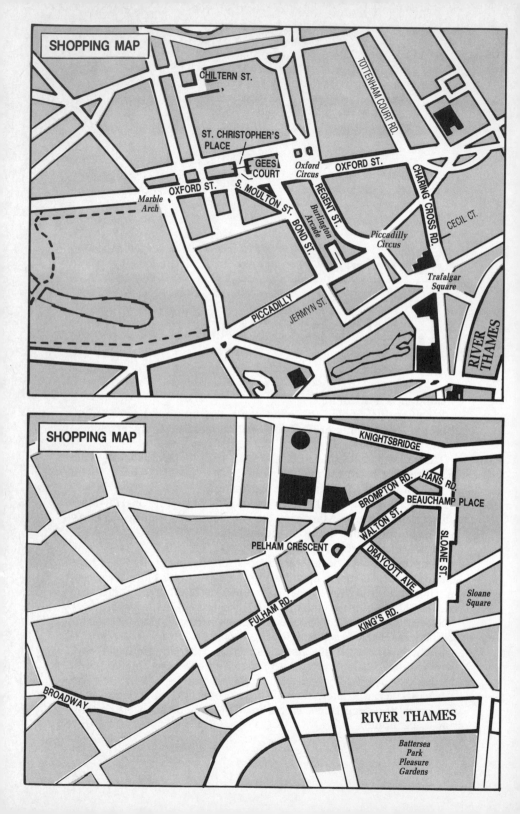

London staggers with her extravagance of shops. She can buy anything at any price.

I watched a wealthy friend buy a nice £ 35,000 Georgian table for her new Belgravia flat, and I watched a daughter get just as much pleasure buying a 50-pence antique watchface at Bermondsey Market to make into with-it jewelry.

London overwhelms with her more than 100 street markets catering to the needs of neighborhood Londoners. Cabbage and "cabbages"—clothes, dearie—are sold side by side at the colorful East End marketplaces.

I confess to having spent the better part of three months in the shopping haunts of London, not, I protest, as a shopoholic but as a professional researcher. (Gloves off, armor on, jaw set, notebook at the ready, and a checkbook at its side . . . just in case. Professional.)

In the company of two daughters and visiting friends, I sampled a zillion street markets, a glut of antique galleries, arcade shops, malls and stalls, every fashion "multiple" (isn't that a nice word for chain store?), most department stores, nearly all the international haute to hautier boutiques, and—*guaranteed*—nary a notable chocolate shop escaped our critical scrutiny.

London also satisfies the wildest possible fantasies. Having considered the possibility of rubbing elbows with the regal and royal as I sorted through the kitchen gadgets at the 'GTC' (General Trading Company)—the Sloane Street emporium that held the wedding lists for both of the Queen's daughters-in-law—it semed perfectly natural that Princess Diana was my table neighbor on a Knightsbridge shopping break.

We stalked the happened-onto occasional Craft Fair at Westminster Cathedral near Victoria Station (Sundays, summers) and Designer Fashions Sales at the Old Chelsea Town Hall.

We sidled into those hallowed shrines for the super-rich, Sotheby's and Christie's, not to bid but to learn more about antiques. We preferred Bonham's Montpelier auction galleries in Knightsbridge because it has a friendlier, more affordable feeling. Phillips on Bond Street has a similar reputation.

Oh, go and look if you've never been. Auctions are free (unless a charity is involved or the collection is of a notable estate).

In any of the auction showrooms, however, you can touch, turn over, peer under and ask questions on preview day, the day before auction. It is a wonderful learning curve. Knowledgeable showroom staff will give you an estimate on what any item is expected to go for. That way, you'll know if you want to return to bid. If you really get serious, buy a catalogue which provides another layer of knowledge.

The Daily Telegraph publishes a calendar of weekly sales every Monday, *The Times* on Tuesdays.

In a separate area of research I read not everything about London shopping I could find—impossible—but a lot. At the BTA or London Information Offices you'll find dozens of books devoted exclusively to the subject, many narrowed to specialties such as antiques, silver, furniture, secondhand clothes, books. There were even books about shopping for books.

I was smitten with *The Royal Shopping Guide,* a directory of over 300 provisioners to the royal household whose royal warrants entitle them to use the phrase "By Appointment" and the royal coat of arms on merchandise, packaging and in advertising. Three hundred of the finest sources for all sorts of things from tea to champagne, dog kennels to diapers, trinkets to tailors.

I eventually settled on a 75-pence "Shopping In London" BTA pamphlet which provides a strip map showing the location of every shop on London's most important shopping streets. My other buy was a £ 3.50 *Time Out's Shopping in London,* a guide to more than 2,000 of the capital's cheapest, most useful and unusual shops with addresses and telephone numbers. It is an encyclopedia of London shopping, slightly daunting, but spot on.

I perused a 1985 edition of Gault Millau's *The Best of London* whose leads were impeccable but whose prices were as obsolete as the 1985 exchange rates.

Living In London: Guidelines, published by the Junior League to help overseas families settle into London easily, led to reliable sources. Copies are available at Harrods.

The serious shopper should buy one of the *AZ* map books which the locals swear by. Several versions exist. The mid-sized *AZ Inner London* version carries simple black-and-white maps for the major shopping, theater and cinema areas in addition to detailed color street maps. Cannot tell you how often I was *lost* on my own, but *found* with AZ's help.

I was further fortified with the suggestions of local friends.

With just a modicum of "hold back," they came out with honed resources, sometimes as tattered newspaper clippings, more often as address books with thumbed thin pages overflowing with names and telephone numbers of their favorite shops.

Throughout the research, I interviewed buyers, store managers, sales clerks and visitors, total strangers asking "What are the best buys in Britain?" Their answers have shaped the focus of this report.

BEST BUYS IN BRITAIN

You can count on the visitor to smell out the best buys: i.e. British-made bone china, lead crystal, silver, the English collectibles and antiques, and fabrics: woolens, designer silks, fine cottons.

London and "bespoke" tailoring for men are synonymous. Made-to-measure shirts, suits and shoes attract the gold credit card set worldwide.

Specialty shopping appeals to a devoted following for fishing and hunting gear, books and old prints, distinctive traditional scents and home accessories in English country prints.

I had, perhaps foolishly, expected to find better value in women's clothes and accessories, especially those from Italy and Germany and France because Britain is part of the European Common Market.

But let us concentrate on those things refined by the Brits, starting alphabetically with antiques.

Antiques

London is a Mother Lode for purchasers of the past.

Certainly, the post-war breakup of country manors has caused heirs, squeezed by debilitating taxes, death duties and lost 20th century economic battles, to dump family heirlooms in significant quantities on the marketplace.

As more and more people began collecting nostalgia, shopping sources have expanded.

What a wide swatch of shopping opportunity London now offers. You can shop for antiques *every* day of the week.

From Monday through Saturday there are the established 9AM to 5PM antique shops.

Somewhere in the city the shops are supplemented by a street market whose focus is antiques. (At one time there was only Caledonia market in Islington.)

As demand for antiques increased steadily, a smart promoter

started the *Sunday* Antique Fair in an upmarket hotel.

What I learned in my Antique safaris was that price and location go hand in hand.

With every change of location, a bit is added to the price.

If you are a serious bargain hunter, you would go outside London like the dealers do and shop the antique markets in Bath (Guinea Lane on Wednesday) or Brighton (south of the station daily), or the many shops in Petworth.

What leaves Bath, for example, will first find exposure in the London street markets like Bermondsey where dealers and their runners also shop.

An object leaves Bermondsey Street Market to find a home in a Camden Passage shop or Fulham High Street or King's Road. Dealers buy for other dealers, knowing of their specialty interests . . . and the price spirals ever upward. High middle-range shops are on Fulham Road or Kensington Church or Pimlico Road.

"We comb the world seeking English antiques to bring back to London for resale," a Fulham Road manager confessed.

If an item makes the top rung it finds itself in a Bond Street or Mount Street antique shoppe and the "bit of a bite" added along the way has made the price of the object formidable.

I found the prices mad.

Whether you are an amateur or expert antique shopper, start where the pros shop in London: at the street markets.

Bermondsey Market: Friday mornings only. Over 270 tables closely huddled in tight rows in a rather grotty desolate area south of the Thames. Known as the New Caledonia Market, it is the successor to the original and where the middlemen who scout all over southern England week after week meet their buyers.

You have to be adventuresome and go early. Dealers get there at 3AM, flashlight in hand to inspect for cracks in the china and the nicks in the crystal. They buy off the lorries (trucks) since stalls are not allowed, by law, to set up shop until 6AM.

The cold, bleak, get-on-with-it attitude of the early morning stall dealers turns some visitors off. No one is rude, mind you. There is just not a lot of jolly rapport. But if you know what you want, and it is there, the price will be right.

Caution: even in summertime, there is a chill in the air at Bermondsey as well. Traders have set up "lockups" in buildings on the periphery, and you might want to duck into the upstairs coffee shop of the Hyper Market just to get warm.

New Trend: there is a five year waiting list for stalls. Because of the rising interest of visitors, stalls are taken over by tourist-oriented traders after dealer-oriented traders pack up and leave. Selling goes on until noon but prices rise by the hour.

Camden Passage a mixture of trash and treasure despite its evolution from a minor to a major marketplace. That's its magnetism. Thirty or so permanent showrooms in a warren of alleyways, arcades and dead-end streets are joined by veteran stall traders with quality "smalls" on Wednesday afternoons and most Saturdays. Fly-pitchers still spread their bric-a-brac on the pavement.

There's an air of gentility and village neighborliness. If you admire the workmanship of an object, the trader takes the time to explain its background.

A bookseller ("Call me Bill") volunteered to deliver a secondhand (not antique) dictionary to our flat across town because "I know how lost writers are without one." Cost, both book and delivery, £1. The tube cost that much.

Yes, it is the ambiance I like as much as the merchandise at Camden Passage. That and the cozy restaurants and pubs intermingled among the tat. (Frederick's is one; atrium room in the back, garden dining in the summer. Book ahead.)

New Trend: a Camden Passage trader assured me, when I asked if England were running out of antiques "Oh, no, Madam. Our antiques just keep getting newer. We're now selling *early* plastic."

Hang onto your Tupperware, ladies.

Portobello Road is legendary. Big. Over 2,000 stallholders dealing in antiques and genuine junk. Hopelessly swamped by tourists after 10AM Saturdays.

A carnival mood prevails; hot chestnuts or baked potato stands and photographers who use parrots and monkeys as props. Most dealers consider the prices inflated. Know your silver and its fair price before you buy at Portobello.

Antiques are traded between Chepstow Villas to Lonsdale Road from about 7AM. Bargains are possible until 9. Collector's Corner, one of the oldest arcades on Portobello, is a scrum of bargain hunters. Claustrophobic shoppers like me who would avoid the Saturday crush should try Friday afternoons (3-5) in the section under the Westway flyover.

New Trend: contemporary art galleries have sprung up all over the neighborhood injecting pulsating new blood into the British art world and offering adventuresome alternatives to the "sporting and floral prints" of the West End art establishment centered around Cork Street. Attracted by space and low rents, these contemporary art crusaders may have started a revolution. Word is that contemporary art is very affordably priced at the moment.

What I discovered on my three months of Antique Indulgence, was the Sunday hotel fair.

It wasn't an original idea.

The enormously profitable ten-day annual Grosvenor House Antique Fair in June must have given inspiration. To discourage non-buyers, a £10 entry fee is charged. If you are in London in June, pay it and go.

This has to be the ice cream sundae of the antique world. Dealers hold back their best for months preceding the fair to woo regular and win new customers. Everything in the show is of museum quality.

The decorative feature of the 1987 production was Queen Elizabeth's Purple Velvet Coronation cloak cascading down two floors. (No, it was not for sale.)

If you don't plan to buy, go at tea time, 4-6PM. It's quieter then; dealers can spend more time with you. If you do plan to buy, go opening day along with the Top Guns whose chauffer-driven Silver Clouds and Daimlers fight for space along Park Lane.

The Grosvenor House Fair—like the Olympic Antique Fair, and ceramics and antiquarian book fairs also in June—are famous international events that draw the top of the market.

What about the rest of the year?

Here is the niche filled by the Sunday hotel fairs.

Three or four private companies now stage Sunday fairs in prominent London hotels year round. The Dorchester, Park Lane, Rembrandt, Tower, Inter-Continental, Royal Garden, the Gloucester, Sheraton Park Tower and the Park Court hotels are regular venues.

The hotel antique fairs are excellent markets for collectibles and jewelry, if upscale. But they are so civilized. The items are arranged on skirted tables, the atmosphere is genteel, the traders friendly, the place is warm and tea is just across the lobby.

Legally, Sunday exhibitors can only sell to the trade, but with a nudge and a wink at the obsolete British law, non-dealers are admitted for a small fee. And with a bit of gracious haggling, you too can extract the same 10% trade discount.

To get in free of admission and more easily negotiate the dealer discount, bring along a half dozen calling cards from an interior designer friend at home.

Oh, yes, you should know that most of the stallholders at Camden Passage or Portobello or the Sunday fairs will have permanent showrooms somewhere else in London.

General antique shopping rules I learned: don't persist if the seller says he has quoted his best price. He probably has. Dealers sell to each other as they are setting up stalls and tables, and there is a 5% to 10% price markup with every transaction.

If you are buying for pedigree, stay with the upmarket shops or with the "datelined" and "vetted" fairs, a guarantee that only genuine antiques predating 1860 for Continental ware, 1890 for English items are offered for sale.

If your comfort zone requires it, deal only with member stores of the British Antique Dealers Association (BADA) or its slightly less aristocratic cousin, the London and Provincial Antique Dealers' Association (LAPADA).

If, on the other hand, you're after collectibles and decorative objects—the smalls that lend personality to a room—and want to buy at the lowest prices, start where the pros start, at the street antiques markets. A well trained eye and a dealer's instincts help but you can have a lot of fun if all you know is what you like and how much you are willing to pay for it.

China & Crystal

Ever since bone ash was added to china clay mixture in the mid-1700's producing a stronger, whiter and more translucent porcelain, "bone china" has been the hallmark of the English potters' trade. Less expensive in England than elsewhere in the world, bone china can be even less expensive in London because competition is keen among the potteries, because there are discount bulk-buy shops, and because of the semi-annual sales in December or January and again in July. Wedgwood, for one, considerately schedules its winter sale in its three London stores in mid-December just in time for last minute Christmas shopping. Discounts of up to 40% are given. Because overseas buyers think so highly of the brand, I started my comparative price research with a couple of Wedgwood patterns. Every store carried *exactly* the same price. Why? I learned that Wedgwood controls its product from kiln to customer, personally operating each of the Wedgwood concessions in London department stores. Of course, every price is the same.

If you love traditional china and crystal and silver and can afford top of the line prices, go straight to Thomas Goode & Co in Mayfair. You can't mistake the place. It has the seven-foot ceramic elephants in the show windows. Made by Minton for the Paris Exhibitions of 1878 and 1889, they are not for sale at any price. But everything else is, including the chandeliers that decorate the ramble of rooms.

Sorry, that's not entirely true. You cannot buy the royal doll house china made exclusively for the occupants of Buckingham Palace. But a nice little souvenir of the shop is a Royal Doulton egg cup for about £ 2 . . . unless you choose to take home an antique Minton dessert service for just under £ 30,000.

The cheapest way to buy china historically has been to seek out "seconds." Today, modern technology has improved firing techniques so much there are few mistakes. The on-sale or price-discounted tableware you buy in London is more likely to be run-of-kiln . . . china that has not been checked before leaving the factory, even though it may be called seconds. There is a good chance you will not be able to spot an imperfection.

Most china and crystal shoppers quickly find the Reject China Shops—not to be confused with The Reject Shop, a Danish modern home accessories multiple. The Reject China Shops offer discounts galore, from a dependable 10% for run-of-kiln quality to 50% for discontinued or bulk-buy items. Cheapest prices for Baccarat crystal in the city are here.

Once spreading like wildfire across Britain, their blaze was extinguished in a 1987 merger with Chinacraft. Now there are only three locations, all in tourist-trod London areas.

Perhaps the merger will resolve the shipping problems that disappointed customers have experienced. The principal stores are on Beauchamp Place, one exclusively for china and, across the narrow street, another for crystal.

Chinacraft, the new parent company, has stores in all traffic areas They sell only top graded china, crystal and giftware—no seconds.

C. Hartley & Sons Ltd, is where the smart American expats of London go—or telephone—to buy their china and crystal. Thirty miles north of London in Letchworth, Peter Hartley gives "substantial" savings on china—*even* Wedgwood—first quality only.

The Hartley range is wide and, best yet, you can order by phone for shipment home. According to very satisfied buyers, they are the *only* store where Waterford is available at discount.

"We only give our overseas customers the price break," Peter Hartley explained. "It is easy to recognize you," he added. "You have a rather distinctive accent."

He quoted a customer as saying "usually when merchants hear my accent, the price goes up."

The telephone number is 04626-79483.

Further discounts can be exacted at the "Pot Banks" and crystal factories in central Britain if you are traveling north or are serious enough about china and crystal buying to do an overnighter in Stoke-on-Trent. (Getting there and back in a single day with time for shopping is difficult.)

The factory outlet shops got their name, Pot Banks, because the several towns comprising the china capital of Britain are fondly known as The Potteries. Savings are as much, or more, as at the annual London sales, up to 50% for some patterns. Spode, particularly, has the reputation for priced-right table/oven/freezer and microwave-safe ware.

If you go seeking a particular pattern, you should call first to make sure they have it in stock. Take along a sponge. The dishes can be dirty and you will want to make sure that defects, if any, are acceptable.

Crystal factories with outlet shops are located in nearby towns. Among them Stuart, Thomas Webb, Tudor, Webb Corbett and Royal Brierley. Savings that will make the trip worthwhile are guaranteed.

Silver

In England, silver must be 92.5% pure and is known as sterling.

Most foreign silver such as Indian or Chinese "white metal" isn't as pure, so cannot be sold as silver.

The "sterling standard" established in 1719 continues today. Previous standards date to 1300; assaying and hallmarking started later in that century.

By law, all but the tiniest pieces of sterling have a hallmark.

Hallmarks consist of four stamps to show the item has been assayed. The first stamp gives the registered sign or initials of the maker. The second is a lion passant to show the silver's purity. The third shows where the piece was made, and the fourth is a letter denoting the date the piece was made.

By law, silver dealers must display a chart showing how the assay system works. Ask to see it and examine the piece you are interested in carefully for the four marks. (The sign for London is a leopard's head.)

Sheffield Plate, artistically the most satisfactory substitute for sterling, was created by Thomas Boulsover in 1743 who accidentally fused silver and copper. Craftsmen worked with it until 1840 when a cheaper process, electro-plating on white metal, was developed.

If you're serious about silver, spend a few pence for *British and Irish Silver Assay Office Marks 1544-1963*. Frederick Bradbury illustrates and describes all registered marks on gold, silver, imported plate and Old Sheffield Plate.

London Silver Vaults is the first stop on many visitors' itinerary. Sometimes it is the only shopping stop, if time is a problem. Located in a still operative Chancery Lane safe deposit company, some 60 underground strongrooms owned by half as many dealers offer the largest array of new and old sterling in the world, as well as contemporary, antique Sheffield or Victorian plate in unrivaled selections.

A silver company's sales agent who covers all of Britain in his rounds got my attention when he said "silver dealers in Central London and the surrounding suburbs work on a 220% markup whereas Silver Vault dealers pare that down to 50% to 60%."

"How is that possible?" I challenged.

"Volume makes it possible; the competition next door makes it necessary." He claimed that a single 8- by 5-foot strongroom in the Vaults would sell as much as—or more than—most major department stores.

Lady Brightman, an energetic lady who gave up her antique shop a few years ago because astronomic prices were so shocking, confirmed the low markup at the Vaults.

That doesn't mean prices are cheap.

Lady Brightman was helping out "old friends" at E & C T Koopman's. The Koopman name is synonymous with quality, the kind of quality that kings and sultans can afford.

She walked me from the £7,500 12-place table setting that stopped my eye all the way up to a pair of royal silver William III wall sconces by Philip Rollos (circa 1700) for a mere £350,000.

But the Vaults deal in every price range. I found good value at Vault 1, the David S. Shure strongroom. Fifth generation silver merchant Sam Bulka, whose family has sold at the Vaults since the 19th century, volunteered that it was the American GI in World War II who parlayed the Silver Vaults into a major retail marketplace.

"The vaults once were used mainly for overnight safe-keeping. Only the 'trade' came into the vaults. But, money was scarce during the war and dealers took to selling to American military personnel direct. That traffic firmly established the public access policy."

Do you bargain at the Vaults? Undoubtedly. Gently and with dignity. Percy's in strongrooms 16 & 17 (old silver on the right, new on the left) even gave a friend an unrequested 30% discount on a wedding gift cake server.

For just a wondrous viewing experience even if you know you won't buy, go to Garrard's in Regent Street. Gorgeous antique silver. Queen Victoria appointed Garrard & Co jewelers to the Crown in the 1840's—and they remain so. Don't expect any bargains.

There will always be a resale market for sterling silver if for no other reason than the weight of the silver itself. Old Sheffield Plate will retain its value as well. But silver plate is a different matter.

Since no laws govern the thickness of silver plating, it is best to buy plate from a reputable trade. Mappin & Webb, silversmiths since 1774, produce a quality plating that far exceeds the British standard and virtually guarantees the life of a table service—with normal use and care—for 60 years.

Antique pieces marked EPNS, or electro-plated nickel-silver, are considered to be quality pieces of plate.

Fabrics And Wearables

Ever since George Bryan Brummell exclaimed at the turn of the 18th century "class distinction is now a matter of cut and the quality of cloth" London has been the world's center for fashion woolens.

Mr. Brummell wore wool.

Mr. Brummell's disciple was the Prince of Wales.

Prior to "Beau's" pronouncement, the dandies of London wore Italian silks, velvets and satins. For which they were called "Macaronis." After Mr. B's example (aided by the Court), and thanks to persuasive self-serving local tailors, "class" supported the local product.

Fact: the wool spun at the Imperial weaving factory at Winchester was "spun so fine it was comparable to a spider's web." The quote is from a Roman Edict written in the third century, AD.

Woolens from throughout the UK still find their way to the big city market of London.

The finest Himalayan cashmeres tailored in the world, top quality camel hair and lambswool are the specialties of the Burlington Arcade shops: Peal (three locations within a single block), Scott and Berks.

Not cheap.

Scotch House (cheaper) and Westaway and Westaway (cheaper still) bring the wool knits of the north to the south with their Arans and Icelandic and Shetland Island sweaters, along with a wide range of garments in classic tartans of the Scottish clans and their own fine cashmeres.

Scotch House's Knightsbridge store has the little green book which matches surnames to tartan clans. They stock both fabric or kilt.

Probably the best value for money in sweaters in London is the St Michael label at Marks and Spencer.

In the fourth annual Best of Britain Knitwear Collection, a juried Design Centre show, a £17.99 "Marks and Sparks" jumper took its place confidently alongside the likes of Pringle, Barrie and Ballantyne, and the even more expensive (£225 to £290) couture knits.

To discuss British fabrics one must put Liberty at the top of the list.

Liberty's pure and mixed woolens are without peer. The firm's worldwide reputation was founded on its magnificent blends of natural fibers in exquisite patterns and colors.

The shrine for the pilgrim to Liberty is the heralded ground floor counters of scarves, large and small, and fabulous fabric accessories that make cherished (and packable) gifts.

Bolts of fabric draped over the Olde World octagonal interior balconies lead you to the second floor fabric department.

Here you'll find, for example, bolts of Viyella. I found the reason for the popularity of Viyella after I bought my first shirt. Warmth without weight or bulk. An addictive sensuousness.

Liberty Lawn cottons are equally peerless. And they last forever. A room to the side of the fabric department has odd lengths of yardage at reduced prices year round; often, a basement "bargain" corner handles the residue from regular sales.

The John Lewis stores and their kissing cousin, Peter Jones at Sloane Square, are other "best buy" fabric sources. Not just woolens. Nor just fabrics for clothes. The spectrum. Excellent home furnishing fabric selection under their own brand, Jonelle.

The stores ardently advertise they are "never knowingly undersold," a slogan backed by a guaranteed refund for the difference between their price and a lower one, with proof of course.

"It's even better than that," a resident says. "I returned a sewing machine along with proof that the same model was priced lower in a suburban store and John Lewis refunded the entire purchase price . . . and insisted that I keep the machine."

You don't think John Lewis has a customer for life?

Everybody's Favorite Store

London is awash with special shops.

Harrods is its most famous. It is to retailing what Lloyd's of London is to insurance. A symbol of London. A symbol of quality. A symbol of innovation.

Like Lloyd's—a society of private investors—Harrods is a gigantic jumble of private shopkeepers with names as famous as Wedgwood, as obscure as Bonsack, and as small as Nature's Sculpture assembled under one enormous roof.

Did you know that most of the 230 departments at Harrods are concessions? Over 65 different "scents" companies compete—and cooperate—in the Fragrance Hall alone. It was Harrods in 1972 who persuaded all their cosmetic houses to outfit their staffs in Harrods own uniform.

Innovation started with Charles Digby Harrod who, facing financial ruin from a devastating 1883 pre-Christmas fire, quickly negotiated with other London stores to fill Harrods' orders, *using Harrods' labels.*

His Christmas sales broke all previous records. The phoenix rising out of ashes image wasn't bad for publicity either.

Harrods installed the first escalator in London and, to calm the qualms of nervous passengers, an assistant offered a tot of brandy. And, no doubt, a PR photographer was there to guarantee a good press.

Harrods, like Lloyd's, is good at promotion.

The store displays more merchandise in its 80 display windows than many a small boutique will have in its entire inventory.

Their motto *Omnia, Omnibus, Ubique* modestly means "Everything for Everybody, Everywhere." To deliver on promise, they operate all services you can name, including a Funeral Service. Their largest cash sale is listed at £ 2,200,000, yet they take equal pride in the sale of six bread rolls, 30p, shipped to New York.

But Harrods is a frustration for the casual visitor.

How so?

The crowds. The store claims to have 50,000 customers *a day.* The food halls are always jammed. You simply cannot find a quiet place to stop, regroup, remember what it was you wanted to buy.

But you have to go, if for no other reason than to see the Doulton-designed tiled walls depicting hunting scenes in the grand Meat Hall. They are fabulous.

A friend who goes every year to the highly rated, gigantic January sale, standing in line freezing for hours with the mob waiting for the doors to open, refers to it as the biggest "bun fight" in the world. She says she has never bought a single item for fear of losing an arm.

Finally, after years of hearing such incredible stories, we were in London on the first day of a Harrods' sale.

People really do queue from dawn or before, friends fortifying them with coffee and rolls on their way to work.

I went at 9:30. Could hardly squeeze inside. It looked more like a refugee camp than a smart department store. People lined in front of signs that promised evacuation: "Credit Card & Send" "Credit Card & Take" "Cash & Send" "Cash & Take."

The scramble in the men's ties section was a warm-up.

The melee in the women's bags section was a punchout.

But the china department!

I decided that if we ever have World War III, it will start in Harrods China Department on the first day of the semi-annual sale.

Combative arms outstretched for the same items. Staff climbed over tables to traverse the room. Foreign tongues engulfed me. I needed another course in survival training.

"The war in the trenches was a great experience," I could hear myself telling grandchildren "but I wouldn't want to do it again."

The Finest "Tuck" Shop In London

Fortnum & Mason also started as a food provisioner.

Had Mr. Fortnum lived today as a stock broker, he might have been prosecuted for insider trading violations. Mr. Fortnum, a retired footman in the household of Queen Anne, put his knowledge of the needs of the Palace household to work.

With Mr. Mason, the partnership imported exotic foods such as "Harts Horn, Gable Worm Seed, Saffron, and Dirty White Candy." They introduced potted foods to Londoners, many of whom when dispatched to the foreign duty, relied on the London tuck shop for regular shipments.

A gentleman needs his luxuries.

It was the Great Exhibition of 1851 that launched the Great Picnic Hamper tradition that still flourishes through pre-ordered baskets or hampers for any occasion.

Earlier this century, the store expanded to include antique furniture, china and glassware, and clothes for the entire family, all expensive. As are many of their food specialties, although vinegars and condiments, teas and chocolates in beautiful packaging are good value and wonderful gifts.

The wine selection is extraordinary. So is the Fountain Restaurant, hard to get into but a delightful place for late breakfast, lunch or tea.

Time your visit to F&M on the hour to see the articulated clock over the 18th century main entrance; in the dress of their day, Mr. Fortnum and Mr. Mason turn to bow formally to each other.

The Fair & Foul Weather Coat Stores

Burberry is another English specialty shop. The to-catch-a-spy trench coat supplier of Haymarket has some new marketing ideas and a little oneupsmanship for its major competitor, Aquascutum on Regent Street.

With your purchase of an all-weather coat, you are automatically enrolled into the Burberry Club. Its advantages: six months insurance for your new coat. Lose it, they replace it.

You also get a monogramed label and half-price off their "valet" service (good for a year). That means your Burberry can go home again for rest and restoration. Basic cleaning is under £15 but add-ons such as new collars, hems, repairs, can jack the price up.

The cleaning incentive is intended for people like us who won't release "catch-a-spy" long enough to get its face washed.

Aquascutum, in its own marketing coupe, dug into its heritage, formally applied for and got its very own coat of arms. This is no easy task. Arms are granted to individuals or corporations by the College of Arms under strict regulations, one of which is recipients have to be leaders in their fields with substantial financial standing.

Your surname does not entitle you to use the crest or arms of a family of the same name, as the Duchess of York discovered when she wanted to incorporate the Ferguson bee into the embroidery of her wedding gown. (The College probably moved faster than usual to secure the Duchess-to-be a coat of arms.)

Aquascutum's new shield, woven into cashmeres or imprinted on buttons and badges, has as its motto *hoc scuto fidemus,* "We have faith in this shield." It's a subtle enough form of advertising.

Designer Clothes At Affordable Prices

We hadn't been in London a week before a friend called and invited me to join her at a private designer sale in a private home.

A week later I saw a sign on the Chelsea Old Town Hall about a Designer Sale scheduled the following week.

At the end of their selling seasons, manufacturers have overruns, returns, seconds, all kinds of odds and ends they need to get rid of. In many manufacturing centers, there are factory outlet stores selling directly to the public.

In London, the practice seems to be more personalized.

The good news is that the merchandise they want to dispose of is of the current season. Anyone can go to the Chelsea Designer Sale at Old Town Hall. You can get on their mailing list to receive their annual schedule by writing to Designer Sale, %Fashion Mail,

2nd Floor, 18 Battersea High Street SW11.

It is possible to buy designer fashions at less than designer prices all year long in London. Not just at the twice annual sales.

Many of the "big boys" of the couture world sell at "knock-off" prices. Not "bargain" prices, mind you, but in the same range that *good* copies—i.e. knock-offs—might cost elsewhere.

In the Bond or Sloane Street shops of Giorgio Armani, Ralph Lauren or Ungaro, you'll find covetable clothes at a fraction of their normal astronomical prices. Clothes that last season were advertised in the fashion magazines for £1,500, or more, could be as low as £200.

These trendsetters market their own "last season" shapes in slightly different fabrics, and, sometimes, under slightly different labels. No fools, these entrepreneurs. If profits are to be made from "knock-offs" they will do the knocking.

Look for alternative names on labels that telegraph the lower priced lines: names like "Mani" at Giorgio Armani and "Sola Donna" at Ungaro. Ralph Lauren's less expensive lines of "Roughwear" and "Classifications" are harder to find without staff help since his three lines, including the very pricey "Collections," are identified, equally, simply as Ralph Lauren.

There are two advantages to buying from the designers direct. As trendsetters, they are so far ahead of the pack that to wear the newest silhouette a mere few months later is probably perfect timing.

Secondly, the quality of the garment will be the same as for the couture outfit.

My best designerwear-at-a-price find is called The Constant Sale Shop. It sells a dozen of the top-ranked European couture lines at sale prices *all year long*. Ungaro, Valentino and Kirzia for women, and Armani and Panchetti for men, among them.

The shop, at 56 Fulham Road, is a sort of an "outlet" store for these haut couture names operating individual boutiques on South Molton, Bond and Sloane streets.

You won't always find your size, or a depth of selection but designer accessories and shoes as well as clothes are perpetually on sale at this one-of-a-kind store.

It knows no peer because each of the designer boutiques that feed it is franchised to a single company, the Aguecheek Group of Companies.

(Wouldn't you love to own franchise rights to five of the best selling designers in the world?)

Fancy Dress Rentals

Don't clutter your holiday luggage with finery for a once-only wearing.

Hire formalwear, as the Londoners do, from stores that specialize in *au courant* attire. Moss Bros (pronounced "Moss Boss") is the London gentleman's favorite outfitter of proper clothes for every occasion, especially wedding but even hunting attire, beginning at about £35.

Simpson's Dress Hire offers reasonably priced long evening gowns mostly (£50 or so) both on Moss Bros's third floor (for family convenience) and in their own store on Piccadilly.

Sasha Hetherington offers 50 or more new women's fashions a season.

Room At The Top lets one-off ladies' costumes only twice and will even alter to fit.

"Bespoke" Tailoring

The "bespoke" tailoring of Savile Row (suits), Jermyn Street (shirts) and St James's (shoes and hats) bespeaks world class. Even frugality, if you accept as gospel legends about customers who have worn a custom-made for a quarter of a century. Jolly good, too, you say after you've priced them.

"When it comes to bespoke tailoring, men fare better in London than do women," Simon Anderson whose "Friends in London" customized tour service includes shopping.

"Shops within a well-heeled walk of each other can outfit a gentleman with made-to-measure suits, shirts, shoes and hats.

"Kilgour, French & Stanbury tailors for presidents, heads-of-state and maharajahs; Huntsman has been the Royals' tailor for over a hundred years. Mikhail Gorbachev shops at Gieves & Hawkes but, it is rumored, buys only off-the-peg."

Elton John and his ilk go to Tommy Nutter whose off-the-rack suits, at a third of the bespoke price, are considered a best buy of Savile Row. Gault Millau's travel guide, *The Best of London,* will direct you to the Emperor Napoleon's court tailor, in business since 1806 in the Victorian building that once housed the Savile Club.

Anderson's shopping tips also included shirtmakers Hilditch & Key, bootmaker James Lobb (he shoes Prince Charles), and haberdasher James Lock whose "prices are no higher than those you'd pay in a good department store."

The going prices, he says, for a three-piece suit are from £1000 (two months to complete); shirts from £60 with a four- to six-shirt minimum order (two months); shoes and boots from £350 and £500 (five months). At least one mid-point fitting required for first-time customers.

My favorite author turned pale at the sound of £1000 for a suit.

Millau also directed us to W G Child & Son in suburban Wandsworth. A more reasonable location produces less staggering prices.

Even Child's £300 for a jacket took a bit of salesmanship.

Here we learned that differences in custom-made menswear are the cut, lining and blind stitching of the collar and facings, the buttonholes and pockets. And such details take time. In our case, two fittings were spaced over six weeks and finishing took another two weeks. (He looks sensational in it.)

Street Markets For Clothes . . . Plus

Street markets, like pubs, continue old traditions of trading despite the growth of supermarkets and multiple chain stores. As long as there is a London, there will be a variety of street markets revealing the local character of its district.

Of the 100 or more, taste at least one during your London visit.

Petticoat Lane is the famous street market for clothes . . . leather and everything else. Sunday mornings only. It is a jumble of countless stalls spilling over Middlesex Street to surrounding alleys and lanes. Bargain jeans, inexpensive baby clothes, a spare piece of luggage to get you home? An alarm clock to wake you up so you won't miss your plane? Good leather purses. All here and much more.

You have to enjoy crowds. And you have to endure sorting through the tat. Centuries ago the Huguenot hangout, today Petticoat Lane's Jewish rag merchants "chat up" regular clientele from The City during the week as well.

Do you want a new shopping adventure? A street market unknown to visitors is the Roman Road Street Market on Saturday mornings in the EastEnd of London. (Take the tube to Bethnal Green stop; then bus #8).

EastEnders have been heading "*dawn* (down) the Roman" for over 150 years to shop for clothes, fabrics, buttons and bows, needles and threads. It is a cut above other street markets for quality.

Massive crowds flock to this very local community market early. The people are the best part. We have friends who cross town to shop here as much for the ingratiating people with their colorful Cockney accents as for the abundant bargains. ("Nearly half what you'd pay in Oxford Street stores for the same quality.")

Nine out of 10 of the 250 stalls sell clothes which are good quality seconds and overages, knits from Marks & Spencer and children's clothes from Mothercare, among other good buys.

Pie & mash with "liquor'—green parsley sauce—is a specialty.

A block or so west of the Market is Laces, a discount shoe store selling fashionable shoes at half of Oxford Street prices.

English Scents

Who has come to London and returned home without an English scent? A bar of soap or bath gel or bath bead, a pot pourri pomander, perfume or cologne? Beautiful fragrances. Perfect, and packable, gifts.

The scent business is big. Selfridges on Oxford Street houses the largest perfumery in Europe. You get an idea of how big it is when you remember that Harrods, not even in the running as biggest, has over 70 perfume concessions in its fragrant forum.

Floris, a family business still operates from the same address its founder hung his barber's sign in 1730.

Juan Famenias Floris might be chuckling over the typically "English" designation since his first scents were based on the fragrant flowers of his homeland, Spanish Minorca.

Czeck and Speake, at the other end of Jermyn Street from Floris, is another traditionalist. Only the company's own fragrances are sold. They come in handsome crackle-glazed porcelain pots. Not cheap but he's worth it.

Penhaligon's is another upmarket perfumery where you can buy unusual gifts. It is richly dark and richly Dickensian. Rich is the appropriate word.

If you, like me, had always thought of Crabtree & Evelyn as English, chalk it up to effective marketing. It's American.

Culpeper's herbal roots were planted in the 17th century by Nicholas Culpeper (not "pepper"). You can still buy a traditional Victorian mustard bath used to ward off chills and colds.

Hottest new line of beauty and fragrances is The Body Shop

. . . expanding everywhere, even overseas. All natural ingredients, biodegradable products are tested on humans, not animals. Simple packaging helps make for *very* fair prices.

Crafts

Some of the best crafts are jewelry and some of the best jewelry is handcrafted. The twain meet beautifully at the hand of designer Wendy Ramshaw who feels strongly that jewelry deserves a visual life beyond adorning its owner. The Electrum Gallery reliably stocks several of her famous "ring" towers made of Perspex and decorated with two or more (one had ten) individual rings, each with a different sized and shaped semiprecious stone. The rings can be worn altogether or separately, or prominently displayed as intriguing sculpture. Priced from £185.

Wendy is one of 70 British artisans represented by Electrum. The gallery mounts six exhibitions a year to showcase its craftsmen.

Reproductions of antiquity Roman, Greek and Egyptian jewelry, and contemporary stylings are found at the British Museum Shop, but some of the best of British crafts are at the Victoria & Albert Museum Shop.

Occupying a tiny corner in the back of the V&A shop, in what is called the Crafts Corner, is the only Crafts Council retail showroom in London where one-off pieces of jewelry, glass, ceramics, handknits are sold. Each artisan represented has been adjudged by the Council as one of the best craftsmen in the country.

It is worth your time to make a trip to the Crafts Council headquarters on Lower Regent street to look at their slides library if commissioning a one-of-a-kind craft appeals.

Or, go to the Design Center on Haymarket for commercial or industrial items. The Centre maintains a catalogue of over 7,000 consumer goods of every possible type.

Lord Roberts Workshop, diagonally across from Harrods, sells quality brushes and military-type chests and small decorative woodenware made by the blind and handicapped. The prices are a lot less than at Harrods.

You have to be alert to find it. Its full name is "The Faithful Order of the Forces Help Society and Lord Roberts Workshop." Whee.

Leather

Mulberry, the leathermaker, belies its 15-year-old history. Belts and bags, leather-trimmed accessories and luggage have the look of centuries old British classicism. Britain's answer to France's Louis Vitton or Spain's Loewes, the prices—while not cheap—are lower and the value exceptional. (Upstairs is a small collection of women's fashion; classic too and well styled.)

Owner/designer Roger Saul started his business as a plaited-leather belt craftsman selling, village to village, from a suitcase. Now, over 100 quality shops in Britain and 500 abroad stock his leather items.

Mulberry operates concessions at Harrods, Harvey Nichols and Liberty stores in London, and has its own shop in St Christopher's Place off Oxford.

Chocolates

Prestat, a handmade chocolate shop on South Molton Street, takes custom orders for one-off designs (can be expensive), or to please a local hostess select from the house specialty truffles. Sinful.

Charbonnel et Walker, Bond Street, are known for their boite blanche, a white box in which a recipient's name or special message is spelled out in foil wrapped chocolates and surrounded with a pick-your-own assortment of plain, cream or nut-filled nuggets. My personal selection of chocolates didn't make it into the gift box. Disappointing, but I ordered and left for tea at three at Browns Hotel at the opposite end of the arcade. Perhaps had I stayed to watch the box filled . . .?

Bendick's After Dinner Mints are still a classic on British tables. Hard to beat. So are their tea rooms.

Harrods has a formidable selection and Fortnum & Mason is no slouch in the gift-boxed department either.

Chocolate Olivers by the makers of Bath Olivers are almost as good as New Zealand Toffee Pops. Almost.

Fishing and Hunting Gear

The Royal Opera Arcade behind New Zealand House on Haymarket has an eclectic assortment of shops. You can buy an expensive antique suit of armor at Peter Dale's or an extremely reasonably priced antique map or print of London at the Old London Art Gallery. Or, if you are a fisherman, you'll find Farlow's and lose yourself among the fishing tackle and rods and reels and fishing clothes.

Around the corner on Pall Mall is the Hardy Brothers emporium. Our fishing friends always volunteer the remark that Farlow's is the friendlier.

For guns, the most famous shop—perhaps in the world—is James Purdy's in Mayfair. A brace of shotguns from Purdy's bespeaks of princely budgets. Of course the price of £17,000 wouldn't deter you but the four-year waiting list might.

Books

At least once on every trip to London I lose my favorite author in W & G Foyles. He always comes back to me, usually with an odd book or two, saying he doesn't know why he goes to Foyles. "It is such a monster."

Disorganized . . . a ramble of rooms . . . frustrating. But still if you want a certain book it is in there somewhere. You should get it free of charge just for finding it. The staff is not much help.

Charing Cross Road is a book lover's Eden. Number 84 Charing Cross Road, immortalized both in book and film, is a record shop instead of the legendary bookshop today. (The Marks & Co street sign is on display in the record store.) But a consolation is, that wedged between the electronic and record stores of Tottenham Road and the National Portrait Gallery behind Trafalgar Square are dozens of specialty book stores—on any known subject.

Cecil Court, a footstep from Leicester Square tube station, is Dickensque with its gas-style street lamps, exclusive pedestrian traffic over stone-paved alleyways. A haven for readers interested in any subject, particularly music, ballet, modern fiction, theater or children's books—new or old.

The high-end antiquarian bookshops are in Mayfair. Bloomsbury (Great Russell Street and Museum Street) and Hampstead where Keats lived are other known book "beats."

The best part: there is no import duty on books. Even if you're not a bibliomaniac, buying a book in Britain is hard to resist.

Shoes

A lot of visitors buy shoes for one reason or another. They like the English styles, the Italian or Swiss leathers, or their feet are killing them and they have to get into low heels, pliable uppers or flexible soles.

My impression about the prices for footwear was that they were the equivalent in pounds sterling to US dollars, which, with the punishing exchange rate, made them expensive. But friends from countries that do not have the volume of production sustained in America assure me that prices are better in London, for the better quality shoes, than they are back home.

Once, I found them so.

Bally is one of those "they're everywhere" multiples. Many of the Bally shoes sold in London are made in England. That is no slur on the craftsmanship of the English, but if you want the soft-as-butter leathers of the Swiss or Italians, head for the Oxford Street or Sloane Street stores. They have the largest selections.

"We sell a lot of 'bunion' shoes," the twinkly young lady at Russell Bromley stated emphatically. She was establishing a rapport with the owner of sore feet. Mine.

"What are bunion shoes?"

"You know, low heels, soft leather . . . the summer shoes are woven strips, and our evening shoes are mesh. They give if you exert pressure on them, but hold their shape otherwise."

What she lacked in logic, she excelled in enthusiasm.

The fact is that they do have recommendable walking shoes for men and women with a lot of style and at reasonable prices (£40 to £60).

Church's men's brogues and Oxfords are as good as you can get without having them hand made (around £100), but their attempt at fashion misses. Many folk vote for James Lobb as the best bespoke shoe and bootmaker.

Toys

Toys means Hamley's, "the world's largest toy store." Six floors are crammed with every toy or game, teddy bear or British toy soldier made for every age. It is more appealing when you focus on a single category, nearly frightening if you try to take in the whole of a floor at a single gaze. Isolate the toy trains that run incessantly or the helicopter flying overhead, or accompany a child into the Teddy Bear (and other fuzzies) Department to see magic in the making.

Under Two Flags, a tiny human scaled shop in St Christopher's Place, specializes in model soldiers, books and military prints. Antique collectors' items at the back of the shop fetch hundreds of pounds.

Pollock's Toy Store is an interior design source for Victorian dollhouse furnishings. They sell old-fashioned toys.

STREETWISE SHOPPING

Oxford Street

Come, stroll London's shopping town with me street by street or, in a couple of cases, block by block.

First, Oxford Street. The golden shopping mile between Marble Arch and Oxford Circus. The clothes-buying mecca for the clothes-hungry populace and shopping visitors.

There is nothing the family needs that Oxford Street cannot provide, and so the world's families flood the street daily. So do the gypsies "giving away" flowers to naive tourists whose delight turns to embarrassment, then anger, when money is asked for. A hassle no city reputation needs.

One also wonders how the fashion industry survives. The street dress is jeans. Tight jeans. Baggy jeans. Mini jeans. Maxi jeans. Jeans jackets studded with nailheads or fringed or laced or beaded. Hole-y jeans. Brand new jeans. Faded jeans. Grey, black and royal blue jeans.

Yes, you see a lot of jeans in the store window displays.

The length of Oxford Street West is chockablock with huge emporiums that sell nearly everything. Here, you'll find the premier stores of eight of England's major department stores, conveniently grouped together. Make that eleven, adding Liberty and Dickins & Jones, actually on Regent Street just off Oxford Circus, and Fenwick's on Bond Street.

None but Selfridges on Oxford Street really fills the American or Japanese concept of department store. Selfridges, one London guidebook said, "rivals Harrods as the world's biggest, best stocked and most confused store."

Marks & Spencer across the street holds the Guinness Book of Records (1987) distinction of being the store with the fastest moving stock *in the world.*

It's where price-conscious Members of Parliament get their suits instead of Savile Row if they wear standard sizes.

"Beautiful fabrics," an MP's wife noted.

"Marks & Sparks" have always gotten top marks for their "knits and knickers."

The store still has no fitting rooms; just a no-questions-asked return policy that's good as gold.

You hold up garments and look in a mirror for visual fit, or try them on over your street clothes, or buy and take them next door to a store that does have fitting rooms. If there's a fit problem, go straight back to M&S, receipt in hand. Home and hoses.

Nearby are two C & A stores, Debenhams and D H Evans and John Lewis in the middle price range, and British Home Stores and Littlewoods in a lower bracket. Unlike most retail stores which clear out inventories twice a year through the traditional sales, Debenhams will *always* have merchandise marked down.

Separating these behemoths are dozens of specialty shops including every popular-priced multiple the British have to offer—clothing and accessories, bookstores and stationers, chemists and scents stores. You won't have to look too far for a bank, fast food stop, souvenir or record shop.

St Christopher's Place

It's nothing more than a passageway between crowded Oxford Street and Wigmore Street via Gees Court marked by a "St Christopher's Place" brass plaque embedded in the Oxford Street sidewalk across from the Bond Street tube.

It is a Londoner's world of chic boutiques and ethnic restaurants, seldom discovered by tourists. Most of the time, it is a quiet browse. Summers, a shoulder-to-shoulder local mob patronizes the popular pubs and cafes that anchor the Barrett Square corner, the link between Gees Court and St Christopher's.

At Christmastime, the square is filled with carolers from the Royal College of Music busking for gift-buying wherewithall. They bring the mobs back to the narrow dead-end alleyway creating a street scene that could be lifted straight off the pages of Dickens' *A Christmas Carol.* It's a sight to warm the heart of Tiny Tim.

South Molton Street

In the same vacinity but abutting the Bond Street tube station, is South Molton, another pedestrian sanctuary that links Oxford Street to the New and Old Bond Streets. For calm window shopping, it beats the the insanity of Oxford Street.

A standout among the British multiples is Brown's, showcasing a dozen pricey international designers in different rooms. Brown's is a Londoner's favorite one-stop designer shop.

Here, also, is that chocolate drop of a chocolate shop, Prestat.

Bond Streets, New & Old

Celebrated Bond Street attracts devotees of the international couture designers and jewelers, the *haut multiples* as I've come to think of them. Every major city in the Free World has a Chanel boutique, or a St Laurent, Lagerfeld, Cartier, Tiffany, Gucci, Loewe, Louis Vuitton, Hermes, Ferragamo, Courreges, Valentino, Basile, Armani, Emanuel Ungaro, Ralph Lauren, Celine, Pierre Cardin . . . ad infinitnum.

They are homogenizing the world in much the same manner as is McDonald's or Pizza Hut.

Yet Bond Street retains its British hallmarks as well. There are the hallowed halls of Asprey for luxurious gifts, Charbonnel et Walker for chocolates, The White House for linens, and Frank Smythson, the Queen's stationer, for all sorts of chic paperware.

Left and right of Bond Street are the hauteur salons of rich men's tailors (Savile Row), fine arts and paintings (Albemarle and Cork Streets), antiques (Mount Street), antiquarian books (Sackville Street), the Sotheby's auction room (Conduit Street) and the Crown's china provisioner, Thomas Goode (South Audley Street).

Burlington Arcade

Parallel with Old Bond Street is the Burlington Arcade which is patrolled by top-hatted beadles in royal blue uniforms to ensure "obedience to the Regency rules against singing, carrying open umbrellas or running" in the arcade.

Its prim and proper countenance hasn't always been so.

Lord Cavendish built the gracefully arched structure in 1819 over an established market lane to keep rascals from tossing rubbish into his garden at Burlington House.

A century later, a second story was added and spaces let to merchants who lived above their stores . . . or let Girls Of The Evening move in to titillate from the overhead windows.

"Oh my, yes, it was a very naughty street," a clerk at one of the three Peal cashmere shops volunteered. He and an assistant bemoaned the passing of an elegant era . . . and the coming of skate boards that have upon occasion violated the arcade.

The shops carry ransom-priced (but top quality) knitwear, antique jewelry, Irish linen and leather. And last-a-lifetime handmade brushes.

Regent Street

The arcade leads to Burlington Gardens. Beyond the Museum of Mankind through the short knob of a street Vigo is elegant

Regent Street. Unquestionably, it is the most graceful high street (main street) in London, perhaps in the world.

Intended as the route for the Prince Regent to travel from his home in St James's to his new palace in Regent Park, the street was conceived by John Nash as a "Royal Mile of shops appropriated to articles of fashion and taste."

The Prince never moved into Regent's Park but the shops continue to live by Mr. Nash's directive. Wedgwood, Jaeger, Burberry, Aquascutum, Mappin & Webb, Garrard, all offer merchandise with impeccable classic British credentials.

Half way between Piccadilly Circus and Oxford Circus en route to Liberty, Dickins & Jones and two Laura Ashleys is Hamley's, the Jolly Green Giant of toy stores.

Piccadilly Circus & Street

Tower Records on the Circus and HMV Records around the corner at the Trocadero Centre blast passers-by with the sound of hard rock. Caution: beware of the seemingly generous semi-annual sale prices; a lot of genuine junk (pirated) is imported exclusively for the sales.

Lilywhite's is a one-stop sports emporium that employs experts in every sport to aid customers. Like, there are golf and tennis pros on duty to advise you. Class, no?

A clutch of shops on the south side of Piccadilly, opposite the Royal Academy of Arts, are legacies of the 18th century. Swaine Adeney Brigg & Sons has elegant gloves and other leather goods, Simpson's forte is classic English tailored clothes (also ladies formal dress "hire" clothes for special occasions), Hatchards is an old world bookstore, and the renown Fortnum & Mason is an exotic grocery-cum-department store.

Across the street is a Pakistani carpet store where I found the best priced Dhurrie carpets in London.

Jermyn Street

One street south of and parallel with Piccadilly between St James and Haymarket Streets is an enclave of shirtmakers and outfitters to the true English gentleman. Many of the stores still have their original 200-year-old storefronts. A stroll along the narrow slow-paced street and a wander into a well chosen store will reward you with the fragrances of a field of jasmine or a forest of sandlewood (Floris), a tobacco plantation (Dunhill), or the aroma of hundreds of cheeses, the best selection in London

(Paxton & Whitfield).

Covent Garden

Covent Garden has cast off its wretched clothes and dirty face just as if Professor Higgins himself had planned the transformation of the grubby girl into a *lover-ly* lady. The people's fruit and flower market outgrew Covent Garden and, finally, in 1974 moved across the river, leaving the once regal piazza and its Victorian cast-iron landmark vulnerable to developers' concrete plans.

It is, after all, valuable real estate.

The hue and cry of conservationists saved what today is one of the best free shows in London. Toney shops, street stalls of schlock, free entertainment, a bevy of interesting restaurants and pubs combine to attract more tourists to Covent Garden than even to the Tower of London.

Knightsgravia

A tube, taxi or bus ride west brings you to the heartland of the Sloane Ranger.

"The shops that serve a Sloane—and why they Really Matter" are included in *The Official Sloane Ranger Directory*. Actually, Sloanies could survive very nicely, you gather, with The *Gang of Four:* "GTC" (the General Trading Company) is a good all-rounder with stylish, eclectic decorative items; PJ (Peter Jones) is indispensable for basics; Harrods and Liberty's are good for everything."

Three of the four are in the area. Only Liberty is not.

Knightsgravia is the Imperial Colony comprising Knightsbridge, Belgravia, and Chelsea.

The British multiples and independent fashion boutiques that dot Knightsbridge from Hyde Park Corner right through to Brompton Road lure shoppers heading for Harvey Nichols at Sloane Street or Harrods a couple of blocks along. Shopping tributaries feed into this malestrom.

Sloane Street is a river of fashion in its own right. The problem is one of musical chairs among the players, the haut multiples.

"Chair, chair, who has a fronting on Sloane Street this year?"

Beauchamp Place (pronounced "Becham"), off Brompton Road, is an unpretentious little street made famous by several top restaurants and a clutch of English designers—Bruce Oldfield, designer to the Princess of Wales, among others.

It has lost some of its luster since the discount china and crystal stores moved into the neighborhood. But probably gained a lot of new customers.

Behind Harrods is the street of Hans Crescent with chic little shops like Feathers which sell Italian and French designer clothes.

Then there is Walton Street, away from the mainstream, just a block west of Harrods, running parallel with Brompton. It is one delightful innovative boutique after another.

Choice are Nina Campbell, an interior decorator whose line of house pretties (a la Laura Ashley) have a fresh look; Draggons for handpainted nursery furniture, toys and accessories; Moussie for handknitted sweaters. Mixed among the decorative print and monogramed linen sellers are small restaurants with big reputations.

King's Road

The young and trendy patrol this shopping route Saturdays as if it were still the high temple of fashion it ascended to in the Sixties. Publishers of tourist literature, including that from the BTA, cannot update shopping maps fast enough to keep up with the retail changes. Boutiques wash in and drift out on the wings of high expectation.

In comparing a 1985 *Shopping In London* with a 1987 version, only a third of the commercial operations were the same, and the majority of the oldtimers were services: banks, chemists, cafes.

The reliable shopping anchors are those antique'n'otherwise markets, Antiquarius and the Chelsea Antiques Market. (The latter is now better known for its rare bookstore, Harrington Brothers.)

Important magnets to Sloane Square are two of the Sloane Rangers Gang of Four: Peter Jones is *the* stylish department store for your home and the GTC dresses your kitchen, dining hall and garden and is a source for inspired gifts.

SEMI-ANNUAL SALES

Twice a year, Londoners swarm the shopping streets like bees forming a new hive. Few stores actually advertise their sales except in house. But, then, they don't have to. The sales are an established tradition. People just know that January and July bring reductions in price for merchandise across-the-board in most stores.

For nearly three weeks, *The Times'* Information Service page lists those stores whose sales start that day, or that week.

The sales are genuine end-of-season clearances, beefed up with some special purchases and some seconds. Each category will be clearly identified. It's the law.

Some sales are better than others. Both Liberty and Harrods are excellent. They mark down most merchandise from 30% to 50%. (The public responds. Sales recorded at Harrods were just over £6 million on the first day of its July 1987 sale; £13 million the first week.)

And immediately after the sales, the fashion season changes. Gone is the last season's merchandise...regardless of the climatic conditions.

Sale time is a rare time to observe the slippage of two national characteristics: "reserve" and "civility." It's no-holds-barred time. January and July are probably the only two months during which a Londoner, or a journalist, dare not mouth the national cliche: "London (or England) is so civilized."

STORE HOURS

Generally, 9AM to 5:30 or 9:30 to 6PM. Oxford Street stores stay open late (7:30) Thursdays; Knightsbridge stores on Wednesdays.

VAT REFUND

Most stores refund from 13% to 15% value added taxes, less a handling fee, if your purchases exceed their allowable minimum and if you are leaving England within three months. You must have your passport to qualify for VAT refund documents. You can shop a store over several days then return, with receipts, to complete the paperwork.

On departing the country, you must have the forms stamped by a Customs official who may want to see your purchases (seldom happens). In that (doubtful) event, and assuming you have packed and checked through the purchases (sensible), take the forms with you and have a Customs official at home verify purchases and stamp the forms.

Check the store's envelop to determine if postage is prepaid if mailed in England.

Theater

12. There's No Biz Like Show Biz In London

It's a love affair that makes the London stage exciting.

The audiences are in love with the talent on stage.

The talent on stage is in love with the excitement of the theater. Movies make money for the talent but the biggest names in England return again and again to the footlights because that is where the art is practiced.

The result is that London theater is a major attraction of the city.

For many people throughout Britain, Europe and the rest of the world it is the leading reason for a London visit.

During the interval, in a theater lobby, the visitor will be mingling with English from the provinces, bus tours from surrounding cities, Germans and Italians, Yanks, Kiwis, Canadians and Aussies. Sometimes you'll even find a Londoner.

Once an occasion of "dress up" (blue suits and dark ties), the lobby crowd today will be dressed in everything from tuxedos to ski jackets, patent leather shoes to sandals, silk gowns to sackcloth. Very diverse.

If you like the theater—any kind of theater—London always provides an extra thrill.

What is playing? What is hot? What is new?

It is like being offered a large box of chocolates. There is so much of it—almost fifty theaters—and it is all *so good*.

Where do you start?

Over the years we have found the most consistent high level theater at Royal Shakespeare Company performances at the Barbican Centre for Arts and the National Theatre Company productions at the National Theatre.

You can write to both theater centers for a monthly schedule shortly before your visit. Or you can become a Mailing List Member.

The schedule gives details for ordering tickets including payment using an International Money Order or any number of credit cards: American Express, Diners Club, Mastercard, Visa.

Instead of the requested *stamped addressed envelope,* obviously impossible for the overseas patron, just clip a dollar bill on the self-addressed envelope and trust the receiver.

Box Office, National Theatre, South Bank, London SE1 9PX, UK.

Barbican Centre Box Office, Silk Street, London EC2Y 8DS, UK.

Getting on their mailing lists for the monthly diaries is one solution for getting advance tickets to a show that will please you.

Another avenue for securing advance tickets is through the largest ticket agency in London, Keith Prowse, which has branches in New York, 234 West 44th Street, New York 10036 and in Australia at 320 Military Road, Cremorne, NSW 2090.

But, let's say, you don't get advance tickets and you arrive in London with no tickets and no idea what is playing—our usual status.

First you have to find out what's on and where. Go to a news agent and buy a weekly magazine called *What's On.* The magazine will give you a day-by-day schedule of everything happening in the entertainment field including theater, opera, ballet, symphony, rock concerts . . . the spectrum. Included will be prices, starting times, running times, addresses and telephone numbers.

The other entertainment magazine is *Time Out.* Both magazines debut midweek, on Wednesdays.

Daily reference is published on the inside back cover spread of *The Times'* first section, opposite the TV and radio schedules. Called the Information Service, it includes theatrical productions that have recently opened. The lower half of the page called "Entertainments" gives complete details also found in the weekly magazines.

In almost every theater lobby you can pick up a free copy of *London Theatre Guide* published by The Society of West End Theatre detailing information concerning current stage shows: theatre, name of the production, cast, times, addresses, telephone numbers.

Of the many ways to buy tickets directly in London, the easiest is by telephone with a credit card. The theater will either mail the tickets to you, time permitting, or hold the tickets for pick up at the box office. You must collect them twenty minutes before curtain time, and you must have your card with you.

If you buy with a credit card, you pay for the tickets whether you show up or not. No refunds. No changes. Charged the minute you confirm the order. But the good part is there is no surcharge.

You can usually get tickets through your hotel concierge. He has sources, particularly for hard-to-get seats.

Or go to a ticket agency. The agency offers the advantage of buying from a seating layout for each theater. You know exactly what you are buying, an advantage lost to telephone buyers. A service charge is added to the ticket.

The concierge is another matter. A friend from Honolulu bought tickets to six shows from her concierge. In every case the price was double that printed on the ticket. Her question to us was "Should I tip him?" "You already have," we counseled.

First Call is a 24-hour 7-day-a-week theater booking service which promises to answer your telephone call within 10 seconds and mail a proper ticket to you. The service is playing on the fact that ticket agents and box offices are often difficult to reach, and that the ticket agents and concierges issue vouchers which have to be exchanged at the box office (which means standing in line) for entry tickets. The cost of the service is relatively small, about £ 1.25 per ticket. The number is 01-240-7200.

You can always go to the box office and buy tickets direct.

Or, for *same day* performance tickets in the West End, there is an official half-price ticket office in Leicester Square operated by the Society of West End Theatre, the same group that publishes the biweekly schedule.

True incident: the Lady Navigator went to a ticket agent for evening tickets. Their per ticket surcharge was £ 2.50. Too high, she decided. She went around the corner to Leicester Square, suffered through a 30-minute line to be sure, but bought tickets for the same show at half price and cheerfully paid an 80p service charge. The Society helps guarantee a good audience by discounting tickets. They are not going to sell you tickets to the hottest shows in town. But you can get tickets to previews, recently opened plays or long standing ones which have not been sold out *for that day only*.

The National Theatre reserves 40 seats (approximately) for *every* performance, matinee or evening . . . even if the production is a sold-out smash. You queue for them starting at 10AM on the day of the performance. You'll meet a lot of Londoners standing in those lines. Remember, there are three theaters at the National.

The Barbican also has a cut-rate day-of-performance policy.

The regular cost of theater tickets, while half or less than tickets on Broadway, is not cheap. People who come in from the provinces, a major portion of the audience in the West End, must be bothered paying £10 to £25 for a single seat. It is one reason you see such long lines at Leicester Square queueing for half-price tickets. Londoners are hungry for good theater but the rising trend of theater prices is reducing the audiences.

At the beginning of summer 1987 five out of the six Shaftesbury Avenue theaters went to dark due to lack of support.

We get confused about seating terminology. English "stalls" are American orchestra seats. English "boxes" mean 1st balcony. Other "boxes" will mean second or third tier balcony. The "balcony" ticket means above the tree line.

If "restricted view" ticket is offered, forget it. The seat will be so far up that you can't see through the cloud layer or you will be tucked behind a post. A large post.

Note: all theaters have bars. Some bars offer coffee and pastries and small sandwiches before the curtain. All kinds of alcoholic beverages available. The most civilized custom is to pre-order and pre-pay for drinks at the intermission, or, more properly, the "interval."

The refreshments then will be placed in a prearranged spot around the bar with your name or number under it so that you can avoid the crush at the bar and escape to a quiet corner, hopefully with fresh air. Cigarette smoking is heavy in England.

Move Over Broadway

In addition to the West End theater, there is lunchtime theater, fringe theater, open-air summer theater in the parks.

What is striking about London theater today is the new ground being broken by musical comedies. In the past it was felt that, yes, the English were quite good with the thunder of Shakespeare and, perhaps, their little Noel Coward drawing room dramas, but for tuneful, imaginative musical comedy, only Broadway measured up.

Today Broadway is almost dormant or importing productions that originated in the West End. Since *Jesus Christ Superstar,* there has been a string of them: *Evita, Cats, Starlight Express, Les Miserables, Phantom of the Opera* and even a 1937 revival, *Me and My Girl.*

The switch was pinpointed by the *International Herald Tribune*: "For the New York Theater, the rise of London as a musical theater capital is as sobering a specter as that of the Japanese automobile industry was for Detroit."

One result is that tickets for musicals can be difficult to come by. *Phantom of the Opera,* the latest of the Lloyd Webber hits, is sold out months in advance. (The original cast was moved on—lock, stock and humpback—to New York.)

What London audiences are supporting these days are lavish musicals or revived classics. Only a handful of new plays are proving profitably popular.

Such times strain the genius of theater managers.

The classic story is of the theater manager whose show on stage drew an audience of two on Monday night. On Tuesday night the audience consisted of one patron.

The producer called in a panic. "What's wrong? What's wrong?"

"Oh," replied the theater manager with aplomb, "It's always slow on Tuesdays!"

Like New York, London theaters are old, houses built in the twenties, or earlier.

The Old Vic, a 19th century theater, one of the oldest existing in London, recently received a £ 2 million refurbishing and is rococo splendid. It sometimes serves as one of the several stages upon which Royal Shakespeare Company troupes perform.

We are keen about RSC productions. Thought anything they did would be near perfect.

Now we know that a RSC performance is no guarantee of a five-star show. Repeat: absolutely no guarantee whatsoever.

We went to see *Kiss Me Kate,* a musical version of *Taming Of The Shrew,* at the Old Vic. Three of the four leads were stand-ins.

Petruchio, instead of the virile, commanding macho male he is supposed to be, was *very* precious, *very* sweet and *very* inept. Near the end of the first act when he physically wrestled with Kate—the only lead who wasn't an understudy—he threw her to the floor, bounced her head on the deck in the process, straddled her and proclaimed his victory. When he stood up and demanded her response—with his glued-on moustache falling off—bringing giggles from the audience—she didn't answer.

And didn't answer.

Now the audience sat up. There was tenseness on the stage. Something was wrong.

She never answered.

Our precious hero had knocked her out cold.

They had to ring down the curtain and declare a ten-minute intermission to regroup and bring on still another understudy.

It was a hilarious disaster.

It happens.

The first post-war theater was the Mermaid, built in 1959 on the site of the old Puddle Dock in a remote location of The City. The converted warehouse was modernized a decade later when the area was rebuilt.

Today it is another one of several stages used by the Royal Shakespeare Company.

But the "official" London home of the RSC is the Barbican Centre, opened in 1982 between two 43-story apartment buildings as part of an urban renewal development fitting 6,500 people into a 20-acre compound.

The Barbican Centre works successfully, all ten stories of it—five above the ground and five below the ground. The London Symphony Orchestra has its home here also, in the concert hall. While the RSC presents the classics in The Theatre to 1,166-seat capacity audiences, a smaller stage, The Pit, stages *avant garde* productions.

In addition there are three cinemas and an art gallery, library, exhibition halls, meeting rooms and restaurants.

The Waterfront Cafe is a convenient place to have a bite before a performance. So-so food but if the weather is nice, and if you are early enough to get an outside table by the pool, it tastes better. Either place, you can enjoy the splashing fountains and the view of the ancient clock tower of St Giles of Cripplegate.

A formal restaurant, The Cut Above, is an English carvery featuring prime roasts, beef, lamb and pork. Dinner from 5:45PM.

The Barbican is easy to reach on the Central Line. Get off either at the Moorgate or Barbican tube stops. On Sundays the Barbican tube stop is closed. Hard to get a taxi after a performance but, if in doubt, follow the crowds. Most people travel by the Underground.

The notable growth of the RSC in recent years with companies performing at the time of this writing on nine stages in London and at Stratford is not without its problems.

RSC's ambitions have not been matched by box office takes. In the summer of 1987 the company, reporting a £1 million deficit, said that unless additional funding were found it would have to close down a theater in Stratford or the Barbican.

Critics have said the RSC is crying wolf again.

Critics have also charged that the giants of the RSC—the Anthony Shers and Jonathan Pryces and John Carlisles—are not matched with other actors of similar stature because the RSC is spread too thin over too many theaters.

We know that there aren't enough Petruchios to go around.

The National Theatre

On the South Bank facing the river and adjacent to the Waterloo Bridge is the South Bank Arts Centre and the National Theatre which opened in 1976.

The opening was exactly 128 years after a London publisher suggested establishing a national repertory center for classic English drama and development of new plays.

The National Theatre Company was given serious debate only after the war and it was not until 1962 that it took form with the laying of the cornerstone for the theater building and the appointment of Sir Laurence Olivier as its first artistic director.

In 1976, the National moved from its "temporary" home in the Old Vic into its new riverfront home.

The National Theatre incorporates three theaters: the Lyttelton, a proscenium theater; the Cottesloe, a smaller rectangular theater; and the open stage, the Olivier. Each is billed separately in newspaper and magazine entertainment sections.

A lobby snackbar is available preceding performances and, usually, there is free lobby entertainment.

You reach the riverbank theater complex via the Waterloo tube station. Follow the signs. It's a bewildering path but you'll find it. Just give yourself plenty of time to get lost . . . and found.

We would not consider visiting London without seeing at least one presentation by the NT company.

An idea of its diversity and quality is our sample of seeing in one month in three different National Theatre theaters, Shakespeare's *Anthony and Cleopatra* with Anthony Hopkins, Moss Hart's chestnut and still so funny, *Three Men on a Horse*, and a new Ayckbourn play, *A Small Family Business*.

Journalistic criticism in London can be brutal on any subject but it seems particularly savage toward the theater.

One reviewer said about an actor "I would be tempted to call him wooden but I don't want to insult the trees."

On the other hand, 1987 was the year of Lawrence Olivier's 80th birthday and he was lionized by the press, shown the courtesy due royalty.

His colleague, Sir Ralph Richardson, was prominently in the news as well. I have an item by columnist Russell Harty of *The Times* that I love to share with theater friends.

Richardson had just returned from New York where he played in Pinter's *No Man's Land* with his friend John Gielgud, about whom he loves to tell stories.

One of them concerned Mercedes McCambridge, an actress with a not altogether un-memorable name. Unique in fact. The two actors went to a party at her house. Gielgud grew restless and approached the hostess. "My dear, I must go now. I have to go to a party by that dreadful woman, Mercedes McCambridge."

"But, Sir John" she moaned. "I am Mercedes McCambridge."

"Oh, darling, no, no, no, it's not you. *It's the other one.*"

Fringe theater is not well known to visitors but it is a fountainhead for London theater's vitality. New plays and experimental productions are born in 70 small theaters, art centers and theater clubs around Greater London, some of which perform as lunchtime theater. It's an enjoyable way to dine.

What's playing where can be researched and booked at the Fringe Box Office, Duke of York's Theatre, 104 St Martin's Lane WC2, Telephone: 01-379-6002.

On the fringe of nature are the open-air park productions in Regent's Park and Holland Park.

We took in a performance of the Regent's Park Open Air Theatre where the New Shakespeare Company presents the classics. Ben Jonson's *Bartholomew Fair* was a bawdy, colorful show played with much gusto by the company.

A cold buffet or grilled hamburgers or bratwurst before the show is optional, but a part of the show that should be enjoyed. The cast stroll the premises juggling, engaging guests in Elizabethan games or songs or dances.

It's all very casual. Complete bar. Permission to take drinks into the amphitheater.

A warm starlight evening would add to the pleasure but rental blankets and hot mulled wine go a long way toward dispelling suffering.

There's More To The London Stage

We tend to speak of London theater as drama or comedy or musical stage productions, but the city offers daily concerts, recitals, symphonies—there are four symphony orchestras—operas, ballets. Look only at the full page of advertising of classical musical productions in the *Sunday Times* to get an idea of the scope of opportunity.

By getting in line early we were able to see a production of *Manon* at the Royal Opera House, Covent Garden. It has to be one of the richest, most opulent opera houses in the world. Its productions careen the imagination. Unbelievably lavish.

There is a scene—a *single* scene, mind you—when Manon and consort attend a festival. So, in the Royal Opera House production, on stage, in addition to the opera stars and chorus, there is a troupe of dancers, another of minstrals and musicians, and a full-fledged circus—jugglers, tight rope walkers, fire eaters—and children galore to add credibility as well as joy to the scene.

Our tickets cost £42 each. If the opera hadn't been subsidized, we subsequently read, tickets to *Manon* and the other productions in the season would have cost £75 each.

We believed it.

Restaurants

13. Sipping & Supping

If you are going to be in London any length of time and are going to be eating out extensively, you should invest in a guidebook of London restaurants. There are several on the market.

We used *Nicholson London Restaurant Guide.* The pocketsized book (£2.95) lists over 700 places to eat, all tastes, all pocketbooks. It is categorized ethnically and otherwise. It leads you to African, American, Chinese . . . on through Russian and Polish to Thai and Vietnamese . . . thirty nationalities total. For good measure, breakfast and brunch, unusual and vegetarian, Open Late and Sunday Eating and Inexpensive Places are tossed in.

Complete information regarding hours of operation, reservation requirements, prices charged and credit cards accepted is given for each listing, along with locater numbers tied to sectional maps, a good idea flawed by the type size of the maps themselves.

Time Out produces a magazine-sized guide, a good reference book but not a thing you want to carry around in your pocket or purse.

Guide to Eating Out in London is a professionally critical, hardcover book by Fay Maschler of the *London Standard*. Highly selective, highly critical but an excellent guide for the gourmet.

Another very good hard-cover book is *The Harpers & Queen Guide to London's Best Restaurants* by Loyd Gossman. Brightly written with observations right on the mark. Only 100 restaurants reviewed.

My problem with the Maschler and Gossman books is that I don't want to pay the hard-cover price for so little. I cheat. I flick their pages in bookstores to compare reaction with restaurants we have experienced or those we are considering. Terrible.

Oh, yes, there is also a *Vegetarian London* book.

The London Tourist Board issues a quarterly guide to restaurants, *Where to Eat in London,* free but bland. A tourist office publication can never be critical.

A change in the restaurant laws went into effect in May 1987. Formerly, a restaurant had to close its bar at the 3PM and 11:30PM licensing curfews. Now you can combine dining and imbibing at all hours. A civilized improvement.

A caveat: before adding a tip to a credit card voucher, read the bottom of the menu to determine if VAT (value added tax) and service are included in the price of your food. It usually is. We have found if service is *not* included that fact is brought to your attention— *clearly*—on the bill. But if it *is* included the credit card form, too often, is presented incomplete for your signature, the hope being that the naive customer will add another 15% tip to the tab. Infuriating.

Most restaurants post their menus in the windows and indicate if VAT, service charge, or cover charge is included. I thought the exterior posting a legal requirement but I've spotted several restaurants without them.

A number of restaurants offer special pre-theater and post-theater set-price menus. Good buys for the most part.

Lunchtime fixed price menus are always good value. The best way to sample the better restaurants without getting economically stamped on.

Dining out in London keeps getting better and better.

There are more restaurants of more variety than ever before.

More ethnic restaurants offering less expensive menus.

More fine restaurants whose impeccable service and crisp vegetables bear the starched prices you'd expect to find. They are not out of line with New York or Paris prices, nor a burden to the expense-account host. To the average tourist these glamorous "in" places are outside the family budget.

The Covent Garden and Soho districts have the largest number of ethnic restaurants concentrated in the smallest area. Prices are reasonable.

The Chelsea, Kensington, Belgravia area attracts the more up-scale restaurants. We counted 30 good restaurants within a 15-minute walk of our Chelsea flat.

More fast food outlets. Pizza parlors are everywhere. Pasta pits are everywhere. McDonalds and other hamburger joints are everywhere.

Pub grub is as abundant as ever. A strong division takes place when diners discuss pub food. From critical palate standards, pub grub is pretty awful, its loyal servants being potatoes, sausage, a little ground meat. One typical dish, for example, is Cottage Pie, a dab of mashed potatoes over a bit of hamburger. Best part of the dish is the title.

You won't starve. Your pint will be nutritious, the food filling and the memory of the pub lasting.

We have many soul-satisfying pubs on our list. Some even serve good food.

If you are in the Covent Garden area, find **The Globe** on Wellington Street. Madhouse downstairs, quieter upstairs if you go early. Perhaps one reason my stage-minded daughter and I found it so fulfilling was because Trevor Nunn, the famous English director, was lunching in the corner.

If you are in Mayfair, find the **Red Lion** at the end of Hays Mews. A 17th century inn where the beef and salmon are from Scotland and pates are homemade.

If you are around Harrods, look for the **Grenadier** at 18 Wilton Row where, it is said, the Duke of Wellington played cards. English food a specialty, Beef Wellington, steak and kidney pie . . . that sort of thing.

Pubs are on every corner in London. There are haunted pubs, singing pubs, riverside pubs, gay pubs. The whole gambit. If you ask a Londoner for his or her favorite pub, it will be the one nearest his flat or home where the pub is like a small private club. You meet your friends there and have a pint and a chat.

Strangers are not usually embraced.

Then there is a matter of ordering. On my first solo visit to a pub I would ask, "A glass of bitters, please."

Of course "bitters" as in Angostora bitters and "bitter" as in a pint of bitter ale are two different things.

Finally a friend trained me to say "A *pynnt* of best *bittah,* please."

The next hurdle was when I thought the barman asked, quite pleasantly, "Slug on the ass?"

This gave me pause. There are some funny bars in London.

The translation finally worked out to the question: "A mug or a glass?" All went well since that indoctrination.

Note: pub hours were under discussion when we left London. It was expected that open hours would be extended. But not on Sundays.

A restaurant classification we see mushrooming is the *brasserie,* a casual cafe import from France. The food is generally wholesome, prices moderate, service indifferent. One sees many brasseries now around London, some of which resemble the French original—tiled floors, cane chairs, overhead whirling fans, brass lamps, and good house wines—in name only.

Our favorite is **La Brasserie** on Brompton Road. Popular. The food is okay, the atmosphere is French-genuine and the service is French-terrible. Reliable house wine.

The most popular might be **Langan's Brasserie** off Piccadilly on Stratton Street where people go to watch people partially because the manager is a character and Michael Caine is a part owner. Smart crowd. The nice surprise is that the food is quite good and the prices are not stratospheric. You can draw a dumb waiter. Sit downstairs for people-watching and the clamorous atmosphere. Upstairs for business.

Note to Americans: if you don't know what "Bubble and Squeak" is, try it here. It is not a mouse steamed in champagne. Would you believe mashed potatoes, onion and cabbage fried? Quite good.

Another is the **Criterion Brasserie** at Piccadilly Circus which was preceded by the Marble Hall, an extravagant neo-Byzantine room with a gold mosaic ceiling which alone is worth the visit. The room dates to 1874. If they ever finish the dreadful construction jungle around Piccadilly Circus, pop in and take a look.

The worldwide trend to lighter drinks has produced the wine bar. A softer atmosphere than the pub and a more sophisticated crowd. Wine poured by the glass from a variety of vintages and menus are a cork above pub grub. A place to sip and chat and have a light meal.

A block down from our flat, a block off King's Road at the corner of Anderson and Bray, **Charco's** is typical. No beer, a buffet table with cold chicken, a variety of salads, three hot dishes, and the inevitable dessert table. Outside tables in warm weather.

In a Soho basement at 44-46 Cranbourn Street, Don Hewitson, a genial New Zealander, runs a corker, the **Cork and Bottle**. Nice atmosphere. All local people. Don knows his wines, having written a book about them. He takes reservations; otherwise get there early.

Don also operates two other establishments: **Methuselahs,** a wine bar and brasserie at 29 Victoria Street, Parliament Square, and **Shampers** at 4 Kingly Street, also billed as a wine bar and brasserie.

At Covent Garden, downstairs in the Central Market, is the **Crusting Pipe** where they serve port in pewter mugs on keg tables. Sawdust under foot. Decent food.

For a strong local flavor step down into the basement wine bar of **Gordon's** on Villiers Street, just a step up from the Embankment tube stop. It's a hangout for personnel from the nearby Ministry of Defense. The men's room graffiti is supposedly the funniest in London.

Ethnically, the strongest growth we have seen is in Indian restaurants usually with Tandoori in the title. Tandoori means cooked in a clay oven. Generally not great ambience but the prices are probably the most reasonable in London.

But there are exceptions. The most outstanding is the **Bombay Brasserie**. An Indian brasserie. That's cute. Excellent buffet lunch. The address, 140 Gloucester Road, is Bailey's Hotel but the restaurant entrance fronts Cromwell Road. Bombay Brasserie is one of London's most popular restaurants, especially for the Sunday luncheon buffet. (Call four days in advance for the Sunday buffet, two days for dinner any night.)

Two other highly rated Indian restaurants are **Last Days of the Raj** (Bengali food, lamb tandoori) on Drury Lane in the heart of the theater district, and **Bombay Palace** (Northern foods) on Connaught Street in Mayfair which also serves a luncheon buffet.

In our Chelsea district we found tiny **Moti Mahal** at 2 Woodfall Court, one block off King's Road. Twenty-five years in business. Lamb chassily and lamb passandra. Delicious.

Berated ourselves for not sampling more Indian restaurants.

The Chinese restaurant industry keeps trading up too. For years, a favorite pre-theater dinery was a tiny, Chinese restaurant called **Dumpling Inn** on Gerrard Street just off Shaftsbury Avenue. Wonderful food. Fair prices.

Gerrard Street has now been "tarted up" becoming an official Little Chinatown marked by overhead lanterns and it is chockablock with Chinese restaurants. Take your choice. We tried the dim sum at **Lee Ho Fook** on recommendation of the Lady Navigator's Singaporean hairdresser. Very good.

Alas, the last time we returned to Dumpling Inn it was a culinary disaster.

We hosted a dinner party at **Ken Lo's Memories Of China** on Ebury Street. Mr Lo, an evacuee of China's Cultural Revolution now in his seventies, is as famous as his restaurants. Two of them. A daily tennis player, author of cookbooks, and owner of a Chinese kitchen store, he runs a fine first-class kitchen. Expensive but memorable. The scallops cooked in the shell were an unusual treat.

Our Chelsea neighborhood Chinese outing was to **Choys,** an old family-owned restaurant on King's Road. Excellent food and service.

The upmarket Chinese restaurants found in most guides will list **Tiger Lee** on Old Brompton Road and **Tai-Pan** at 8 Egerton Gardens Mews.

Wherever you are in London, there is a decent Italian restaurant near you.

If you are looking for the glamor-setting, people-watching restaurant, go to **San Lorenzo** on Beauchamp Place. I had heard about the so-superior attitude in the service at San Lorenzo and declined to try it. Who needs that with your pasta?

But attitudes don't faze the Lady Navigator who took a friend to lunch there during which she glanced at an adjacent table and then turned back to her London guest and asked, "Do you think that pretty young woman cuts her hair that way so she will look like Princess Di?"

Her companion leaned over and hissed, "That *is* Princess Di."

Neither of them are coffee drinkers but they had two after-lunch expressos to prolong the experience, sneaking peeks. When they reluctantly left, they found the Beauchamp street jammed with people who had heard that the Princess of Wales—not the Lady Navigator—was having lunch inside.

We tested **San Frediano** (affectionately called "San Fred's") on Fulham Road and returned to stage an important birthday dinner with Italian-raised daughters who thought they were back in Trastevere in Rome. Yummy tagliatelle with mushroom sauce. Crowded and boisterous. Fun waiters when you are with smashing looking women.

Beccafino on Draycott Avenue, comparatively new, was tested and passed. Has already picked up a following. In the same Chelsea area is **The Pasta Connection** on Elystan Street. No pass. Decent, fresh daily pasta, but cold, non-personality service. (I think there must be a school in how to be a bad Italian waiter.)

When we sought a restaurant near the Old Vic Theatre for lunch before a matinee, we found **La Barca**. Excellent. The Lady Navigator had a lovely chicken in wine sauce; I had an herb-rich grilled veal chop.

French restaurants, as a whole, tend to be more expensive. Why this is I don't know. Somewhere in one of the London newspapers I read an article on French restaurant prices. When the owner of a popular restaurant was asked how he determined his prices he smiled and wet a finger with his tongue and held it up to the wind. *Voila*. Whatever the traffic will bear.

Small French restaurants that will leave your limbs and wallet intact include, in our experience, **Au Bon Accueil,** just up the street from the Pasta Connection. Sinful mushroom starter in garlicked olive oil. Overcooked asparagus was sent back. The contrite manager was indignant that it had happened. "I'm sorry. I don't know what is wrong downstairs today." The indifferent service didn't help but still a good *boite* that has been in the neighborhood a long time.

Better was **La Poule au Pot** on Ebury Street. Now this for lunch has the right atmosphere. The manager, jovially bellowing in French, sets the tone. The food is very good. No menu at lunch. Just bellowed items. My boeuf bourguignon—huge portion—was excellent.

Never seen before: the house wine, red or white, is served in magnum bottles and you are charged for what you drink. A place you want to go back to with a great and good friend on a rainy day and finish the magnum. And carry on.

Getting into the expense-account bracket we have **Ma Maison** on Walton Street. It usually makes everyone's Best Ten list. Unimposing exterior, the small restaurant is somewhat pressed for space inside. Specialties of the day are recommended. Or try the pork fillet stuffed with prune and onion cream sauce.

New to Walton Street is **Turner's.** John Turner was the chef at the highly respected **Capital Hotel Restaurant** until he opened his own eatery in 1987 to rave reviews and the following of an established Capital clientele.

Tante Claire on Royal Hospital Road is also well known and respected and worthy of your best client. Perhaps the best French food in London. *Mais tres cher*.

In the same category, across the river in the unchic Battersea area is **Chez Nico** on Queenstown Road. Reservations a must. Exceptional, we've been told.

In most guidebooks English restaurants are separated as a distinct category, which we have difficulty understanding. "Carveries" *are* typically British. But those elegant establishments that wheel trolleys laden with huge silver salvers filled with roast beef or lamb to be sliced to order at your table are becoming rare.

By the criteria of one guidebook we have eaten at three English restaurants.

Rules on Maiden Lane has been a long time favorite because it looks like an historical London restaurant should. Established in 1798 by Thomas Rule, it has enjoyed an illustrious literary and theatrical clientele. The likes of Lillie Langtry who was frequently entertained by Edward VII in a private dining room. The management even cut a special door so he could enter unseen.

The walls are covered with a collection of prints, pictures, playbills and cartoons. Set luncheon menu is reasonable. The service personnel in white aprons are quite efficient. Last time, we had a waitress, a major change. I have read that Rules is on the tourist circuit but we've seen no evidence of that being true.

The **Tate Gallery Restaurant** is also listed as English. I think that means that there aren't any French sauces. You go to the Tate for the wine list and an omelette.

Simpson's-in-the-Strand we did find to be touristy. Specializes in true English fare: smoked salmon, carved beef, treacle roll and a slice of Stilton cheese with a glass of vintage port. Correct dress is essential.

Recommended by several London friends, **English House** on Milner Street in Chelsea has a Victorian dining room in a private house. Excellent reputation. Chicken mousse poached in cream, excellent steak and kidney pie. Trifle, that sort of thing. Expensive.

Also listed as English (it offers an array of French cooking) and expensive is the **Savoy Hotel Grill Room** on the Strand. *The* elite businessmen's luncheon spot. Packed daily.

On the other hand the **Savoy Restaurant** for Saturday lunch is serenely superb. We were taken there on the first day of Spring and it was a spoiler for every restaurant that followed. The table overlooking the river through budding trees was all starchy white and crisply neat. The service was attentive and unobtrusive. The food was perfect. Fortunately, I didn't see the bill.

Fish restaurants are common in London today. Gone are most of the fish-and-chips shops of yesterday found in every block. The reason, we were told, is the high price of fish. Reduced catches in the North Sea have put the price of the meal outside the purse of the people.

But there are exceptions.

Geale's on Farmer Street near Notting Hill Gate, is a special exception. The best of the old style fish-and-chips shops we found. Inexpensive and very satisfying. Fish-and-chips is *all* they serve. It is deservedly popular. No reservations. Tea room atmosphere. Paper napkins. Menu on the wall with prices changing minute by minute, like an old-fashioned daily stockmarket board, as the size of fish available changes.

Rock Sole Plaice at Covent Garden on Endell Street, a continuation of Bow Street, is both cheap and good fresh fish. Sit outside in the summer. No license. BYO.

The Lady Navigator stumbled across a pub, **Flanagans** on Rupert Street between Shaftsbury Avenue and Leicester Square that had really fresh fish-and-chips. Best outside of Geale's she had in London, she said. Not to confused with the hokey **Flanagans** with the song-and-dance waitresses on Kensington High and the other on Baker Street.

For local color find your way to Berwick Street in Soho between Poland and Wardour. Amidst a busy open street market near the top of Berwick Street at number 20 is **The Dining Plaice.** A grotty looking place but its fish-and-chips are exceptionally good.

(It is the favorite fish-and-chips shop of an airline executive who led me there and ordered two slices of buttered bread with his haddock. He took chips and laid them out on one half of a slice of buttered bread, folded it over and ecstatically ate it. The starch-on-starch sandwich is known as a *butty*—famous in Manchester where it is pronounced *booty*.)

Scott's, a traditional favorite for fish diners, is still an "in" place. Once in a gracious old Edwardian setting in Piccadilly, now in modern premises on Mount Street. Everything is Scott's is reliable from the oyster to the fresh salmon. Excellent wine list. Sometimes lofty service. We liked the former ambiance.

Bentley's Seafood Restaurant And Oyster Bar has been at Piccadilly forever, just across from Selfridges on tiny Swallow Street. Has its own oyster beds. Recommended fresh fish. Seating suggestion: downstairs for color, upstairs for quiet.

Not to be confused with **Bill Bentley's.** Three venerable fish specialty eateries (French style) at Bishopsgate, Baker Street and Beauchamp Place just a block down from Harrods.

Poissonnerie de l'Avenue on Sloane Avenue is another French-style restaurant high on the lists of Sloane Rangers and companions. Next door to a fishmonger's shop, suggesting absolute freshness. Recommended bouillabaisse.

All of the above are expensive.

Not cheap and not good is **Wheeler's** on King's Road. We have long been addicts of the Dover sole at the quaint Wheeler's restaurant, corner of Duke of York and Apple Orchard Yard, off Jermyn Street near Piccadilly. But the experience of the King's Road Wheeler's made us shudder. A chef's salad, wilted, tasteless. Overdone salmon. *Lonely* service. A bad, bad show.

American tastes are synonymous with McDonald's. The red-and-yellow signs abound around London. Lots of McDonald's.

The upmarket version of McDonald's is the **Hard Rock Cafe,** bordering on legendom, at Old Park Lane. Stand in line to get in. Stand in line to buy a T-shirt. Lots of folks there just for T-Shirts. "Why don't they practice a little American ingenuity and walk along the line outside selling them?" a friend with a teen-ager wondered. Rock music, ceiling fans and pool lamps, hamburgers, steaks and shakes. Dreadful. One daughter walked in and walked out. "I didn't come to London for this," she said.

On the other hand we tried **Joe Allen,** a block south of Covent Garden, a simple brass plate marking its basement entrance at 13 Exeter Street. Blackboard menu, checkered tablecloths, attractive theatrical posters line the bricks walls. Paper napkins and ketchup bottles on the table. Some nice looking people as at the Joe Allen's in Paris. So-so food. Casual service. Chili? Brownies? Pecan pie? All here.

Maxwell's is listed as an American cafe. We tried the one at Hampstead Heath on a holiday. Crawling with children. Lots of children. Loud children. There is another one, crowded with older children, at Covent Garden.

A new American entry is **Tony Roma's** on St Martin's Lane. Part of what is becoming an international chain—with chain decor—but the best babyback pork ribs in the world.

American food backs into Tex-Mex cuisine and Dallas-born localites gave us their list of favorites to chose from: **Cafe Pacifico** facing Leicester Square, **Break for the Border**, a take-off on the popular restaurant "On the Border" in Dallas-Fort Worth which sued and lost, **Texas Lone Star Saloon** on Gloucester Road (bad food, good music). Lone Star Beer, partner. **ChiChi** on Leicester Square, very good but not cheap. **LocoBoco**, new and untested, also in the Covent Garden area.

La Cucaracha, Greek Street, Soho, was London's first Mexican restaurant.

Other restaurants we have tried:

Clarke's on Kensington Church Street. We found Sally Clarke's upbeat restaurant in the International Wine and Food Society's annual publication. Very imaginative kitchen. All pre-set menus. Professional presentation. Long on quality and short on quantity. The grilled tuna—main course—was barely a tasting. Expensive. Sally Clarke gives you the impression that you are lucky to be there.

Nineteen on Mossop Street next to the **Admiral Codrington** pub, colloquially referred to as "The Cod." Open on Sunday. Reservations suggested. Observe the British habit of stopping off in the pub for a Sunday pint or two and then go next door and have a fine meal at a modest cost and then go home and have a nice nap. Very civilized.

Tui, a charming Thai restaurant on Exhibition Road near Albertropolis. New. Two story. One daughter found it and wanted to take it back to Carmel with her. Modest prices. Tui is next to an Italian restaurant which, in turn, is next to an Indian restaurant.

Foxtrot Oscar on Royal Hospital Road. The name needs explaining. A smart-crowd hangout in the Chelsea area. Blackboard menu. Stiff drinks. Eggs Benedict on Sunday brunch. Make reservations and ask for a table on the ground floor. Don't go into the basement.

Launceston Restaurant on Launceston Place in lower Kensington. New. Good reviews. We gave it about an eight. Expensive.

Dan's on Sydney Street just off of King's Road. Inside or outside in nice weather. Great sauces. Pleasant atmosphere and service. Expensive. Lots of Sloane Rangers who dress in anything.

We had the good luck to be invited to the **Overseas Bankers Club** in The City behind the Bank of England. The menu listed a long variety of unusual English cheeses together with a description and the dairy or farm or cheese factory from which it came. Incidentally, the *de rigeur* biscuit to be eaten with cheeses is Bath Olivers (Since 1775).

Another experience was being taken to **Harry's Bar,** a private club restaurant, ultra chi-chi, in Mayfair.

Our last and best restaurant experience was the **Gay Hussar** on Greek Street, favorably reviewed in every restaurant guidebook. Small, *intime*. Luncheon rendezvous for publishers and politicians. The 70-year-old proprietor is Victor Sassie, a personal jewel who knows the basic lesson that any food is enhanced by the personal attention of the proprietor. We went and loved it. Loved him. Let Sassie order for you. Reasonable set-price lunch. No credit cards.

Despite the increase of hundreds of restaurants to the London scene, the problem in London is the same throughout the world. Where do you get a nice place to eat with memorable food, reasonable prices, good service, and a come-back ambiance? It is not easy.

Hotels

14. Where To Lay One's Head

In times past we have enjoyed London on expense accounts, stopping at such hotels as Grosvenor House, the Hilton and The Dorchester, all on Park Lane.

We have stayed at the Cumberland at Marble Arch and the Washington and the May Fair, both in Mayfair, and, in Knightsbridge, the Capital and what is now the Hyatt just a couple of steps from Harrods.

Overnighting at Heathrow we've slept at the large sound-proofed Sheraton and the functional Post House.

When we are paying the bill out of our own pockets, we have stepped down economically to test the Strand Palace on the Strand and the Willet, a bed-and-breakfast hotel off Sloane Square.

With the luxury of a week in London which, by law, should be the *required* minimum length of stay in London, we have booked into Dolphin Square in Pimlico, a massive block of residential apartments (1250) built for the gentry and members of Parliament in 1937 when it was the largest block of flats in Europe.

One wing is reserved for transient guests who have privileges to the year-round, Olympic-sized pool and racquetball courts in the basement for a small fee. The leased studios and one bedroom flats are not furnished in a gentry fashion, but there is the adequate kitchen for breakfasts and snacks, and a variety of ground floor food, wine, pastry shops to erase the necessity of leaving the building to shop. A ground level restaurant—the Dolphin Brasserie had gained a fine reputation lately—theater ticket and travel agency, and a concierge provide the services of a hotel. Not cheap.

Once we tried the Nell Gwynn on Sloane Avenue for an even longer stay. The apartment required a 21-day minimum, the typical length of stay for serviced flats in tourist neighborhoods. The two bedroom apartment was shockingly expensive and darkly depressing. Its shoehorn kitchen was so small the waste pail had to sit in the living room in order to open a cupboard. We consoled ourselves with the thought of how spacious it would have seemed on a yacht. But we moved out on the 21st day.

The Lady Navigator had scouted neighborhood estate agents with furnished flats to let. Most of them required a three month minimum and a "company" lease, i.e. guaranteed by a company operating in London. (Later we learned why such precautions are taken. Under English law, individuals cannot be evicted. Landlords find dealing with companies a safeguard.)

She finally found our *maisonette* (meaning two levels) in Chelsea which was a third less in price than the Nell Gwynn, still expensive but it was substantially bigger, lighter, more modern, and with a cheery spacious fully-equipped kitchen. It was one block from Safeway Supermarket, three blocks from Waitrose Supermarket, the library and the nearest tube station.

While there are several new hotels under construction and constant refurbishing of older hotels, the accommodation situation in London is difficult and visitors should not be surprised to pay more for less than in other major cities of the world.

Six hotels were being built in 1987 but travel authorities expect that the number of *overseas* visitors alone will increase from 13 million annually to 26 million within ten years. Another 12 million Englishmen travel to the capital annually. You can see the problem.

If price is no problem, London is no problem.

Big hotels with big tariffs are not in short supply.

Sheraton, Hilton, Hyatt are all here with the usual big chain characteristics. Along with Inter-Continental and the Four Seasons Inn on the Park.

The Dorchester was bought by an oil-rich sheikh who installed his own management. Avoid the Grill.

The Grosvenor House is now part of the Trusthouse Forte Group, the nation's largest hotelier, who have upgraded most of their properties exercising great care in redecorating. We had an overnight stopover in the Grosvenor recently to find, under those lovely high ceilings, rooms with brightened interiors and a staff to match.

Traditional luxury hotels in London include The Ritz, Savoy, Claridges and Connaught. Claridges has been ranked one of the top ten hotels in the world by the *Travel & Leisure* magazine.

Both Browns and Britannia are also favorites of the well-heeled. Tea at Three is a "must" at Browns despite its somewhat lackadaisical service.

The Sunday tea dance in the sumptuous dining room at the Ritz is a high hoot.

A new wave of boutique hotels asking luxury hotel prices has become the favorite stopover for jet-setters thinking small. Like 7 Down Street, a hotel with only six suites, each exquisitely decorated.

Or Forty-Seven Park in Mayfair, the London address for Tom Selleck.

There's Dukes at St James's Place where every room bears the name of a duke. Some dukes are smaller than other dukes. Ask for the upper floor rooms. Big dukes.

The Stafford Hotel near St James's Palace where the Queen Mother often dines is a favorite of Honolulu friends. It is said that in calling the Stafford dining room to make reservations, the Queen Mother asks if there is space for her. Silly question. Her popularity is reflected by the dish named Castle Mey, another of her homes.

Or stay at a private club, the St James's Club. You are permitted one visit, with an advance reservation, without being a member.

Next to the Capital in Knightsbridge is L'Hotel by the same management with only 12 rooms. Twelve tiny rooms. Down Basil Street, another 12-room hotel, Hotel 28, gives its guests pause for thinking small. The rooms are so tiny that even the promotional pictures focus tightly on twin beds and a door to the "loo" to give the illusion of space.

In Chelsea, 11 Cadogan Gardens is a good buy in the luxury small hotel price bracket for old world British tradition. Victorian period furnishings in an 1897 building unmarred by a commercial hotel sign. A small unfurled flag marks the address and guests ring the doorbell to enter. Tea in the salon poured by liveried attendants, handwritten bill upon departure. Best buy: the ground floor double with the adjoining solarium.

Blakes Hotel in South Kensington is owned and decorated by Anouska Hempel and is one of London's most talked about hotels because she is a much talked about decorator. Every room (100) is different.

Near Buckingham Palace is the Goring Hotel, a rarity among London hostelries, because it is an older hotel (1910) which is still owned and run by the same family. Retains its own private garden, too. Claims to have been the first hotel in the world to have central heating and a bathroom in every guest room.

Price is a problem. Where do you go?

We checked out the several moderately priced hotels in the Chelsea-Belgravia-Mayfair areas and scouted accommodations in Bloomsbury, Kensington and South Kensington. Moderate meaning under £ 100.

A friend told us about Green Park Hotel on Half Moon Street, a block off Piccadilly. Recently remodeled, it has a cozy bar and decent restaurant, individual character to the bedrooms, and rates include breakfast. Our friend paid more at the Flemings across the street for a "tired" room and had to buy her own breakfast.

Green Park is one of the nine Sarova Hotels in the heart of London, each deliberately different from the other. They also manage a health and fitness accommodation, the Aquilla, and the Rembrandt Hotel in Knightsbridge. The Rembrandt's frumpy exterior conseals its gracious, old but modernized interior. It has a respectable carvery restaurant.

The Grosvenor Hotel adjacent to Victoria Station (not Grosvenor House on Park Lane) the Lady Navigator found surprisingly old-world pleasant and a favorite place to stop for tea on the way home. The Millau London guidebook describes the Grosvenor as "a monument to the age of the train in the age of airplane (350 rooms)."

"They are trying to come into this century," defends the Lady Navigator, "through an ongoing renovation program, floor by floor." She admitted that, without a map, you could end up on a train to Bath instead of your room . . . such is the maze of corridors and fire doors and dead-end nooks.

A block northeast of Victoria Station and the National Coach station is Ebury Street, a quiet, gentle street like its Belgravia neighbors. Two blocks of what once were residential terrace houses are now almost exclusively small hotels and B&Bs. A couple of dozen side by side, by side. Most of them are dreadful. Rude or indifferent staffs. Overpriced for what you get—average range, £35 to £40 *per person* per day—which mostly does not include an *en suite* bathroom. Maybe breakfast, often just a "Continental" placed in your room the night before.

The London bed-and-breakfast accommodation is different from that in other countries where your bedroom is, most likely, part of a family dwelling and breakfast is served by them if not taken with them. To the London accommodations industry, seemingly, a B&B is a converted residence offering a bedroom and an impersonal breakfast service.

Ebury House came closer to being acceptable. The owner-manager made the difference. We met him polishing the brass doorknob . . . a gesture denoting good maintenance and a sense of caring. He is personally involved with his guests, he cooks English breakfasts to order. A frequent guest volunteered she thinks of Ebury House as her "home away from home" which is the kind of feeling a good B&B generates.

If we were booking into a B&B in London, we would write to David Davies, Ebury House, 102 Ebury Street, Westminster, SW1W 9QD and plead with him to fit us in. Or find us something of the same caliber.

The Ebury Court, at the top of Ebury Street (No. 26), has 38 bedrooms, a good table by reputation, a small lift to the 3rd floor and a porter. Some rooms have baths, some don't. You pay twice the going rate of other Ebury Street habitats, and the management couldn't care less if you come.

"We don't want inquiries," the receptionist told the Lady Navigator haughtily, "we just have to turn them away."

They will never have that opportunity.

We looked at and liked the Royal Court Hotel on Sloane Square for its location, its staff, its remodeled rooms and the most charming hallways—some with skylights—in London. Corridors, lined with theatrically oriented prints in support of the Royal Court Theatre next door, are quite the cheeriest in town. The mood extends to a popular restaurant on the ground floor, a bistro in the basement and a pub on the corner.

The 69-room Cadogan Thistle Hotel on Sloane Street has a charm that dates back 100 years when Lillie Langtry, then the rage of London theater, sold her home to the Cadogan Estate and moved to Monte Carlo. She is remembered in Lillie's cocktail bar but it is the secluded lounge where tea is poured afternoons you feel the old world grandness of another era.

The Fenja, at 69 Cadogan Gardens, shares the same quiet residential neighborhood with 11 Cadogan Gardens a block off Sloane Square. The 13-room hotel, revamped under new management, retains the feel of an Edwardian townhouse. No lobby. No dining room. Just a charming young woman at a desk to answer questions, arrange for afternoon tea or any meal you request to be served in your room but from their own kitchen.

By comparable standards, Fenja is a bargain now (£78 double) but it probably won't be once word-of-mouth exposes it.

Two South Kensington hotels in a residential area get accolades from Londoners who book family and friends in them: Sixteen and its across-the-street neighbor, the Alexander Hotel at 9 Sumner Place. Sixteen is a big "little" hotel with a bigger room tariff than its neighbor which seems to capture Sixteen's guests on return visits.

"The Alexander cannot, in our opinion, be bettered," says Ashley Courtenay *(Let's Halt Awhile in Great Britain)*. It has a rentable cottage in what is considered one of the best hotel gardens in Chelsea.

In the Lady Navigator's opinion, the best buy on Sumner Place is Aster House at the end of an early (1848) Victorian Terrace. It is owner occupied and owner operated, always a good sign of management. Peter and Rachel Carapiet won the "Best Guest House In London" award in 1987 and the hearts of many guests who were made to feel as if No 3 Sumner Place was their home. There's no hotel sign; you have your own front door key, an individually decorated room, access to a tranquil garden and breakfast with the family. At £52 to ᴸ68 double, it's a steal, but don't expect porters and doormen and elevators.

The Kensington High Street area has a cluster of hotels catering to tour groups. The Royal Garden is first class. The Royal Kensington farther on is moderate.

There are literally hundreds of small hotels and guesthouses in the Bloomsbury district, along Cromwell Road and off Bayswater

Road but the small buildings housing them are beginning to be turned into smart condominium apartments by investors seeking a quick profit. The future of these establishments is clouded.

The British Travel Authority publishes a free booklet listing hotels under £50. In London, £50 doesn't buy a lot.

Flat Letting

The record price for a rented apartment in London is £10,000 per week, but that particular Park Lane penthouse was large enough to house a Middle Eastern potentate, his family and half a dozen retainers.

The estate agents (real estate companies) locally thought the price cheap. The only comparable accommodations for short holiday lets are the Dorchester Hotel apartments which would cost the Arab a lot more.

The long and short of flat letting in London is tricky.

For a "long" let—a year or more—canvass the neighborhood in which you would like to live, look around for an estate agent with "for let" signs under property photos displayed in the window. One estate agent will lead you to another. There is no multiple-listing system as in the USA, thus, the estate agent in the vicinity is your best bet.

You can try to do the same thing for a short—called holiday—let, but with unpredictable success. Most agents deal *only* with "company" lets.

The better idea is to contact John Birch, chairman of the Association of Residential Letting Agents (1821 Jermyn Street, SW1Y 6HP). He can wire you into the 50 or more ARLA companies with twice that many offices throughout central London whose business is to find tenants for their apartment clients.

Mr Birch says that finding a flat or house is free to the tenant, the fee being paid by the property owner.

That was not our experience. But our landlord is an American...and we do things differently, don't we?

Two types of "holiday" accommodations are available:
(1) the service flat (read that to mean sterile hotel quality furnishings, with kitchen) requires a minimum 21-day stay;
(2) the individually owned apartment which can be for a negotiated length of stay.

Many of the 21-day minimum apartments must have paid off

the mortgage many times over. Such is the price they extol. Mr Birch confirmed that surcharges of 50% (minimum) are added in summer. That drops to about 25% in spring (April/May). Winter (mid-October through March) prices are the cheapest, and availability the highest.

Average price for a small space one-bedroom service flat in central London during the high season is £500 a week. Prices increase annually, just as hotel room rates. A rule-of-thumb for both is 10%.

Another rule-of-thumb after shopping many service flats is, if you find the apartment advertised in national or inflight magazines or in a large display ad in the London telephone yellow pages, it will be top priced. If it has an "800" number in the USA, float a loan before you come.

A private home or flat is a more satisfactory experience. It will be better furnished, probably cleaner, certainly more personal. And you will be in a residential environment. According to Mr Birch there are always large properties for short "holiday" lets during school holidays (mid-July until early September). Give plenty of advance notice and expect to pay the entire rent in advance plus a full month rental as a deposit against breakage and damage.

Short term rentals are like small space leases in big office buildings; they are either a godsend or a G-D nuisance. For this reason, the estate agent who found our Chelsea flat recommended following the same routine as for locating a long-term let.

"Check into a hotel then shop the estate agents in the neighborhood desired. You get to see what you are renting instead of relying on a photograph—never totally satisfactory—and the agent, with a tenant on hand, may be able to convince his client to take a holiday let as interim income."

For a flat in Chelsea we would go back to Mr Allister Bowe of Mistral on Sloane Avenue, SW3. Highly efficient and reliable.

Week Or Less Flats

Among the few holiday let apartments willing to accept guests for under the 21-day period we found are a couple of "keepers." They are in different price brackets, to be sure. One bedroom and studios at Clifton Lodge (45 Egerton Gardens, near Harrods) are being remodeled unit by unit in the English tradition. Small but manageable for two. At about the same price of an acceptable hotel room (£85 per day plus VAT for a one bedroom), the advantage is having a kitchen. Ask for a flat with a recent face-lift.

202 (202 Kensington Church Street, W8 4DP) was bigger and more reasonable. We looked at airy, self-contained, fully equipped studios and two room apartments ranging from £43 per night (sleeping two) to £68 per night, (sleeping four to six). All in, as they say. Daily maid service. Minimum stay in high season, one week. One week's rent deposit paid in advance required. Good location for transportation. Hundred yards from Notting Hill Gate underground.

The apartment building has only 21 units. The manager wished he had 400. The occupancy is 85% year round.

Private House Hotels

Remarkable values prevail in the "paid guest houses" that dot Gower Street in Bloomsbury. With breakfast but without private bath, these private house hotels, a form of B&B, charge about £15 per night per person. The area is owned by the Duke of Bedford who sets quite high standards of maintenance and cleanliness. Hard to get. They are even hard to see.

The farther out from the city core one goes, the better the buy in flats or bed-and-breakfast accommodations. For example, one such accommodation recently featured in the *International Herald Tribune* is the home of Paddy and Judith O'Hagan at No. 52 Mount Park Road in Ealing. (It is also included in *The Historic Hotels of London* by Wendy Arnold, £ 5.95.)

Ealing, the Victorian era's "Queen of Suburbs," today is served by two underground lines, the Central and District lines.

The O'Hagan home is solidly Victorian with huge high ceiling rooms, wide staircases and a large rose garden. The rooms—there are two only—are large and well furnished. A vase of flowers, a bowl of fruit, a bottle of mineral water and a tin of homemade biscuits add to the home-away-from-home touch.

The cost was £22.80 and included a hearty English breakfast. Dinners can be arranged for 7 including drinks before, wine with and cheese after.

Is it any wonder that first-time visitors change their itineraries and schedules to come back to No. 52?

The O'Hagans belong to a marketing group of similar accommodations called Wolsey Lodges with 97 such homes from Scotland to Cornwall. Contact Wolsey Lodges, 17 Chapel Street, Bildeston, Suffolk 1P7 7EP, England for their booklet, *Welcome To An Englishman's Home,* which is distributed by the British Tourist Authority.

Note: I have found a warning to B&B clients from New Zealand that British homes may differ from that which they know at home. I think the tour operator was saying that the British home might be old, in a cheek-to-cheek neighborhood of buildings. Or maybe it is, as we discovered in Ebury Street, the charmlessness of London B&Bs.

Incidentally *Nicholson London Guide* warns readers of hotel touts at railroad stations.

Rental Tips

Talking to different travelers reveals different systems for finding the best buy in low-cost accommodations.

A Honolulu friend goes to the London area she likes and surveys the glass enclosed bulletin boards in candy shops or tobacconists to find neighborhood B&Bs and small hotels.

The lady is partial to the Holland Park area and recommended Abbey House and Observatory Hotel.

We tested the theory in several communities. It seems to be universal in the non-posh neighborhoods.

A small publishing associate also canvasses the neighborhood where he is going to be doing the bulk of his business or attending a convention until he finds what he wants. His last discovery was the Concord Hotel on Cromwell Road. Clean, neat, inexpensive.

One of our tennis playing friends said he found the Portman Court Hotel (28 Seymour Street, Marble Arch W1) when he came to London to attend Wimbledon and now all the members of the Kailua Racquet Club who come to London stay there.

Another innovative system offered by a New Zealand travel veteran is to call tour coach companies who book blocks of hotel rooms and ask if they have a "surplus" room for that week.

"You have to take what you are offered, but the price is right."

The Lady Navigator discovered that "business" hotels, i.e. those typically used by visiting British businessmen during the week, offer substantial weekend discounts (about 40% off) and accommodate children under 16 free if they share the room with a parent. The Mount Charlotte Hotels with a dozen central London hotels is one example and the offer is in effect the year round. Weekends may start on Thursday. Two night minimum.

Another reliable source for low-cost housing is the newsagent's bulletin board in the Royal Opera Arcade behind New Zealand House on Haymarket. Often the listings are for flat sharing but some B&Bs appear.

Students flood the hostels in London in summers, some of which are in beautiful settings. One such is in Holland Park in the former mansion, but you have to belong to the hostel organization. The membership fee is modest.

At East Acton, six miles west London, (Central Line) there is a tent city for young people. Restaurant and showers. Dormitory-style tents for 3, we hear.

Literature

Hotel guidebooks that looked useful were: the Red *Michelin,* the AA and RAC guides on *Where to Stay, England, Nicholson's London Guide* and *Ronay.* (The *Where to Stay* books are also available for Scotland and Wales at bookshops and major tourist Information Centres.)

There is not yet a satisfactory official hotel directory breaking down accommodations into categories according to set standards and prices.

There is a strong feeling among several honest travel writers that the hotel situation in London is tough. Fewer amenities for more money that anywhere else in the world.

We set out to disprove it. We couldn't. And we really tried, scouring neighborhood after neighborhood in desirable areas.

London has led the international market in continually setting higher and higher rates and the public keeps paying them and paying them.

To pay US$100 for a grim hotel room is discouraging.

For current prices to any of the standard hotels mentioned above, check your travel agent.

In the final analysis, the first-time visitor to London should take advantage of the experience and the bulk space contracts offered by tour operators to get the best buys in accommodations.

The Social Scene

15. Highlight Events

Whenever you go to London, you will find year-round special events.

By long standing tradition, the 'season' occurs in early summer.

After the busy summer season, however, the list is just as colorful. To cherry pick The London Visitors Bureau's annual list of traditional annual events (85 all together):

The Horseman's Sunday in September.

The Costermongers' Harvest Festival Service in October with cockney Pearly Kings and Queens wearing traditional pearl button covered suits.

The Opening of Parliament with the Queen on parade in late October or early November.

The Lord Mayor's Show the second Saturday of November.

The Christmas tree lighting ceremonies in Trafalgar Square in mid-December.

Charles I's Commemoration Day period costume parade in January.

Chinese New Year Festivities highlighted by the dragon parade in Soho late January or early February.

The Oxford-Cambridge boat race on the Thames in March.

The Queen's Birthday on April 21 and Maundy Thursday when the Queen distributes purses of specially minted pennies to as many poor people as the years of her age.

But the great social season of London is, and always has been, in the late spring and early summer when the weather is likely to be kind. At that time starts a roster of must-go, must-dress, must-be-seen-at events.

These include the Chelsea Flower Show, the Glyndebourne Opera season, a trio of military parades—Beating Retreat, Sounding Retreat and Trooping The Colour—the Royal Ascot races, the Royal Regatta at Henley-on-Thames, the Wimbledon tennis championships, and, finally, the start of the "Proms" or the traditional Promenade Concerts at The Royal Albert Hall.

If you plan a trip to London to enjoy the social events of the spring/summer season, you need to do a little advance planning. (Local friends who know the ins-and-outs help. They might even find tickets which is more difficult.)

Spring's Herald: The Chelsea Flower Show

The Big Season starts in late May with the Chelsea Flower Show—or more properly The Great Spring Show—held on the grounds of the Royal Hospital in Chelsea. It is sponsored by the Royal Horticultural Society which has over 100,000 members. Nowhere is the British love for a bit of green and a potted plant more evident.

Normally the hospital grounds are a quiet scene of gravel lined wooded paths, open lawns and tennis courts. Suddenly, eleven acres are given over to tents and canopied stalls, *House And Garden* picture perfect garden pavilions and ideal backyards.

The show is supported by equipment and greenhouse manufacturers, nurserymen and landscape architects. It encompasses every aspect of the horticultural world. In the Grand Marquee—grand is the right word for the three-and-a-half acres under canvas—there are 160 exhibits.

It is rather gigantic.

Tradition is that the Chelsea Flower Show be held on the Royal Hospital grounds, as it has been since 1913 with interruptions for the war years. It is contracted to stay until 1990. What the directors will do to meet the demand for more space remains to be seen.

Tradition is strong that it remains. Space requirements make an equally strong case to move to enlarged quarters.

But as a visitor we don't concern ourselves with that.

Do we go to look at the flowers? Oh, yes. But above all we are attracted by the people. Those *real* English types.

In doing the tourist rounds we are mostly looking at fellow tourists. Running shoes, open shirts, bedraggled golf jackets. We are an awful sloppy lot. We justify it by saying we are at leisure.

At the Chelsea Flower Show you see the English at leisure. Old shoes, the patched jacket, the doddering country squire and his tweedy lady, the upmarket yuppie with his leggy lady, the strange, the skinny, the pipe puffer, the bloated beer swiller, the dear little matrons. Oh, what a cast of characters.

Another piece of theater.

Of course one takes in the roses, the orchids and begonias, the fuchsias and pansies . . . those tiered floral arrangements around the perimeter of the Grand Marquee that say Spring Has Arrived.

Of course one wanders down aisle after aisle to examine the alpine and rock gardens, the royal wedding bouquets (very crowded), the bonsai plants, and the hanging baskets.

One stops at the scientific and educational exhibits. Did you know there is a Carnivorous Plant Society? The Hardy Plant Association?

Exhibitors come from throughout England to show their plants and from as far afield as the United States, Belgium, France, the West Indies and South Africa. And plants of the entire world find plots large and small to appeal to the casual or careful eye.

Fringing the central exhibit tent are displays of classic gardens, window box arrangements and hothouses. Merchants are promoting their lawn furniture, stonework and statuary, garden books, sprays, fertilizers and lawn mowers.

The National Trust sells tea towels.

The National Trust for Scotland sells tea towels.

The *Daily Express* sponsors a show garden.

The *Daily Mirror* sponsors a show garden.

The *Daily Telegraph* sponsors a show garden.

The *Sunday Times* sponsors a show garden.

Hundreds of would-be exhibitors apply for space and can't get in.

Food halls dispense hamburgers and scones and tea and spirits and beer. If you haven't been introduced to Pimm's Cup—a beverage—now is the time to meet. It is *the* social drink at large spring-summer social events.

The show opens on a Monday for the judges and press, Tuesday for members, and Wednesday for the public. It closes on Friday. Hours are from eight to eight except Friday when it closes at five. The admission after four is half price.

The crowds are enormous. Over 200,000. Shoulder to shoulder. In the main tent, overhead arrows direct the traffic flow: "Go ahead." "Do not enter." "No left turn."
But then the crowd is the best reason to go.
Flowers: gorgeous. The people: divine.

Do go. The Queen does.

Things you learn: you can become a member of the Society for the cost of a first public day ticket. The membership gives you the chance to go the first day—Members' Day Only—plus another day. The routine seems to be that members use their second entry to go on closing day, late, to buy the exhibited flowers and plants. The sidewalks of Chelsea late Friday afternoon look like a marching floral shop with people staggering under loads of trees, shrubs, buckets of flowers. It's a riot. But then the whole thing is.
For membership or ticket information write The Royal Horticultural Society, 80 Vincent Square, London SWI 2PE (834-4333). No children under five are admitted.

What Are You Wearing, Drinking, Eating At The Glyndebourne Festival, My Dear?

From late May until the middle of August, in the middle of the afternoon, couples in formal dress and floaty gowns, wicker baskets and champagne buckets from Harrods or Fortnum & Mason in hand, line up at Victoria Station to board trains south.
You always suspected the English of being a bit formal, but black tie and chiffon at midday—on the train—is a little much, no?

They are dressed to the nines for a most unusual musical experience. Their journey will end at a country manor house 54 miles south of London when the early evening curtain goes up on a first-rate opera performance, one of a series in the Glyndebourne Festival Opera.

Formal dress is recommended although, I was told, I could have gotten by in a dark suit.

The Glyndebourne Festival was started in 1934, the effort of John Christie, a wealthy 48-year-old bachelor whose marriage to a young opera singer inspired him to build a proper stage and theater seating 300 patrons. It was Mr. Christie's suggestion that the audience "take trouble" to dress for the occasion as a compliment to the artists, train travel notwithstanding.

A new tradition was born.

The 300-seat opera theater built at his estate at Glyndebourne, 11 miles north of Brighton, eventually was enlarged to accommodate 830 and three restaurants were opened for diners without hampers.

From the beginning, the operas concentrated on quality and were tremendous artistic and social successes. The management didn't try to hire name singers but singers' names were made at Glyndebourne, among them Pavarotti and Joan Sutherland in early career performances. Rudolf Bing was its general manager before leaving for the Metropolitan Opera in New York.

The May-to-August Glyndebourne Festival Opera mounts half a dozen productions.

The social high point of the evening of opera is the 75-minute Long Interval. Audiences in all their finery spread around the estate's green lawn in the long gentle English summer twilight popping corks and munching picnic fare, twittering like the nearby birds. Not to be missed. Remember tickets are at a premium.

Public booking by post opens 31 March. Telephone inquiries are accepted from 28 April. Overseas visitors without pre-booked tickets may call at 10:00 on the day of a preferred production to inquire about returned tickets. (Check the *Sunday Times* or the entertainment magazine for schedules.) Cost will be between £40 and £50 per ticket. Train travelers are advised by the box office the time of the best train to catch for Lewes which will be met with a shuttle bus to the estate.

Information on future schedules is mailed at the end of every season, about a year in advance. To get on the mailing list, send £2 (£2.50 overseas) to Glyndebourne Festival Opera Box Office, Glyndebourne, Lewes, East Sussex BN8 5UU, UK. Telephone: (0273)541111.

Royal Ascot

This is the time of *My Fair Lady*. Gentlemen in gray formal attire with gray hats—required dress for the Royal Enclosure—mostly rented from Moss Bros—and the ladies in the newest Spring fashions with a special emphasis on the millinery. Hats that sweep and swoop, feathers that flutter in the wind, hats that tilt, cling to the head, blow off the head, graceful hats, crazy hats. One lady wore a hat box with a hat on top of it. The winner at Ascot is not a horse but the lady with the most photographed hat. Starting on Wednesday during the third week of June, the racing schedule covers four days, four days of Pomp and Pimm's with Champagne Charlies, and as the *Daily News* reported, with a thousand imitations of Rex Harrisons.

Its social face aside, Ascot is the best festival of flat racing in the world and takes an army of organizers to stage. Just hauling away the rubbish costs £15,000, part of that to pay 180 extra staff to keep the place all neat and tidy.

Oh, well, it is just money, especially for one lady who reported that the fresh flowers for her husband's private box cost £8,000 a day.

She is now divorced.

Nigel Dempster, the *Daily Mail's* social arbiter, used to host a party for over 130 friends catered by Scott's of Mount Street in the reserved car park. But, deciding it had all gotten to be too much, he reported to his readers he would be watching it all on television.

"Ascot is just rabble everywhere nowadays," Dempster wrote.

"Just a great social climbing gathering and it's just ludicrous. You can't walk anywhere because there is no room. If you get up off a seat, someone else sits on it . . . even Dukes don't go any more because they don't want to be in a freak show."

Ahhh, but the Queen goes and enters the track in a carriage. So does the Queen Mother and Princess Di.

It is a royal show.

And it is best watched on television where you get to see all the hats—hours of hats over the four days of four hour broadcasting per day from BBC—and the best seats of all if you want to see the races.

Trooping The Colour

Another June event is the Queen's official birthday which is celebrated by Trooping The Colour. (Not Color, nor Colours; not Trooping of The Colour. But "Trooping The Colour.")

Trooping The Colour takes place at the Horse Guards Parade. The ceremony originated in 1755 and has been going on continually since 1805.

The stands surrounding the Horse Guards Parade Ground seat 10,000 spectators and you cannot get a ticket. They are snapped up months in advance.

The public can witness a rehearsal but, of course, that is without the Queen, the star player in the pageantry.

You can join the throng along The Mall parade route from Buckingham Palace and watch the Queen, the Queen Mother and the Princesses roll by in their fairy godmother carriages, followed by Prince Phillip and the Prince of Wales on horseback. You might even get an over somebody's shoulder look into the parade ground itself but you won't see much.

It's fun to be on the scene and part of the crowd and see the Royal Family in the flesh. But you miss the broad spectrum of the event.

Again, it is much, much better on television.

You are assured of a dry seat, a refreshment at hand and the comfort of close-by facilities.

You see everything. Everything, from the parade of Royals to their appearing at the balcony overlooking the parade grounds, the Queen's facial expressions, the precision marching. Everything.

Even better, you have authoritative commentary to tell you the significance of what you see.

In 1987, for instance, a tradition was broken. The Queen, resigned to giving up the riding of her favorite horse and sitting sidesaddle for the hour or so the ceremony takes, rode instead in a carriage. Gone was the uniform of the regiment and the tricorn hat of former years. In their place a simple blue frock with a matching hatband on her straw hat.

The colorful Household Cavalry preceded the carriages transporting the Queen Mother and the lovely Princess and son William, followed by the Queen in a dainty black trap with ivory panels. Real ivory.

She waves gently to the crowd which she was could not do from her horse.

The regiments are already at the parade ground and make their appearance from either side to the sound of martial music. Huge sound of martial music from some 360 marching musicians.

The regiments take up their positions, the Queen's carriage enters and circles the parade ground. She alights at a small reviewing stand where she alone will review the regiments and take the salute.

Watching from a window directly behind her in the Horse Guards building are the feminine members of her family and her grandchildren. You get the odd TV glimpse of giggling royal children pushing each other.

There follows an hour of music and precise marching maneuvers so perfectly drilled—the result of three months of rehearsals—that they look exactly like little wound-up toy soldiers.

Finally comes the review and the moment when the single Colour bearer carries the Colour (read the flag) to the Queen, lowers it horizontally, (the only time the Colour is ever lowered), the Queen nods her acceptance, the Colour is raised and returned to the regiment.

Trooping The Colour is a tradition rooted in practicality. When wars were fought by foot soldiers, this drill burned the colors of the regimental flag into the brains of the troops so that, in case of disorganization during battle, they would reassemble around their familiar Colour.

The performance is flawless.

The carriages arrive, the Queen departs and the regiments leave the field.

And the curtain falls on yet another act in the ongoing London play.

The preceding week we had gone to a similar ceremony at the Horse Guards Parade Ground to witness, in a slight drizzle, the annual Sounding Retreat by the massed bands and bugles of the Light Division.

Sounding Retreat, now ceremonial, once served as a communications exercise, giving fair warning that the gates to the fort were to be closed. Its origins are of the 16th century.

Historically, the formation of the Light Division dates to the time of conflict with America when it became painfully evident that red and white uniformed soldiers advancing forward in tight formation to the sound of drums made the loveliest of targets for colonials shooting from behind trees.

The men of the first unit were specially trained soldiers picked for their intelligence and durability and dressed to blend into the surroundings. They were able to move at double time on the signal of a bugle instead of a drum, and encouraged to use their own initiative to scout and skirmish.

The first Light Company was so successful that the company grew into a regiment and then into a division.

"They are," our host who is a Light Division man, "the equivalents of your Marines."

The ceremony today is a social and sentimental gathering time for past and present members of the regiments and their friends who assemble at sunset to watch and take pride in the display of traditional military drill and music, including a short concert.

The evening ends with an evening hymn and the playing of "Sunset."

It is a colorful, tuneful, sentimental and moving ceremony.

You can buy tickets to Sounding Retreat and to the preceding week's Beating Retreat, a military marching and musical spectacle of the Guards Massed Bands under the floodlights of the Horse Guards Parade grounds.

Tickets for these events may be purchased from ticket agencies or at the Souvenir Shop of the Guards on Birdcage Walk, or by writing as early as January to Ticket Centre, 1B Bridge Street, SW1.

Tickets to Trooping The Colour are, democratically, allocated by lottery. You can try for tickets (only two per ballot) by sending a self-addressed envelope (with postage money included) prior to February 28 to The Brigade Major, Headquarters Household Division, Horse Guards, Whitehall, SW1. A fee is charged.

Local residents say they send in several ballots.

The Royal Regatta

July issues in still another gathering-of-old-friends event that is so much part of the "season." The Henley Royal Regatta.

During the first week of July, the little town of Henley-on-Thames is abuzz with yachts, canoes, skiffs on the river, hordes of people of every age group toting thermos bags of champagne and picnic hampers. Women will be dressed in elegant sportswear—little silk dresses and brimmed straw hats—and many, many of the men will be wearing rowing club blazers. It borders on high hilarity. There is music in the air and...oh, yes, and rowers on the Thames.

There is a hint of Mad Hatter-ness about it all.

Henley is to rowing what the Chelsea show is to gardening...a social tradition. The Henley gives the men a chance to drag out the old rowing club jacket, stow the boot of the car with liquid and munchable goodies and drive to Henley-on-Thames for five days of Old Tie seeing and partying.

An American lady living in London summed it up as "the College Homecoming."

"I am the wife of a rower," Jackie, our gracious hostess, said. She wore the *de rigeur* flying saucer white straw. The dear lady had been up until three ayem assembling a small repast of cold salmon—the whole salmon served on a silver platter—pate, and three salads, plus strawberries and cream. A case of still and bubbly white wines had been chilled and crystal glasses set out on a linen covered table decorated with flowers and protected by an umbrella.

The car boot concealed all of the storage containers. We were, you see, in the members' car park. Row after row of cars were focal points around which other Henley reunioners had assembled to eat and drink.

"I do the lunch and Patrick gets to watch the rowing."

"You see all your old friends at Henley," Patrick told us. "Actually they are not necessarily your friends but you saw them here last year, you know, and the year before that so you smile and wiggle your fingers at each other."

In 1839 at a Town Hall meeting at Henley-on-Thames a resolution was approved to establish an annual regatta "under judicious and respectable management...which would be a source of amusement and gratification to the neighborhood, and to the public in general."

It has been blossoming for 150 years, growing successively from one afternoon of racing to five full days and attracting the cream of rowers from throughout the world.

Almost every country in Europe has been at Henley at one time or another. Schools and clubs from America and Canada have traditionally offered strong challenges although, when we went, the rowers of the Soviet Union were dominating the races.

"They look so much older somehow," murmured an English companion.

Program events involved clubs from Yale, Dartmouth, Harvard, Tufts.

The Americans come with their families and try to look more British than the British but they are too neat somehow, too scrubbed. And they look as if they just had a glass of milk instead of a Pimm's. And then there are those cameras around their necks.

This is a straw hat day. Men wear boaters and the women wear straws sashed with pink tulle, or wide garden party straws wreathed with silk blossoms. This is not a Royal Ascot type of dress day. The men, if not in striped boating club jackets, wear dark jackets with white trousers. The women tend to silks and silk pretenders.

We have decided that the English are better than any other race in the game of Let's-Play-Dress-Up.

The place to be is in the Stewards' Enclosure where dress codes are as strict as those once set by the Crown for Presentation at Court.

A pre-Regatta bulletin carries this important paragraph: "Members are reminded that, in accordance with tradition, gentlemen are required to wear lounge suits or jackets or blazers, with flannels and a tie or cravat. Ladies should wear dresses or suits and will not be admitted wearing skirts above the knee, divided skirts, culottes or trousers of any kind. Similarly, no one will be admitted to the Stewards' Enclosure wearing shorts, jeans or denim skirts."

"They mean it too," Jackie had cautioned the Lady Navigator.

"A friend of ours showed up one year wearing a divided skirt. It was a handsome outfit. She looked smashing. The gate attendants prohibited her entry. She was angry, but resourceful. She found oversized safety pins and pinned them on the front of the skirt, marched up and through the gate defiantly. We all felt like applauding."

The Stewards' Enclosure is intended for Members (£ 50 a year) and their friends primarily. A five day reserved parking place in the car park is another £ 45.

Once inside, there is a reserved seating stand for Members and another grandstand for guests and overseas crews and their families.

One drinks at Henley. Behind the grandstand are several bars where one gets champagne and Pimm's.

"Pimm's is like drinking through a hedge," said a friend explaining the undergrowth of cucumbers, sprigs of mint and slices of lemons and other bits and pieces floating to the top of the glass. A time-bomb on a hot day. Pimm's tastes like soda pop but the base is gin. We ordered a "large" not realizing it would be a pint-sized mug (US$5 each). One is all a stranger needs.

"Cloakrooms," the most civilized of temporary facilities, are considerately located between the Garden Bars.

The serious business does not take place on the racing course but in the car park where tables are being set up, chairs laid out, buckets and glasses arranged and all made ready for lunch.

"I always try to see one race before lunch," said our hostess. Now relieved of her duty, she would not see another. And she would be one up on many of the attendees.

We had a delightful repast. My camp chair companion, Sir John, was celebrating his Silver Jubilee of Henley attendance. He had rowed at Oxford and served professionally in the diplomatic service spending much time in Turkey.

My other companion was Roger, a former banker in Egypt before the war, still indignant that King Farouk's men had stolen his elaborate door knockers when he was on a vacation. He was a member of the Leander Club, the leading club of Henley and he worn pink socks, the colors of the club, as did Patrick who also wore the traditional pink tie. They were most proud of their socks.

Oh, yes, the races.

Because the Thames is narrow, only two boats can race at a time. Therefore, it is match racing and somewhat unique making Henley that much more attractive to oarsmen.

New races and new silver cups have been added over the years.

In 1841 the Stewards' Challenge Cup was instituted for fours where the shell carried a coxswain. In 1868 a clever crew plotted that on signal of "Go" the coxswain would jump overboard and the shell, relieved of the weight, could go on to an easy first. It was disqualified. Sorry, chaps.

The distance of the course is one mile and 550 yards, the distance of straight water on the curving Thames that could be laid out in 1839 on Henley Reach.

I estimated that there must be hundreds of rowers involved in the 82 races scheduled for that Thursday. The first race starts at 9 AM, the last race at 7:05PM. Before one race ended, another race began.

By the time the shells and sculls have reached the grandstand the race is pretty well determined.

"I can remember only one photo finish," Patrick recalled, "and then the judges must have been too old or too drunk to call it."

The river bank in the Stewards' Enclosure is lined with lawn chairs where one can curl up if the day is sunny and sleep away the Pimm's.

At four is tea. To be correct you should have tea at the Leander Club, the rowing club next to the bridge. But you must be with a member who also has to have made a reservation because tea under the huge temporary silk parachute canopy is terribly popular: finger sandwiches, fruit cake, tarts and eclairs after all that lunch which we had just finished an hour earlier.

A small number of tickets are reserved in the Stewards' Enclosure for overseas visitors. You write—after May 1—to The Secretary, Henley Royal Regatta, Regatta Headquarters, Henley-on-Thames, Oxfordshire, RG9 2LY. Or call (0491) 572153. Because Stewards' Enclosure tickets are so popular with foreigners living in London, tickets must be posted to a foreign address.

Beyond the Stewards' Enclosure is a general admission section if all else fails.

The train back to Paddington Station with a change at Twyford gives you a little over an hour to digest food and drink.

The bright green fields captured by tall trees with an occasional church spire saying "The village is here" is so peaceful and so quietly correctly English.

It is a calm painting after the crazy kaleidoscope of Henley.

The Holy Of Holies—Wimbledon

This is the strawberries-and-cream sporting event of the year.

Some 400,000 tickets were sold in 1986 which was voluntarily reduced by the All England Club in 1987.

Hundreds of only the top ranked players in the game from 42 countries are in contention.

Untold millions around the world are glued to television sets as the drama between the highly publicized protagonists unrolls.

It is an event for big stakes.

In 1877 the first "Lawn Tennis Championship on Grass" was held at the All England Croquet Club on the grounds situated off Worple Road, Wimbledon.

In 1884 a ladies' event was added. '

The name of the club, incidentally, which moved in 1922 to Church Road, is now The All England Lawn Tennis and Croquet Club. It is not "Wimbledon." The complex includes the Centre Court, the enclosed Court No.1 and another sixteen outside courts.

In 1967 the championship became open to all categories of players, including professionals.

Since that early time more than a hundred years ago, the tournament has steadily grown into the most prestigious tennis event in the world, the huge amount of prize money being far less important than the real payoff—winning the title.

Wimbledon is now very professional. The two week event offers around £2.5 million in prize money, and even with the payout of prize money, overhead and tournament staff, the tournament earns another couple of million annually. It goes into the profit pot which had exceeded £6 million by 1986. The money is used to promote tennis throughout England.

(With all that money to spend the press was asking why England hasn't won a Gentlemen's Single Title since Fred Perry in 1936.)

Preceding the Wimbledon event there are important warm-up tournaments at the Queen's Club in London for men and Eastbourne in East Sussex for women when the hype starts to build.

Classified sections in newspapers are filled with ads asking for tickets, mostly by touts. The asking price from a tout for Centre

Court tickets for a final was around £1,000 in 1987, according to the street talk.

There is a limited number of tickets for the Centre Court, No. 1 and No. 2 courts available each day at the turnstiles from 10:30 AM. People sleep at the gates overnight to get them.

A small amount of standing room is available on the main courts. Don't plan on going to the bathroom once you get sardined in.

Unreserved seats are available for the other courts for £5 during the first week and £4 the second week when there is less action on the outer courts.

There are no refunds in case of rain.

Once upon a time while touring England and Scotland, we celebrated my birthday at Gleneagles and our friend, Alan, flew in for the party. Over the cake and the singing of the Italian waiters—happy *birzday* to you—Alan threw me an envelope. It contained airline tickets for transportation to Heathrow, a chauffered Jaguar to pick us up, Centre Court tickets to watch Bjorn Borg rifle down his opening opponent, return Jaguar to Heathrow, and the flight back to Edinburgh.

We had to pay for the strawberries and cream out of our own pocket.

It was such a perfect day that I've never wanted to spoil it by going back.

The Lady Navigator went out at noon on the second day of play. The first day had been rained out without one match being played.

She waited until four o'clock and play finally started and she stayed in the English late summer light until nine o'clock.

I remained in the London flat with my private store of strawberries and cream, my own private facilities, and television. BBC coverage—so good—was on two channels for the first two hours so I could switch back and forth to watch different matches. One channel continued to broadcast until eight in the evening. Lots of convenient tennis.

It is not the same as being there.

One way is to go out late. People leaving will give you their tickets and you can watch some excellent late afternoon tennis.

Nearby the courts are hospitality tents erected by the megacorporations to entertain important guests.

I'd still settle for the TV in the flat.

"Coward!" said the Lady Navigator. "You stay home and watch television and you can't buy a souvenir T-shirt or tennis visors or tennis balls or umbrellas. Okay, they ran out on the second day, still, you missed it. You don't see the star players arrived by chauffered limos to the dressing room doors and the young things queueing for the autographs of the bright young stars of tomorrow. You miss the wild fashion parade, and the crowded food tents.

"You miss the feel and the color of it all."

And what are you're suggestions?

"One, go the *first* week while everybody is playing and you can see many of the top players on accessible outside courts. You can roam from court to court.

"Go by tube on the District Line taking a Wimbledon-bound train but get off at Southfields station and follow the crowds.

"Go at noon to avoid the earlier queues. I walked right in.

"Beeline for the top of the bleachers at Court 3 so you can also watch play on Court 2, which is now reserved seating, as well as other courts.

"Take binoculars.

"If you buy tickets from a tout, don't take the first price asked. Bargain. He expects it.

"Ticket prices are reduced after 5PM which sounds too late but isn't. Especially the first week.

"If you know you'll be in London for Wimbledon, write the All England Club for tickets prior to January 31. You might get lucky.

"I, for one," she said drawing herself up into the superior air reserved for Lady Navigators and Queens and God-Loves-Us-Editors, "wouldn't miss it."

Wimbledon tickets are also allocated by lottery—two per entry. Same drill as for Trooping The Colour tickets. Address: All England Lawn Tennis and Croquet Club, Church Road, Wimbledon SW19.

She later discovered the Savoy's Strawberries-and-Cream Tea which brought her around to my way of thinking. A giant TV screen on which to watch the action and a liveried staff who cottles, replenishing tea and cakes and scones with frequency.

"The Savoy's cozy lounge is a the next best thing to being at Wimbledon," she pronounced. "Very civilized."

It is nothing more than a catered version of my routine but, in front of my own TV set, I own the control buttons.

The Exuberant "Proms"

"DO YOU PLAY TABLE TENNIS?" yelled the standing audience on the floor of Albert Hall.
"PING!" boomed the gallery.
"PONG!" responded the floor.

What in heaven's name was this?
We were seated in an Albert Hall box waiting for the second concert in a sixty-six day series of nightly Henry J Wood Promenade Concerts, a major event in the midsummer social-musical calendar.
For the series, floor seats at Albert Hall are removed leaving space only for the "Promenaders" i.e. people willing to stand for the evening's offering of classical and semiclassical music for the price of £2.
An alternative for the music hungry, and even lighter on the pocket, is to stand in the fifth floor gallery for £1.50.
We suspected the Proms were in the mode of the informal and enthusiastic Boston Pops series . . . but "PING!-PONG!"?

It wasn't surprising to read in our Proms booklet before the concert began that the seed of the Proms had been planted in a pub-cum-music-hall, the Crown and Anchor, in 1839 where "the musical public can regale themselves with the spirited musical performance going on there."
Price of admission was one shilling. Reserved seats: two shillings.
Early ingredients of the first concerts were a number of short pieces with encores, cheap prices, a festive atmosphere and the availability of refreshments.
Moving to a larger hall, the idea of a series combining all of the same ingredients continued at Covent Garden Theatre, now the Royal Opera House, where seats were removed and the floor raised to the level of the grandstands. A writer at the time described the scene as one where nine-tenths of the audience didn't know what music was being played but "the place is a great mart for flirtation. Venus meets her Adonis here..."

In 1893 the Queen's Hall, 2,127 seats, became the venue for the popular concerts. Two years later a young conductor, twenty-six year old Henry J Wood, first brought down his baton.

One shilling was still the magnetic door price for arena standing room. Smoking was permitted but audiences were asked not to strike matches during the performances.

Keeping to the earlier tradition, the musical fare was light—a sprinkling of marches, overtures and dance pieces with an obligatory cornet solo.

Over the next forty-five years Henry J Wood stiffened the fare to a more serious side although Saturday's concerts remained dedicated to lighter programs—and still are.

We were there on a Saturday night. At the end of the overture when the piano was first brought on stage for the evening's featured performer, the promenaders in a coordinated burst yelled "HEAVE!"

Back from the gallery came "HO."

It was obviously a well-rehearsed ritual.

During the war the Queen's Hall was destroyed and Henry J Wood, then in ill health, wrote to give British Broadcasting Company the right to continue using the title "The Henry J Wood Promenade Concerts." Three months later, August 19 1944, he died. The BBC has been the successful force in keeping the Proms vibrant ever since.

The venue changed to The Royal Albert Hall and the series was expanded by bringing in many foreign orchestras although the various BBC orchestras now make up the backbone of the series. International vocalists and instrumentalists, choirs, dancing troupes and a host of guest conductors—I counted 43 for the season—add variety to the series.

So popular are the Proms that one of the hottest spring publication in the bookstores is the annual edition of *PROMS*. It contains the programs for the entire season starting in July, sketches about the guest soloists, background on the series, and ticket ordering information.

Prices vary according to the concert, graduating from "A" to "E." We had an "A" concert with a £ 9 price tag for a box. The last evening—and impossible to get into—featured Leonard Bernstein conducting and Kun Woo Pai at the piano. That "E" category concert cost £30 for the same box seat.

Our evening was forecast in the daily *Times* as being "undemanding." The program admitted the featured pianist had never won a competition which he dismissed as being "a pernicious influence." Definitely "A" level stuff.

In the *PROMS* publication, which the Lady Navigator was first in line to buy, we found an advertised package including box tickets, pre-concert refreshments with canapes, champagne at the interval and a post-concert seated supper in the same private room behind our box.

Fortnum & Mason advertised Prom Picnic Boxes for pre-ordered and day-of-performance pick-up in the same publication.

Well, you can't go to a London "Event" without eating and drinking, can you?

The Lady Navigator bought the refreshment/champagne-supper package for £38 each.

We joined our party of only 26 in the Prince Consort Room for a glass or two of red or white wine. The fancy canapes, the organizer announced, were totaled when they fell off their trolley departing the elevator. Replacements were peanuts and potato chips.

Not a great omen.

The amenities were catered by Brookes, the official contracted caterers for The Royal Albert Hall who operate a buffet restaurant on the balcony level two hours before every concert. Brookes also work the Paris Air Show and the Henley Regatta.

Our seats, three and four in Loggia 30, were on the edge of the balcony, overlooking the audience.

Said the Lady Navigator, "I *like* boxes."

Returning to the elliptical Royal Albert Hall was a nostalgic moment for me because it was here I went to the Central School of Dramatic Art in the summer of 1945. The classroom was located behind the gigantic pipe organ on the fifth floor gallery level.

In the morning, walking around the gallery to class, I used to look down in the semi-darkness at the symphony rehearsing on stage under suspended overhead lights. Was it the London Symphony? Was it Sir Thomas Beecham? No matter. It was all quite romantic and appropriately theatrical.

In those days The Royal Albert Hall was rather war-weary

dreary but now, looking around from Loggia 30, seat three, how grand the old girl looked.

After all, the huge building was completed in 1870 with a seating capacity of 8,000, now reduced to 7,000 by safety regulations.

The pipes of the vast organ were now a gleaming pewter color and the wood accented with butterscotch gold.

Flying saucer discs have been suspended to eliminate the echo that plagued the Albert initially. It was said of earlier day acoustics that this was the only auditorium where a composer could hear his work played twice at the same concert.

Three levels of boxes were curtained in plush red velvet.

Indirect lighting created a soft amber tone everywhere, hiding the hall's wrinkles and crinkles.

It was an evening of grandeur with the heritage of the "festive air."

In the last half or our program the floor audience swayed together to the swooping of the Viennese waltzes and in the last piece, Johann Strauss II's *Thunder and Lighting* polka, the floor audience broke out colored umbrellas and bobbed them up and down in rhythm with the music, looking like car pistons. At one interlude they bellowed in a rehearsed yell, "DON'T WE HAVE FUN!"

In the last quick polka the entire audience broke into rhythmic hand clapping and was then led by the exuberant conductor with gestures to clap softly . . . Now A Little Louder . . . NOW LET IT GO!

He received three encores. Lots of fun.

At the dinner after—a free glass of wine was poured to make amends for the dropped canapes—we sat next to Stuart Harding, managing director of International Arts & Music whose company organizes Proms Evening Out packages including rail-and-hotel arrangements for out-of-town clients.

We learned that the "pops" atmosphere of that evening's performance occurs only during the first Saturday night concert when there is an annual Viennese program, and on the final evening of the season.

The last half of the final program is wild, he reported. Signs are lowered from the balcony, balloons rise, the PING and PONG verbal exchanges are expanded.

"Yet, Mrs. Harding said and the table diners agreed, "during the performance itself, they are respectively quiet."

And you can't get in. To even qualify for the raffle to buy a ticket for the last night you must have purchased tickets for five other concerts during the season.

Standing-room-only Promenaders and balcony ticket purchasers will start standing in line two weeks before the last concert to get tickets, which can only be bought on the day of the performance.

The annual *PROMS* booklet tells you how to book by post, telephone and credit card or by person. An order form is contained in the booklet. Ticket applications are not dealt with before June 1.

For information about Proms Travel Bargains, write International Arts & Music, P.O. Box 1, 30 Culver Road, St Albans, Herts AL1 4ED.

Out of Town

16. Day Trips & Overnighters

Surrounding London are dozens of rich exploration opportunities. Which to take depends upon your own interests.

Do you want archaeological history?

Tours to the Treasure Houses of England or private romantic estate gardens?

Do you want to go to the time of the Druids in a visit to Stonehenge and ponder the "why" of those great stones in a circle?

Would you rather make a nosegay of the architectural wonders in cathedrals like York and Canterbury and Coventry?

How about castles? You can visit Leeds and Warwick and Windsor, or great houses like Castle Howard in York where *Brideshead Revisited* was filmed?

You wouldn't want to leave England without a visit to the university towns of Oxford and Cambridge or a cultural dip in the Avon waters at Stratford to see a Royal Shakespeare Company play.

And you must see the Roman Baths in Bath and the beaches at Brighton.

So much is available within a hour's train ride or coach trip from London.

You can even enjoy the solitude and beauty of Scotland and the pubs of Dublin in one direction or Paris in the other on overnight trips. Each so close by air.

The opportunities: abundant. The selection: difficult.

DAY TRIPS

Brighton
Victoria Station.
Travel Time: 55 minutes.

Colchester
Liverpool St. Station.
Travel Time: 52 minutes.

Guildford
Waterloo Station.
Travel Time: 35 minutes.

Greenwich
Charing Cross Station.
Travel Time: 12 minutes.

Hampton Court
Waterloo Station.
Travel Time: 32 minutes.

Kew
Waterloo Station to Kew Bridge.
Travel Time: 20 minutes.

Rochester
Victoria Station.
Travel Time: 55 minutes.

St. Albans
St. Pancras Station.
Travel Time: 18 minutes.

Thames Barrier (Charlton).
Charing Cross Station.
Travel Time: 20 minutes.

Tunbridge Wells
Charing Cross Station.
Travel Time: 1 hour.

Windsor
Paddington Station(change at Slough)
Travel Time: 35 minutes.
Waterloo Station.
Travel Time: 47 minutes.

Winchester
Waterloo Station.
Travel Time: 1 hour 10 minutes.

Arundel
Victoria Station.
Travel Time: 1 hour 17 minutes.

Bath
Paddington Station.
Travel Time: 1 hour 20 minutes.

Bournemouth
Waterloo Station.
Travel Time: 1 hour 38 minutes.

Cambridge
Liverpool Street Station.
Travel Time: 1 hour 15 minutes.

Bristol
Paddington Station.
Travel Time: 1 hour 40 minutes.

Canterbury
Victoria Station.
Travel Time: 1 hour 20 minutes.

Chichester
Victoria Station.
Travel Time: 1 hour 37 minutes.

Dover
Charing Cross Station.
Travel Time: 1 hour 26 minutes.

Norwich
Liverpool Street Station.
Travel Time: 2 hours 15 minutes.

Oxford
Paddington Station.
Travel Time: 1 hour.

Portsmouth
Waterloo Station.
Travel Time: 1 hour 30 minutes.

Stratford-Upon-Avon
Euston Station to Coventry
(joins Guide Friday coach to
Stratford-upon-Avon).
Travel Time: 2 hours.

Salisbury
Waterloo Station.
Travel Time: 1 hour 30 minutes.

TRAVEL AND STAY A DAY OR MORE

Cardiff
Paddington Station.
Travel Time: 1 hour 55 minutes.

Chester
Euston Station.
Travel Time: 2 hours 40 minutes.

Edinburgh
Kings Cross Station.
Travel Time: 4 hours 50 minutes.

Plymouth
Paddington Station.
Travel Time: 3 hours 30 minutes.

York
Kings Cross Station.
Travel Time: 2 hours 15 minutes.

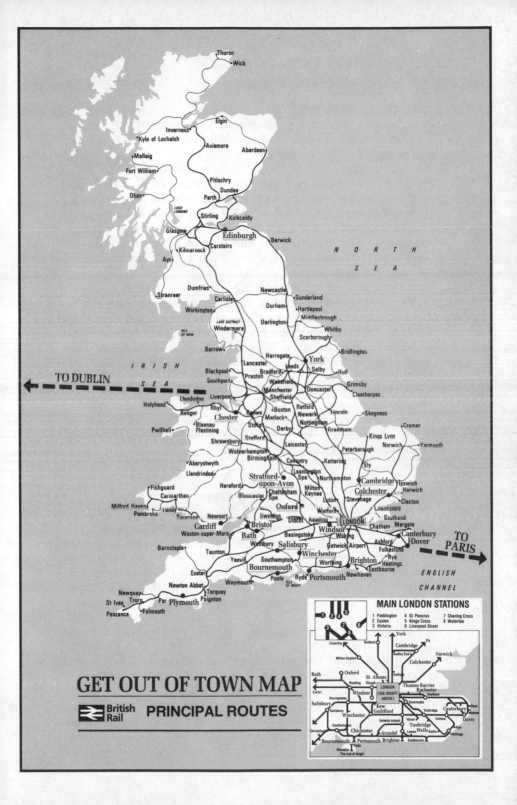

GET OUT OF TOWN MAP

British Rail — PRINCIPAL ROUTES

Stonehenge I wouldn't miss because it is unique in the world. Was it an agricultural clock? A solstice measurement? A temple? Or all three?

We sent a visiting daughter off on a guided day trip which stopped at the Salisbury Cathedral, Stonehenge and Bath and waited up for her report. Admittedly exhausted but brimming with enthusiasm, she would have done it all again. A fine tour.

She also elected to do a self-guided overnight trip to Glastonbury, site of Tor Hill, one of the ancient mystical legends of Britain where Chalice Well's water flowed red after hiding the Chalice of the Last Supper.

This is the land of legendary King Arthur and Camelot.

Stratford, too, can be done in a long day. Visiting Ann Hathaway's cottage and Shakespeare's birthplace is a school dream come true for many and seeing a Shakespeare play by the Royal Shakespeare Company is a huge dollop of cream on top. The Lady Navigator thinks that the superb talent of the Company makes Shakespeare as understandable as the "Dallas" or "Dynasty" TV shows.

Friends who made the coach trip to Stratford and nearby Warwick Castle reported that the castle has been taken over by Madame Tussaud's waxworks and is now a hokey, artificial presentation. Too bad.

Take a Pint Of Water At Brighton

You need to look at an ocean wave and breathe in sea air.

Bright Brighton and its sister town, Hove, are just an hour away from London by train.

The resort has been popular with the British as a vacation spa since a doctor in 1750 recommended drinking a pint and a half of sea water daily and a swim in the ocean as a cure for glandular diseases.

Royalty came; the fashionable followed royalty; the artisans followed the aristocracy.

A principal object of attention then and now is the Royal Pavilion, an oriental flight of fantasy created by the spendthrift George, Prince of Wales, later Prince Regent and finally, finally King George IV.

As Prince Regent, he instructed his favorite architect to create a lavish Indo-Chinese palace near the sea. John Nash did that.

Exterior: pure Raj. Interior: psuedo-Oriental. It is one of the rarest, most bizarre palaces in Europe.

The pavilion is open every day, fully furnished in its original style. Save your "ohs" and "ahs" until you see the table setting of Regency silver in the Royal Pavilion's Banqueting Room. Set for an intimate dinner for twenty-two.

Nearby are the former stables of the Prince Regent, now housing the Brighton Art Gallery and Museum.

Or seek out the local YMCA to see where his mistress, Mrs. Fitzherbert, lived.

Shopping is a high sport, especially in the "Lanes" and in Gloucester Road for antiques, a Brighton specialty. But explore the chic shops in East Street and the Regent Arcade. We bought a handknit sweater in Brighton for a daughter a few years ago and it remains a favorite to this day.

Upper Gardner Street has a junk market Saturdays. The open market is near The Level.

Rock candy is to Brighton what salt water taffy is to Atlanta.

The favorite shopping area is in the maze of Lanes that once was a fishing village. The crisscross of narrow, red brick alleys are filled with shops, pubs and cafes.

Offshore, the Palace Pier which was built in 1899 is known for its live entertainment, promenading, and amusement. The "beach" is not one you curl your toes into. Rocky.

Being a better class resort, there are several first class restaurants including Berkeley Brasserie, Parks and Le Grandgousier.

Swimming, windsurfing, horseback riding, golf, tennis arc sporting pursuits to entice you to stay longer.

But the biggest sport is seeing the Royal Pavilion.

A Worthwhile Long Trip—York

The city of York is most satisfying for visitors.

Situated on the winding River Ouse, the pretty city's towering gothic cathedral boasts the finest mediaeval glass windows in Europe.

A museum recalls the time when York was a major Roman fortress and the second largest city in England.

A page of economic history is permanently on display in the National Railroad Museum. Its major collection of locomotives and carriages traces a means of transportation pioneered by the British.

To flavor the visit you can walk the ramparts built to guard the city a long, long time ago.

Can all this be tucked into a day trip from London, we wondered. Yes, it can in the summertime when day's light lingers on until well after nine o'clock.

We bought a 'Cheap Day Return' ticket at King's Cross Station for a leisurely 9:35AM departure, arriving just before noon. After a pleasant lunch at the Bess Restaurant in the classic Royal York Hotel next to the station, we walked across the Lendal Bridge, passed the Yorkshire Museum and in ten minutes we stood before the cathedral, the star attraction of the city.

York Minster is the largest Gothic Cathedral in Northern Europe.

"What does 'minster' mean?" asked the Lady Navigator.

A free pamphlet picked up at the Information Desk at the train station told us that it was a mission center from which the surrounding country was evangelized.

The Minster is also a cathedral—its proper name is Cathedral and Metropolitan Church of St Peter in York—and as such it has one of the two archbishops of England. Its capacity is 5,000 people, standing room only.

We have visited cathedrals all over the world but the intense beauty of daylight filtering through regal colors of millions of bits of stained glass panes, falling on woods mellowed by centuries of time is one that we will remember forever. That high vaulted nave imparted the same ethereal feeling that you get upon entering a forest of gigantic redwood trees.

The booklet takes you on a walk-through of the cathedral and gives background on some of the highlight painted and stained glass windows, but reading distracts from looking. You want someone to tell you about it personally.

We inquired about guide services and were assigned David Kempley, a delightful retired RAF type, needing only a splendid white moustache to fit Central Casting's image of the MGM retired squadron leader.

"The cathedral nave in which we are standing was started in 1291 and took 60 years to finish," he said.

"The vaulted roof is of wood and the bosses, those carved wooden fixtures at strategic points in the vaulted ribs, are all of individual designs and tell different stories.

"For example, look up that pillar, go half way across the roof and you can see St George slaying the dragon. His sword has not only gone in the dragon but has come out the other side."

We wished we had brought binoculars to better see the ceiling decorations.

"When the ceiling was being cleaned for the first time during the Victorian period, they discovered one boss depicted Mary breast feeding the Christ child. *Shocking,* to the Victorians. If you look now, Mary is bottle feeding the baby. It was decided to retain the edited version because it so typified Victorian attitudes."

David Kempley pointed out details in the window graphics we otherwise would have missed and tossed in history lessons to boot.

"Keep in mind that there was not a lot of written communication in those days. The windows told religious stories first, but local legends crept into them also. Here, in the central pane, is St Peter flanked by the pilgrims. But look closely at the bottom border and you'll see a local legend depicted by animals. A cock preaching the sermon at a monkey's funeral, next is a hunting scene. There, a monkey eating and drinking before the funeral is over and, in the corner pane, a monkey already coveting the widow.

"You have to read your own morality play into the art work."

The North Transept's Five Sisters window (circa 1260) is a geometric pattern of 100,000 pieces of grey and green glass known as *Grisaille*.

Over a period of time, David Kempley explained, the lead in stained glass tends to disintegrate. The Five Sisters window was taken down after World War I and reassembled with fresh lead. The money came from funds subscribed to the memory of British women who lost their lives in the war.

He directed our attention to an astronomical clock dedicated to the members of the RAF who flew out of northern airfields and never returned.

You cannot miss the Great East Window—the size of a tennis court—the largest area of mediaeval stained glass in the world.

"We know when it was made, who made it and how much it cost which is rather unusual for mediaeval stained glass art.

"The Minster has the contract for its construction by a John Thornton of Coventry in 1402 which stipulates that the work was to be completed in three years. The artist's total compensation, with bonuses for meeting the schedule, was £ 57.

"But that was a fortune. He lived in a grand house in town while working on the window, paying 10 shillings a year in rent."

(A book on sale at the bookshop describes the details of the vast masterwork.)

We had made our way around to the south side of the East Transept. Kempley stood in front of a statue of the Archbishop Lamplugh by the famed carver Grinling Gibbons.

"Look at it closely. It has two right feet." It does.

Only in parting from David Kempley did we learn that all guides in the Minster are volunteers. No payment. No tipping.

After leaving York Minster we turned down Petergate to South Petergate which leads into a Tudor-like street called Shambles where half-timbered stores—once houses—have overhangs that nearly touch each other over the narrow, tourist-crammed lanes.

Note: all the people we found in York were so kind and cheerful. And their accents tinged with burrs and rolled verbs were delicious. It is a region of great pride. Families residing abroad and in other parts of England have been known to return home in time for the birth of their children so they, too, would be natives of Yorkshire.

After first ducking into a street market to buy four succulent peaches to take back to London, we returned to the Museum Gardens and the Yorkshire Museum. The special attraction was a new exhibit, "Roman Life." On the right side of the garden is the remaining structure of a Roman tower.

Just beyond the entrance is a transept wall of the old St Mary's Abbey.

York, during the time of the Romans, was the most important city in the north and second only to London. As a pivotal fortress, it was visited by three Roman emperors, Hadrian in the 2nd century, Severus in 3rd and Constantine in 4th century.

Little remains of the fortress except the tower wall in the garden.

The exhibit, however, brings alive through copy and memorabilia the emergence of towns, the dress and designs of the Romans, their cuisine and houses, the commerce and industry of the time.

Visitors learn about the time of changes including the invasion of the Jutes, Angles, Saxons and Frisians from Germany who took command of the area.

Anglo-Saxons in turn gave way before the Danish Vikings who captured York in 866, producing in time a new wave of prosperity through craftsmanship and trade.

The Anglo-Saxons recovered York in 954 but lost it again to William I, the Duke of Normandy, who ravaged the town and the countryside after winning the Battle of Hastings in 1066.

We retraced our steps to the Station Road and followed directions to reach the National Railway Museum, opened in 1975.

If you are a railroad buff, here is heaven.

The saga of railroading unfolds in this gigantic former railshed complete with turntables.

The history of railroading, pioneered in many aspects by the British, started with the use of ore cars riding on crude tracks, taking the metallic dirt from the mines to the wharves or to the smelters.

Metal rails replaced wooden rails, steam engines replaced man and horse power, diesel replaced steam as engines grew more and more powerful and trains hauled bigger loads to more places and went faster and faster.

It is all here. The quaint, the crude, the cute, the sleek.

The progress of locomotives is followed chronologically around two genuine railroad turntables displaying 44 original and many famous locomotives.

You can walk under the locomotives or get an overview from a nearby balcony.

A sound track in the background simulates the huffing and puffing of a steam engine departing a station.

Even the non-locomotive-oriented visitor can find pleasure in looking in the passenger carriages.

There is, for example, Queen Victoria's private railroad coach. She was so pleased with this opulent carriage that she contributed £ 800 to its £ 1800 total cost. You can mount a window-high walkway and peer at its interior, as you can with most of the carriages.

Or there is the Duke of Sutherland's saloon. He had the unusual privilege of being able to hitch his private car behind any train traveling on the Highland Railway, a right awarded for his generous monetary contributions.

(The Duke of Sutherland also built a private railway line 17 miles long over which he personally drove a private locomotive to his own private railway station.)

Pullman cars, first class carriages, second class compartments . . . all are on display under the museum roof.

What comes to mind is that we had more style in the old days of shining brass and gleaming wood and starched headrest doilies.

Slide shows, lectures, and rows and rows of exhibits of old uniforms, posters, dining car place settings, tickets and the other associated memorabilia of railroading are part of the vast complex.

Buffers, with waitresses in turn-of-the-century starched uniforms, is the most attractive museum restaurant we had seen in England. It recalled the former days of railroad elegance.

We made a six o'clock train back to London.

What we missed was the luxury of taking one of the many coach tours and guided walking tours in this living museum of a city.

We didn't, for starters:

1) See the Castle Museum and its cobbled village.

2) Experience the Jorvik Centre where the time of the Vikings is recreated in sights, sounds and smells.

3) Go on an hour cruise on the River Ouse to the Archbishop of York's Palace.

4) Walk all of the city walls or enjoy all of the views from the ramparts.

5) Go outside the city to see Castle Howard, the mythical Brideshead of television fame, or tour the Yorkshire Moors and Dales.

Would we go back to York and spend more time?

Oh, yes.

Bath—On The Orient Express

Bath is a delight.

Situated less than one hundred miles due West of London, it has been a popular spa retreat for two thousand years.

First popularized by the Romans who found its hot spring waters beneficial, and revived in the 18th century under the Georgians, Bath is an ideal holiday destination today for English and overseas visitors alike.

The historic attraction is in the archaeological remains of the Roman baths. The architectural attraction is in the charm of the

Georgian terrace houses.

Although Bath deserves an overnight stay, it is within easy reach—one hour, twenty minutes—of London's Paddington Station and is economical with a "Cheap Day Return" ticket.

After the trip to York and the whiff of graciousness we witnessed at the National Railroad Museum, we were ready for a bit of yesteryear elegance on the rehabilitated carriages of the Orient Express.

The Orient Express runs one-day tours out of Victoria Station once a week to Bath or on to Bristol and other one-day destinations. The current schedule is on Wednesday which coincides with the antique marketplace in Bath.

The Orient Express is so yesterworld opulent. At Victoria Station there is a separate check-in and waiting room with carpeted floor at trackside.

Many passengers come dressed in costumes befitting the transportation. The tea-party flouncing hat, the striped jacket, the pink furled umbrella.

It is not an inexpensive trip but the tour in the restored carriages of the most luxurious train in the world includes a champagne breakfast, coach tour in the city and a winey supper on the return trip. Oh, my dear.

Our car, one of nine, was the *Lucille* built in 1928. Our reserved places were at a table already set with white-on-white table cloth, starched napkins, engraved glassware with VSOE (Venice-Simplon Orient Express). The fresh red rose in the slim silver vase matched the small red lamp shade on the brass lamp which, in turn, matched the brass overhead luggage rack.

The dark polished paneling was of holly wood and inset with art deco Grecian urns in a lighter wood. The side lights were protected by tulip-shaped Lalique crystal shades.

Each of the nine refurbished and restored cars has a different motif and a distinctly separate history.

The *Audrey* "Carried the Queen, the Queen Mother and the Duke of Edinburgh to review the fleet."

The *Cygnus* "Reserved for Royalty and visiting Heads of State."

The *Phoenix* "Used by General de Gaulle. Favorite carriage of Queen Elizabeth."

The first gesture of the immaculately uniformed stewards—we had two—was to pour a "Buck's Fizz," half fresh orange juice and half champagne, leaving out either half if you desired.

What decadence. What snobbery. What fun.

The easy ride to Bath through the pretty green countryside was blissful.

At Bath we were met by coach and local guide and toured through the some of the Georgian residential communities, the terrace houses and gardens and over the Pulteney Bridge, the only bridge in England that is completely lined with shops on both parapets.

First stop was at the Assembly Rooms and the Museum of Costumes.

The Assembly Rooms, designed by John Wood in 1771, were used for concerts, for gambling and for sipping tea when tea cost £ 124 a pound, and to be seen drinking it—out of a saucer—automatically established one's economic importance. The crystal chandeliers are fine examples of England's early crystal cutting and craftsmanship.

What one wore in the way of finery to the Assembly Rooms in Bath's heyday of social prominence is the core of the Museum of Costumes and is well done.

But the star of Bath is the Roman Baths, one of England's most important archaeological sites.

What strikes you, after touring the series of sophisticated hot and cold baths, steam baths and saunas, was the incredible building ability of the Romans.

Still visible are the Great Bath, the King's Bath, the Circle Bath, and springs still pouring out gallons of steaming water.

Models show the baths as they were in Roman times and fragments of stone carvings and artifacts from the originals. Again, you shake your head at the engineering talent of these original conquerors.

Upstairs a most elegant Pump Room with a breathtaking cupola, now the Four Seasons Restaurant, is a vast room with a magnificent bar—and a small side bar where you can sample the curative waters.

Towering over the Roman Baths and the Pump Room is the adjacent Bath Abbey, a masterpiece of the late Gothic architecture begun soon after 1500.

Beneath the Gothic edifice lie the remains of an even greater Norman cathedral built at the beginning of the 12th century by Bishop John of Tours, then one of the largest and most impressive churches in the country.

The present abbey has a vaulted roof that soars to God and is famous for its East Window, an immense work of art that depicts the 56 scenes from the life of Jesus Christ running sequentially from the bottom left corner to the top right corner and topped by 30 figures of saints.

One of the legends of Bath is of a person who developed a terrible skin disease so severe that he removed himself from society and became a pig farmer. The pigs then picked up his rash. But one day in the fields the pigs came across a batch of mud in which they wallowed and came out pure of hide. The farmer followed and also was cured. The miraculous mud and curative waters of Bath, known to the Romans, were re-discovered.

Near the middle of the town which straddles the River Avon an obelisk stands in a small patch of green with a sign that says "Obelisk was erected in the memory of the happy restoration of the Prince of Orange through favour of God and to the great joy of Britain by drinking Bath waters, 1734."

There will always be a Chamber of Commerce.

With such royal publicity, by the late 18th century the city had become the most fashionable spa in the country. The wealthy came from throughout England and Europe requiring housing. The result was the magnificent Georgian stone terraces, an architectural legacy for the city.

In June the city holds the annual Bath Festival, one of the most attractive music festivals in England. On opening night the crowds swarm into a upland park to hear madrigal singing. All of the street lights are turned off and a lighted candle placed in each window of the Georgian terrace houses encircling the park.

Part of the joy of Bath is to roam the little side streets and arcades of this most Georgian of cities.

One of the tourist sites is Sally Lunn's, the oldest house in Bath, built in 1482. Sally Lunn lived there in 1680 and was known for the Sally Lunn Bun which was eaten with curd cheeses and ham or with cream mixed with beaten egg whites and fruit. It's now a teahouse restaurant and the Sally Lunn buns are part of the menu, to eat or take home.

A favorite shopping item is the Bath Oliver biscuit, the only biscuit to eat with cheese and the chocolate covered biscuit which is a calorie skyrocket to nibble with tea. (The Bath biscuits are now made in Reading.)

Of the favorite shops I found, one was for lengthy ladies called Long Tall Sally and another for crystal called A Touch of Glass.

Canterbury, A Modern Pilgrim's Tale

It could not have happened—but it did.

At dusk, time for Vespers, on December 29, 1170, four knights belonging to the court of King Henry II burst through the door of the Canterbury Cathedral and slew Thomas Becket, the Archbishop of Canterbury, cutting off the top of his head.

The execution had resulted from a quarrel between Becket and King Henry II who, vexed, cried aloud, "Who will rid me of this turbulent priest?"

A king's wish was a soldier's command.

One dramatic sequel was that Henry II, king of England, in an act of penance ordered by the Pope, fearing eternal damnation, walked barefoot through the streets of Canterbury in hair shirt and pilgrim's gown to Becket's tomb where he confessed and asked forgiveness.

Baring his back, he submitted to enough lashings from the monks to have killed a weaker man but not Henry II. He walked back through the town, mounted his horse and rode away.

But the greater drama was to come.

Miracles were ascribed to the sick, lame and blind who came to visit the fallen archbishop's tomb.

Becket became a saint.

With his martyrdom and sainthood, Canterbury and the tomb of the fallen archbishop become the object of pilgrimages never seen before—nor since—in Northern Europe.

His tomb was moved from the lowly crypt to a grander new chapel then on up to an elevated cathedral addition.

Pilgrims came from throughout the civilized Western world to pray for a miraculous healing—or to witness one. And Canterbury became the topic of poems, stories, novels and plays from *Canterbury Tales* by Geoffrey Chaucer to *Murder in the Cathedral* by T S Eliot.

Canterbury is only 50 miles from London, almost to Dover.

What could be more tempting to a visitor in London than a small pilgrimage to this southeastern city, just an hour and twenty minute train ride away? The city itself is quaint—it really is—and its cathedral not only historic but the mother church of the Anglican Communion.

We left Victoria Station for Canterbury at 9:20AM on a Cheap Day Return headed for the East Station because it is closer to the Cathedral. By 11AM, we were standing in front of the Information Office in the town center to rendezvous with our guide whom the Lady Navigator had prearranged through the Canterbury Guild of Guides (Tel: 0227-459-779).

Our guide was Grenville Harmer who had been a professional engineer and a teacher until 1969 when he began a third career as a guide. A tall, grayed gentlemen with an easy manner, he imparted lore of Canterbury not easily found by the casual visitor. Our morning of walking the old ramparts, cutting through quiet gardens and narrow lanes and touring the grounds of the cathedral with Harmer-the-Teacher was much too short.

"I'm going to take you along the main street to the west, outside the walls, behind the cathedral to places you won't see on the cathedral tour, back to the center of town by way of one of the more historical streets and get you back here in time for lunch. Does that sound satisfactory?"

Perfect.

We began our tour at the the corner of Prince Street and Mercery Lane. The main street goes through four name changes in a mile length.

Across the street was a Boots Chemist shop. Built in the 14th century, it once was occupied by Simon, the Mercer. The lane, now lined with gift shops, took its name from his trade.

"In the Boots' basement is a crypt," said Mr Harmer. "Crypts were common in that century; what is uncommon is that the crypt still exists. If you go down to the basement of the store where they sell pet supplies and that sort of thing, and if you inquire very politely, and if a cooperative clerk is on duty, you could go down the few steps to the ancient crypt where you'd find a well. Still there. It was an emergency water supply for the monks in the cathedral. An underground passageway linked that house with the church.

"Mercery Lane is the Tudor street of Canterbury, much like Shambles in York, with ancient buildings snugged together along a cobblestone lane. Overhead there is an iron lamp which I didn't see for several years after moving to Canterbury. Wouldn't you like to have it?''

He directed our attention down to Westgate, the only remaining original gate to the city. There used to be six but, ''fortunately, the city ran out of money before they could tear down this last one. Westgate is considered to be one of the finest mediaeval gates in Europe.

''See the Elizabethan building jutting out into the street? Once it was a weaver's cottage for Huguenot refugees who settled here in search of religious freedom. Canterbury being only 38 miles from France, they first settled here and practiced their weaving trade.''

We walked to the east and came to a dividing line where the German bombs in the reprisal ''Baedeker Raids'' of 1942 had fallen erasing much of the old city. What remained was only the old church tower of St George's where Christopher Marlowe, who was born near here, was baptized on February 26 1564. A colleague of Shakespeare, the famous playwright was killed in a tavern brawl near Greenwich when he was only 29.

Part of the post-war redevelopment was a large theater named for Marlowe.

Our next stop was on the city's ancient wall.

''The walls of the city were built in the era between the 11th and 12th centuries and were built on Roman foundations. Oh, yes, this was a major Roman city. One result of the 1942 bombings was the discovery of a giant Roman amphitheater, probably the largest in England. The archaeologists were given three months to explore the site before a major shopping development was built over it.

''From here you can see a bastion sticking out from the wall and if you went the same distance you'd find another bastion and so forth all the way around the city. What determined the spacing between bastions? The length of an arrow's flight.

''Across the way is St Augustine's Abbey and through this gate, Queensgate, is the Cathedral.

''Although both institutions were run by the Benedictines, the two houses did not get along. At one point the monks from the abbey paid a monk from the Cathedral to steal some of Becket's relics so they, too, could profit from the pilgrimage trade.

''After Henry VIII's taking over the churches and abbeys, the Augustine Abbey became a royal residence and Queen Elizabeth stayed there when she came to meet the Duke of Alencon, with the idea of marriage.

"You see the two windows over the gate. Charles I stayed there when he came to meet his French bride.

We entered Queensgate which Mr Harmer said had been the route Queen Bertha used in the sixth century to attend services at St Martin's, said to be the oldest parish church in England.

Beyond the gate was Kent Memorial Garden, once a bowling green for the monks and now a memorial to servicemen killed in WWI.

We wandered among the aged buildings, some of which had been hospices (hotels) for pilgrims, others the living quarters, bake house, brewery, and other service buildings for the monks.

Mr Harmer pointed out the former hospice, Aula Nova, or New Hall where Chaucer stayed and complained that the food was cold.

Most of these buildings now house King's School Canterbury, one of many established throughout England by Henry VIII who converted the Catholic abbeys into public schools. (Read that private schools.)

The best known piece of Norman architecture in England is the staircase (circa 1180) at the King's School that leads into a library.

Somerset Maugham, the famous novelist, attended King's School, didn't like it, but in his will dictated that his ashes be sprinkled on the green adjacent to the Norman stairs.

"There are reputed to be two ghosts in the Cathedral." We were standing in an automobile service road behind the Cathedral.

"One is Thomas Becket and the other is Nelly Cook, the pretty maid of the abbey's master. Why such a pretty maid was employed was a subject of gossip. One day an even prettier lady came to the door and claimed to be his niece. Nelly was very suspicious and her suspicions were confirmed when the bedpan she put in the visitor's bed was undisturbed for ten nights in a row. Nelly poisoned the pie she served to the two of them.

"She was convicted of the crime and walled into that wall. You can see a faint silhouette of what is supposed to be Nelly. Workers many years later during reconstruction found the skeleton in the wall of a woman with a pie pan in her hand.

"They say today if you come into the garden at nine o'clock on Friday night you'll see the ghost of Nell Cook walking the wall.

"Of course you'll never know because they lock the gates to the garden in the evening."

In preparation for our afternoon tour inside the Cathedral, we learned that King Ethelbert married Bertha, a Frankish Catholic who brought with her monk missionaries in 597AD. Augustine became the first Archbishop of the new "Cathedra."

After the Norman conquest the church was rebuilt on a magnificent scale and rebuilt again in a Gothic style in 1174 after a major fire. Additional building occurred in other Gothic styles before Henry VIII ordered the tomb of Thomas Becket destroyed, and the monastery dissolved. The Puritans under Cromwell later vandalized much of the church, pulling heads off statues and smashing priceless stained glass windows.

We had left the cathedral grounds and nearly reached Mercer Lane again when Mr Harmer pointed out the Mayflower restaurant where Robert Cushman lived. He was one of the organizers of the Mayflower voyage to America.

We thanked Grenville Harmer muchly for the tour and went to lunch at the Queen Elizabeth Restaurant and ate in the second floor room where Good Queen Bess entertained the Duke of Alencon during their meeting. The Duke, like all the others, didn't pass the test.

The restaurant was the Crown Inn from 1424 to 1774.

The original plaster ceilings are among the finest in the country, done in 1572 by pargetters. The initials 'ER' and the crown can be seen in the ceiling plaques.

(The restaurant was non-licensed but the low prices—after London— were marvelous.)

Before entering the Cathedral grounds, look up above and see twelve angels each carrying a shield showing on element of the twelve Stations of the Cross. The dice of the soldiers on one shield, the cross on another, the shroud on another, etc.

Inside the gate there is a map of the grounds and an information center. I wanted to know the most common question asked of the information center staff at this most famous cathedral, the Mother Church of the Anglican Communion.

"The most common question? 'Where are the toilets?'" said the lass as the booth. (They are down at the southeast end of the grounds.)

Frequent guided tours of the cathedral are available at only £ 1 a person. You need a photographer's permit to take pictures inside. Easily arranged, but nonetheless, a permit.

Having prearranged for a guide, we were met at the entrance by Kitty Ridout whose forefathers came over with the Huguenot settlers.

Kitty was a volunteer guide, a small lady with short hair and an infectious smile, who was a member of the congregation.

She led us to the relief figures of King Ethelbert and Queen Bertha on either side of the southwest porch entrance. Then inside.

The nave of the church goes up and up and up. "Too high, some people have said," offered Kitty.

"Look at the colored window on the west end of the nave. This is the West Window, containing 13 figures from the genealogy of Christ dating from the late 12th century. You can see the figure of Adam in the center of the bottom row after he was sent out of Eden."

Going down the steps to the left of the nave at the transept, known as the Martyrdom Transept, we came to the spot where there now is a simple, bare roped-off altar, the *Altar of Sword's Point,* theatrically lighted and quite dramatic. On the wall behind the altar is a modernistic black cross shaped like jagged lightning. Two black swords on each arm of the cross point down to the spot where Becket was murdered.

In front of the altar slab is the simple word THOMAS. Here on May 29, 1982, Pope John Paul II from Rome and the Archbishop of Canterbury, Robert Runcie, knelt together in prayer.

From the Martyrdom Transept, we descended from Norman architecture into a Romanesque crypt where signs request silence. The column carvings of the 12th century are rare, and beautiful.

First is the chapel of Our Lady Undercroft and behind it the site of the original Becket tomb from 1170 to 1220. If you look up to the wall overlooking the site, you will see windows where the monks kept constant vigil over the first shrine.

Kitty led us into the choir for its stone vaulting, the delicately carved pointed arches, the stained glass windows.

And then into the Trinity Chapel which once held the new tomb and shrine of Becket, before the tomb was destroyed by Henry VIII. The body was never found. The site of the tomb is marked on the floor by an inscription and a burning candle. You feel he is still there.

Henry's rout failed to find the top of the saint's head, kept as a separate relic by the monks. To enshrine the relic, the last Gothic chapel was built behind the principal shrine, called the Corona, now rededicated to the Saints and Martyrs of our own time.

At the entrance to the choir, look up at the great central tower known as Bell Harry from the curfew bell at its summit, a noble effort with intricate fan vault.

Before leaving, stop at the chapel of St Michael's, the warriors' chapel. Curiously, it is also the tomb of Archbishop Stephen Langton. When the chapel was rebuilt, they didn't leave enough room for his entire tomb with the result that half of it is sticking out the far wall of the chapel. You can go outside and see.

If there were a third ghost at Canterbury, it could well be Archbishop Langton insisting that his feet be taken in from the cold.

Canterbury is a charming town. An overnighter or more here could be quite pleasant. A respectable museum, a river boat ride, the Marlowe Theatre, many restaurants, small hotels, many B&Bs are among its offerings. The main street is nicely paved in brick and reserved for pedestrians.

You'll not want to miss it and, having gone, you'll resolve to make another pilgrimage.

A Day In The Country—Windsor And Runnymead

A day of paradox. It includes the contemporary glitter of the today's modern monarchy set against a historical event which pulled the teeth of the ruling monarchy in the 13th century and established a precedent of liberty and freedom for all.

You can go in one pleasant day to Runnymead where the Magna Carta was signed and travel on to nearby Windsor where the Queen lives four months of the year and visit the State Apartments she uses for entertaining when she is in residence.

To visit Runnymead you either need a car or need to take one of many available coach tours.

Northwest of Staines, less than two hours out of London off Highway A-308 is a flat plain next to the River Thames.

Two stone pillars mark the entrance to the meads, or meadows, engraved with the words "In these meads on 15th June 1215—were provisions formulated for the preservation of peace and every individual perpetually secured in the free enjoyment of his life and property."

It was a scene of high drama.

King John was the perfect blackhearted king. Murder came to him easily. Waffling was his second nature. Unlike his tall, blond brothers, he was stocky, feral of face. The people hated him.

However, faced with King John or the armies of France, he was the lesser of two evils. But he needed the allegiance of the barons.

Stephen Langton, the same Archbishop of Canterbury whose entombed feet protrude from the walls of Canterbury Cathedral, found a document of basic rights signed by Henry I. The archbishop organized the barons in pressing John for the same concessions.

And so the meeting was set for a hillside at Runnymead.

King John came to the rendezvous area with only his staff and kin. On the opposite side were all the barons of the country. They made the king an offer he couldn't refuse. Sign or else.

It took four days of drafting and re-drafting the document. Finally John signed it.

The Great Letter covered many resolutions including rights extended "to all freemen of our kingdom" declaring that no freeman could be exiled, outlawed or imprisoned but by the lawful judgment of his peers, or by the law of the land. (The British Museum displays many of the pertinent documents pertaining to the Magna Carta.)

Rising behind the meadow is a small hill and on the side of the slope is a small open shrine, perhaps ten feet wide, marking the site of the signing of Magna Carta by King John. The temple was erected by the American Bar Association. Inscribed on the dome is "Magna Carta—A Symbol of Freedom Under Law."

Nearby on the same hillside and reached by a cobblestone path is another memorial to freedom, a plain marble monument inscribed "This acre of ground was given to the United States of America by the people of Britain in memory of John F Kennedy."

The reason for the gift here at Runnymead is contained in a speech Kennedy gave on January 20 1961. "Let every nation know whether it wishes us well or ill that we shall pay any price, bear any burden, meet any hardship in order to assure the survival and success of liberty."

On a summer's day, on a hill of fresh-mown grass, overlooking the Thames, it is a peaceful piece of ground to celebrate what we take for a granted, a freedom from tyranny, a freedom that started in Runnymead.

Windsor is easy to reach by train.

Its accessibility makes it a popular out-of-town target for tourists so be prepared in the high season to encounter a million of your countrymen no matter what country you come from.

Note: the State Apartments are closed when the Queen is in Official Residence from late March to early May, during most of June, and at Christmas and New Year's. Open hours are 10:30AM to 3PM in the winter and until 5PM in the spring-summer seasons.

The castle was started by William I shortly after his victory at the Battle of Hastings as one of his outer ring of fortresses to protect the strategic central fortress of London. Over the years it expanded from a wood and dirt fortification to the grand, crenellated castle that you see today.

Approaching from the south side, the road crosses the avenue leading from the 4,800-acre Great Park to the castle. The avenue is three miles long and is open only to pedestrians and horse drawn coaches. At the top of the avenue is the vast, turreted, picture book castle.

It closely resembles the castles in the fairytale books of your childhood.

Parking is a bear. If you drive, get to Windsor early.

The first thing to see, after passing through the walls, is St George's Chapel. Small entrance fee.

For 10p buy a guide to the most important elements in the chapel.

By this time in our touring the churches and chapels of England, we understood that Perpendicular Gothic meant a series of tall slim perpendicular columns with fan vaulting, like fingers of a hand, that supports the roof, relieving the walls of weight bearing, thus permitting the use of more glass. The effect is to give the interior more light and a greater sense of space.

Work on the chapel took fifty years and was finished by Henry VII.

It was virtually rebuilt beginning in 1920. Every stone was removed, inspected and replaced where necessary. The structure was cleaned. The ceiling bosses were repainted. The job took nine years but, as a result, lucky visitors today see a chapel that looks much like the one finished by Henry VII.

In the second bay of the nave is the tomb of George V and Queen Mary. An effigy of the pair in white marble atop the tomb captures a remarkable likeness. It comes as a shock, after seeing three hundred effigies of English nobility, starting with the

Knights Templar, to be confronted with faces of people you remember from pictures in your childhood.

Farther on, set back in a small chapel, is the tomb of King George VI. A bas-relief of his head is spotlighted.

Beyond the nave is the Choir of the Order of the Garter, a most commanding room.

On each side of the room are beautifully carved stalls, carved in the 15th century.

Three rows of dark wooden pews line each side of the choir. The upper tier contains the stalls of the Knights of the Garter. The middle tier is for Military Knights. The lowest tier is for ordinary members of the congregation.

Behind each knight's stall is a canopy with a helmet surmounted by his crest, and above it hangs a banner bearing his coat of arms.

When a knight dies, his helmet is removed, his banner is lowered and his coat of arms is reproduced on a metal plaque and attached to the back of the pew.

Enclosed private balconies at the altar end allowed queens to watch the ceremonies at a time when the Order was exclusively male.

According to legend, the Order started when King Edward III was dancing with beautiful Countess of Salisbury. Her garter slipped to the floor—on purpose, it was suggested. The king gallantly replaced it and the members of the party tittered. "If you think naughty, you are naughty," said the innocent king and started the Order of the Garter with the motto, *Honi soit qui mal y pense.*

"The problem with the legend," said Ben Tyler, an amiable parishioner who serves once a week as a volunteer strolling information officer, "is that research shows that men wore garters in those times but women didn't."

There are two types of knights in the Order of the Garter, and only 26 seats.

Hereditary heads of state form one part. Emperor Haille Selassie was a knight. So was Queen Juliana of the Netherlands.

The other sector is appointed by the ruling monarch. Former prime ministers usually are knighted, but not automatically. When a knight is appointed, he receives a coat of arms from the College of Arms which is imprinted on a flag and flown over his place in the choir.

Among the flags flying were those of Harold Wilson with two ships on his banner because he enjoys ships. James Callahan, recently knighted, had no flag yet flying. "It takes time to research, design and fabricate the flags," Mr. Tyler noted.

"Could Mrs. Thatcher become a knight?"

"Oh, my, yes," said Mr. Tyler. "But she would have to wait until somebody died."

"I think she could easily arrange that," a member of the party was heard to murmur.

The Choir of the Knights of the Garter is also a room of former kings and queens.

To the right of the High Altar are the tombs of Edward VII and Queen Alexandra. Inside the door is buried Edward IV and across the room in a bay is his victim, Henry VI, whom he probably had murdered in the Tower.

In the aisle in front of the altar is a tomb cover leading to the Royal Vault where King George III, George IV, and William IV are buried together with other members of the Royal Family.

In the middle of the room is a marble slab marking a vault containing the bodies of Henry VIII, Jane Seymour, his third wife who died a natural death, and the remains of executed Charles I.

"With his head?"

"Including his head," was the answer.

Leaving St George's Chapel, which is part of the Lower Ward, you pass by the Round Tower of the Middle Ward, and proceed to the Upper Ward and the State Apartments.

From the North Terrace you get a lovely view of the valley below and the famous school of Eton in the distance.

Windsor Castle has 750 rooms and you are can visit 16 of them in the State Apartments.

You couldn't stand more than 16. You are drained visually by too much of too much.

But you must experience the State Apartments, first visiting the Doll House. A miniature castle in its own right with tiny, perfectly detailed furniture. A fantasy come true. The Lady Navigator had to be bulldozed away. Surrounding shelves have another ton of miniatures, even playing cards.

A catalogue of the art work, paintings, tapestries, sculptures, precious furniture has addendum after addendum, reflecting the constant changes in the State Apartments. It is not easy at Windsor to keep visitors informed about what is where.

From the Grand Vestibule to the King's Drawing Room, the 16 State Apartments where the Queen entertains formally during her stays, is a magnificent combination of architecture, furnishings and art.

Grandeur on a royal scale.

My favorite room was the Waterloo Chamber with its grand ceiling looking like the interior of a great galleon.

The Lady Navigator voted for the State Bedchamber where Empress Eugenie and Napoleon III once slept.

The chambers are impressive and exhausting.

We fled Windsor for the comfort of a simple country pub.

The Visitor's Oxford

Oxford is an hour's ride from Paddington Station in London.

The temptation to visit the English speaking world's oldest center of advanced learning is too tempting to resist—and one shouldn't.

Oxford is a rose, but a thorny rose.

The classical university town has a Town and Gown division but Oxford also has in its suburbs an automobile factory so you find a Town and Gown and Factory city swarming with 200,000 shoppers, shop keepers, students, factory executives and workers and their wives. Add a daily tide of tourists to the attendant number of cars, taxis, buses and bicycles and you have a hodgepodge community.

You'll enjoy the cluster of academic Gothic citadels more if you are prepared in advance for less than ivory-tower tranquillity.

In previous visits to England we had walked through the Oxford quads and watched the punts on the Thames and lunched in a tucked away, oak-beamed pub. All very satisfactory.

A visiting daughter's day trip visit had enthralled her. She was ready to throw away a travel career and start anew in the heady atmosphere of Oxford's academia. She reported that to miss Blackwell's Bookstore on Broad Street was to miss Oxford and recommended a visit to the basement for the bargains.

Our return to Oxford was stimulated by a newspaper report story that Bodleian Library, long closed to visitors, was experimenting with morning tours. Bodleian Library. Second in size only to the British Library. A repository of five million books. Original manuscripts: 5,000. Total number of maps: 985,000. Footrun of occupied shelving: 81 miles. Number of reading rooms: 24. Number of seats for readers: 2,078.

We couldn't miss that. Upon arrival we taxied directly to the library. A half-hour tour was just leaving (£2 each). The volunteer guide, Rosarie Nolan, was well informed and charming and, best of all, there were only two of us signed up for the tour.

We started in the Divinity School, the oldest surviving building of the library complex, finished in 1488. The splendid Perpendicular Gothic structure serves as an exhibition area for some of the library's treasures.

The year 1988 will mark the 500th anniversary of this library building.

The adjacent Convocation House is a dark, oak-paneled meeting room where the House of Commons had met at one time and was now used for a variety of University functions.

Part of the Convocation House is a small courthouse, no longer used but a reminder of the days when the Chancellor held court and administered justice to the disobedient.

We followed Mrs. Nolan upstairs to the hallowed halls of the Duke Humfrey's Library where you can only go with a guide, where massive pre-17th century manuscripts filled the bookcases. In one section there were private areas for special researchers while the other side of the room had readers' alcoves sectioned off with windows at the end. (Electricity was not installed until 1929.)

The ceiling was timbered and elaborately decorated. The atmosphere was solemn, serious, time-stopping. The Humfrey's Library had the same *sancti sanctorum* feeling as the Old Library in Dublin's Trinity College.

Great libraries feel like churches.

The best news is that the Bodleian Library tours have met with such success that tours are being extended to two hours in 1988.

We just had time for a pub lunch before joining a guided walking tour of the city with 21 others, having failed to find an individual guide by telephone the day before.

Oxford was a market town long before students attending the universities at Paris and Bologna returned to England in the 12th century and were organized into teaching halls by learned masters. The halls grew into separate independent colleges.

Today there are 35 colleges of which 28 are for undergraduates only. Each college has a library, a chapel, dining hall and living quarters but students from all colleges attend common faculties scattered around the township.

Lectures are held at 17 different faculties around Oxford but each college student has a tutor with whom he meets weekly and discusses his or her work. A normal undergraduate career takes three years.

The most surprising figure is that 40% of Oxford students are now women.

We visited or peeked into Christchurch, Oriel College, Merton, Corpus Christi, Magdalen—pronounced "Maudlin."

Not to be missed is the Sheldonian Theatre designed by Christopher Wren where, in an elaborate ten-page ceremony, recipients of degrees are bumped on the head with a Bible signifying their elevation to graduate status. Nor should you miss the Chapel of Christchurch which, officially, is the Cathedral of Oxford.

Yes, we visited Blackwell's and peered at travel books, later bought a jar of Oxford orange marmalade, another must.

In the summer the college students are gone and are replaced by foreign language students in special summer sessions sponsored by universities from many other countries.

On our next trip we'll finish reading Jan Morris's book *Oxford* and secondly take a picnic lunch and go to the Magdalen Bridge and hire a punt and go out of the Thames and look at the spires of the colleges from the distance. That would be the best part.

No. The best part would be to be a student. The daughter was right. What a wealth of learning to wallow in. Five million books.

Cambridge—The Newcomer (1284)

It all started when students in trouble with their Oxford authorities ran away to the monastery schools of Cambridge.

Creating Town and Gown problems with the local officials from the beginning, they were all finally gathered together into a college, Peterhouse, founded by the Bishop of Ely in 1284. Cambridge University had begun.

Today there are 24 colleges, two exclusively for women.

Cambridge is bigger than I had thought. What I expected to be a quick stroll from the railroad station to the Information Office took a full half hour. I found a bustling city of 100,000 people and 50,000 bicycles.

Had to have a refreshing pint at Fountain Inn (1749) to make it all the way.

Having decided to go to Cambridge on the spur of a sunny morning, I had made no pre-arrangement for a guided tour. The Information Office receptionist said she would try to find a guide for me (£18). Mrs. Joan James, a pert thing with a straw boater tilted on her grey hair, wore a striped jacket and carried a furled umbrella. She looked as if she might break into an 'Off to Buffalo' tap dance any moment.

We started at the St Bene't's Tower dating to the early 11th century—pre-Norman, pre-University. A curio about the church: it is the burial place of a Mr. Hobson whose large stable of horses made him a fortune and the town mayor. The thing about Hobson's Stables was that the customer got whichever horse had had the longest rest. No choice. The universal expression "Hobson's choice" means there isn't any.

We stopped in front of Cavendish Laboratory, founded in 1874, where Lord Rutherford, a father of nuclear physics, was once head and where Watson and Crick discovered the double helix leading to DNA, the foundation of life. They received the Nobel prize in 1962.

Each of the 24 colleges is separate, independently financed and administered, but Cambridge University pays teachers' salaries out of an annual £ 40 million government grant and administers several institutions such as Cavendish Laboratory.

A British student will pay only for his food and lodging, about £ 1600 for the scholastic year from October through June. An unsubsidized foreign student would need about £ 6,000.

Around a court—not a "quad" as at Oxford—each college has living quarters, a hall for dining, a chapel for praying and a library for studying.

The most valuable library probably is at Corpus Christi college. Matthew Parker, Archbishop of Canterbury, organized a great movement to collect books for educational purposes—and then kept them! The books, including the *Anglo-Saxon Chronicles,* are in the library.

The most noted chapel is King's College Chapel, a magnificent Perpendicular Gothic structure. Rubens' *Adoration of the Magi* adorns the altar. The Christmas Eve services from the chapel have become internationally famous via BBC.

The richest college is Trinity, founded by Henry VIII. It is said that you can walk from Cambridge to Yorkshire and never leave land endowed to the Trinity College. The container port of Felixstowe is owned by Trinity. Prince Charles went to Trinity. Porters wear their bowlers even during the summertime at Trinity.

You enter the courtyard via Trinity Great Gate, over which is a statue of Henry VIII. When first built, Henry's statue had him carrying the Orb and Cross in his left hand, a scepter in his right. One night the scepter was replaced by a leg of a chair. Unamused college officials replaced the scepter. It was only a short time until the officials found the scepter gone again, the chair leg back. This ping pong of scepter-cum-chair-leg continued until the officials retired.

Recently, the Great Gate underwent a major renovation. It was covered with tarpaulins for months and months. Prior to the unveiling, everybody in the concentrated university town titillated "Would it be —?" "Or would it be—?"

It was a chair leg, a varnished chair leg.

Stones for King's Chapel were floated via the River Cam to the back of the college. Today "The Backs" for the King's Backside, is that stretch of river frontage linking several of the colleges. It is a peaceful, idyllic riverfront. Punts leisurely slide over the smooth water and under the bridges, one of which is the Bridge of Sighs, a reproduction of the Venice bridge so named because it led to the prison.

The students at St John's probably heave the same sighs, but for different reasons.

The famous run against the clock in the film *Chariots of Fire* which was supposed to take place in Trinity courtyard was actually filmed at Eton. There are cloisters seen in the film. There are none in Trinity which would not allow a film crew in the college. But they did film the Trinity clock.

The hands were missing when I was there but it struck five anyway; struck the hour twice, as it always does, which was a signal for me to return to the station and catch the milk train back to London.

Note: the colleges are closed to visitors during the examination study period of May and June. Do not disturb the animals.

During summer months, college facilities are rented out to other universities, like UCLA, for special sessions. Cambridge, like Oxford, is filled with language students from abroad.

Scotland

The lasses of Scotland with the fairest of skin and the most enchanting burr of speech, are delectable things.

And then there is the heather, the lakes, the golf courses, the distilleries.

And then there is Edinburgh, a distinctive city, a city of education, kings and castles.

All of the above are reached in four and a half hours by train or an hour by air.

We've toured Scotland by car and would seize on the chance to do it again. But we ran out of time and, by proxy, recaptured the charm of northernmost Britain through the eyes of daughter number two, she of the fairest of skin, reddish hair and the hint of a California drawl in her voice.

Her first stop was Edinburgh Castle where the hilltop position gives the best spot for viewing and photographing the city. It was where she got the first clue of the Scottish character.

The national motto is *Nemo Me Impune Lacessit,* Touch Me Not With Impunity. Or, in her translation, "Punch me in the nose and you'll get punched back."

She noted that the rampant lion that adorns many things shows four claws if a king is on the throne, three if a queen. "Also, things are often dismissed as 'modern' if they are only a century old. The guide thinks 200 years is barely worth noticing."

The castle has only been taken by siege, never by force.

She found St Mary's Chapel, known as the Scottish National War Memorial, a heartbreaking place devoted entirely to Scots lost in war: "soldiers, sailors, airmen, nurses, civilians and 'the tunneller's friends'—canaries and mice."

The small chapel of St Michael, patron saint of warriors, contains a casket in which rests a scroll listing the names of 155,000 dead soldiers. A rather dramatic presentation. The memorial stands atop the highest spot in the castle.

She found the Royal Services Museum "brimming over with pomp," a wealth of medals, flags, badges and buttons of incredible lavishness.

On Carlton Hill she visited a monument celebrating the end of the Napoleonic Wars. It gives the visitor another glimpse at the Scottish character. The monument required £ 2,000 to build but the city could raise only £ 1,000. So they built half the memorial.

"The citizens wouldn't have it otherwise; it is symbolic of the pride and poverty of Edinburgh."

She visited only the courtyard of Holyrood Palace because royalty was in residence. Normally the tour includes the interior.

"In the grounds," she reported, "is a small structure known as Queen Mary's bath house. In her time, taking a bath was commonly an annual event, usually in May. (It launched the annual May Bank Holiday.)

"After the scrub down, people were sewn back into their clothes, adding more layers as the weather cooled.

"June weddings were also a result of the May bath. Although the wedding party was relatively clean, the bride who had had a customary prenuptial bath, carried a bouquet of posies to ward off the scent of the assembled group."

Was that the origin of the wedding bouquet?

Her tour included a look at the site of Lithgrow Castle and Stirling Castle, the "Gateway to the Highlands and Guardian of the River Forth" and fantastic views along with the more buttons and badges displays.

"Passed the remains of Buchanan Castle and reached Loch Lomond, Britain's largest inland body of water, 24 miles long, and picked up a lake-washed pebble said to be good luck for a year.

"Although May usually is spring in the northern hemisphere, it is winter in Scotland. I could have used heavier gloves and sweaters. Laycring is a must. The coach was quite warm.

"I took seven rolls of film and could have used more."

Paris Or Dublin?
An Hour To The Right, An Hour To The Left

The temptation while in London to stretch beyond England for just a short visit is almost irresistible.

And why not?

You can fly to Paris or Dublin in just an hour.

We took a short excursion to Dublin, a city we know well and enjoy.

What do you do in Dublin?

You go to the Old Library in Trinity College, a most beautiful wood-and-books room and look at the Book of Kells.

You go to Phoenix Park and drop a quid on an Irish race horse.

You shop O'Connell Street, much more upmarket today.

You look up your ancestors and buy a mug or tea towel or plaque with your family coat of arms. Were the McDermotts Irish kings? Of course, of course, of course.

You go to the old pubs with brass bar rails and drink cool Guinness and talk about the price of lambs and the *darty* this and the *darty* that.

If you are really into Guinness, you go out to the St James Brewery, the first in today's mega company, and sip a free glass straight from mother's bosom and enjoy the brewery's museum.

Oh, 'tis a *fyne, fyne* city to visit.

Or you can take the hour's trip to Paris on British Airways.

Warning: secure your French visa before leaving home.

Since September 1986 the French have required visas, a move that has been implemented with their famous concierge mentality and courtesy.

In London it took an entire morning to progress through block long lines and complete our visa application plus a return trip to pick up the stamped passports. And that was at a relatively light time of year.

A pleasant part of a return to Paris is that, unlike London, there are many hotels of medium price range which are clean, colorful, and touched with French charm that gives a weekend in Paris a special appeal.

We stayed at the Grand Hotel des Gobelins at 57 Boulevard St-Marcel on the recommendation of friends and it was all of the above. The cost for two nights was US$100.

It was in an area devoid of any tourists and surrounded by typically French brasseries and restaurants. Not a camera in sight.

Our primary mission was to visit the new Musee d'Orsay—and it is the reason that you must go back to Paris.

On the left bank of the Seine, opposite the Tuileries, was a bombed out railway station, Gare d'Orsay, which since the war had remained an ugly blackened pile of rubble.

The former museum of the Impressionists, the Jeu de Paume at the corner of the Tuileries, had long been too small for both the collection and the crowds lined up to get inside.

The solution was to take the former railroad station and convert it into a modern museum.

Today it is a miracle of architecture.

The great glass arched roof, no longer grayed by railroad engines, casts a pleasant changing pattern of light over tiered floors of varying heights exhibiting classical statues. On either side of the principal lobby are three floors of galleries containing the best of the former Jeu de Paume Impressionists, the Neo-Impressionists, plus a host of other artistic masterpieces.

Two lookout towers over the far end give you a chance to fully enjoy the greatest exhibit in the museum . . . the museum itself. The credit, incidentally, goes to a lady from Italy, architect Gae Aulenti.

Just to walk into the museum is a thrill. Note the ornate overhead lamps and then turn around and look at the magnificent, massive, gilded, restored railroad clock. What a joy. You could fly back to London now and the trip would have been a success.

Then you can stroll among the works of your familiar friends:

Delacroix, Millet, Corot, Courbet.

Manet, Monet, Renoir, Whistler.

Pissarro, Degas, Sisley, Van Gogh, Cezanne.

Bonnard, Vuillard, Vallotton, Seurat, Signac, Toulouse-Lautrec.

On and on and on. A treat. A veritable feast.

There are salons devoted to architecture, Art Nouveau, sculpture, and a marvelous gallery on furniture.

There is even a grand railroad station restaurant.

Our smart move was to get to the Musee d'Orsay when it opened which varies according to the day, usually 10:30AM but 9AM on Sunday and *closed on Thursday.*

Across the river, there are revolutionary things going at Le Grand Louvre. I. M. Pei, the renown Chinese-American architect, is creating a controversial glass pyramid at the new entrance to the museum of classical art. Also an extension is being added to the Louvre but it is underground.

At the Place de la Bastille a new opera house is under construction to be opened in time for the 1989 bicentenary celebration of the storming of the Bastille in 1789.

The Pompidou Centre, created by the same architects who did

the revolutionary Lloyd's of London headquarters, is drawing more visitors than the Eiffel Tower or the Louvre.

Even more exciting is the new Cite des Sciences et de l'Industrie which costs a staggering £ 500 million to build and £ 60 million to run. Like the Science Museum in London it is overrun with gangs of schoolchildren who enjoy learning about gadgets of today and tomorrow, particularly in participatory exhibits.

The museum itself is as large as an airship hangar while its feature building is a giant silver sphere, *La Geode,* inside of which is an "Omnimax" cinema theater.

While I was happy just walking the streets on the Left Bank and sniffing the trees and drinking in the atmosphere, the Lady Navigator went shopping and returned, eyes glistening with satisfaction, arms loaded with "fantastic bargains."

That evening we celebrated a birthday with a glorious, expensive dinner at E Marty's and drank too much wine and held hands and told each other how much we loved each other. Like you are supposed to do in Paris, France.

Hints

The most painless way to go on out-of-London tours is to build them into your schedule with your travel agent before you leave home.

You know what the cost is in your currency. The transportation, the guides, the bags, the tips, the meals, the itinerary details are all taken care of.

On the other hand there is abundant help in London.

Package tours can be selected from London travel agents or you can go to one of several Information Offices and find out about the city, castle or area you want to visit and pick and pay for customized tours.

Lots of cars to rent, and buses, trains and planes to chose from.

We have found great satisfaction, when on a tight time schedule, in prebooking local guides by calling the local Information Offices in advance.

The Nitty Gritty

17. Details: Before You Go . . . When You Arrive . . . And, Of Course, The Weather

England is like an independent minded woman; she just refuses to be predictable.

Be prepared for a variety of weather.

Be prepared with your warmest clothes in winter, but don't be surprised if you also need them occasionally in spring and summer.

In that regard, she is predictable.

You must *always* be prepared with hat, raincoat, and umbrella at any time of year. (Not to worry if you forgot to pack your collapsible brolly, London specializes in them.)

Although the city has a reputation for moisture, it gets only 25 inches a year, less than the 32 inches received in Rome every year.

Summers can be warm and muggy. You'll want your lightest clothing but—just in case—pack a sweater (jumper).

Because buildings and pavement hold the heat, London is usually several degrees warmer than the surrounding countryside.

Dress depends upon your length of stay and your social obligations, but a sensible rule-of-thumb is to do a trial pack, then remove half of what you packed.

I hold this advice sacred. I preach it to the Lady Navigator before every adventure and she listens intently . . . then packs seven bags. And doesn't unpack any of them.

The average traveler today is dressed for comfort and usually looks sloppy. If you look the gentleman in coat and tie, you will blend easier into the London scene.

But, for comfort's sake, wear pliable flat shoes for cobblestone walking.

Entering The Country

You need the usual passports but few visitors need visas.

You may stay six months without any fuss on a visit. No working for wages, though, without a permit.

After passing immigration, you claim your baggage at a turntable where there are lots of big, sturdy handcarts available and porters if you need them.

Customs clearance is easy. If you have no more than a bottle of spirits and a carton of cigarettes, follow the green signs to the exit. If you have items to declare, follow the red signs.

Airports

Great improvements.

Gatwick in the last several years has become a major international airport with connecting flights to anywhere in England or Europe or the rest of the world.

A new terminal in Gatwick will relieve present congestion.

You can plan on having airline personnel ready to answer your questions, a bank open to change money when you arrive, places to rent cars, desks to help you find hotel space if by chance you came—brave but foolish—without reservations. After passing through multiple time zones, who wants to worry about a place to stay?

The nicest thing about Gatwick is the convenience of the train to Victoria. A train leaves every fifteen minutes from an "in-terminal" station. You wheel your luggage-laden cart onto the elevator, go down to the train level, roll the cart to the train where there is plenty of room to store your luggage. The train is air-conditioned.

Within thirty-five minutes, you have arrived in Victoria Station in central London where heavy-duty carts await to ease the pain of getting to a taxi, bus or underground. Again, porters are available.

Heathrow also has seen dramatic changes in the last few years. British Air and KLM now share a separate facility, Terminal Four, which is considerably separated from Terminals One, Two and Three where the other major airlines are bunched together.

The extension of the Underground (Piccadilly Line) from all Heathrow terminals to London is a major bonus to the independent traveler. Stations are located below each terminal but don't plan on traveling with seven bags on the Underground. Especially during travel-to-and-from-work hours.

The increase of taxi fares to about £15-£20 plus tip to central London makes the Underground much more attractive.

At the present time a share-a-cab scheme is being tried but is not meeting with much enthusiasm on the part of the drivers.

If you want the deluxe treatment, you can arrange for limousine service with companies like Friends in London who meet you with either a Rolls Royce or, less expensively, a Jaguar, take you to your hotel, hold your hand for an hour answering any questions you want to pose.

This company also conducts tailored tours anywhere on any subject. Nothing is too esoteric. The owner, Simon Anderson, a Kiwi, has conducted photo hunts for railway bridges, shopping sprees, pub crawls in and out of the city, and picnics in the country. (A wonderful solution to a Glyndebourne Festival evening or a day at Royal Ascot.)

Write Friends in London, Ltd. P.O. Box 163, London WC2N 4NJ, telephone 01-240-9670.

Three other airports serve London.

Luton is reached by train via St Pancras or subway and bus; Stansted via Liverpool Street Station. The newest, London City Airport, in Docklands is mainly for STOL aircraft (Short Take Off and Landing) and when opened in 1987 was reached by bus, taxi and swinging through the trees. A shuttle-bus service is planned.

All airports around London are—or will be—serviced by airport buses with central pick-up and drop-off points. If you are an economically-squeezed student, they are the best buys.

Getting Around in London

You don't need a car.

You don't want a car.

Getting around the corkscrew streets of London is difficult enough for a taxi driver much less a visitor.

Taxis are lovely.

The FX4 is the big, square, turn-on-a-dime boxy car that has earned London its reputation for having the most comfortable taxis in the world. Its distinctive four-cylinder diesel engine clatter soothes the nerves—one of the sounds that sets London apart—in harmonious fugue with similar engine sounds from the buses.

Note: a new Metrocab model with a plastic, non-steel body, looking un-London sleek, is being introduced slowly into London's fleet of 16,500 taxis.

Every city in the world should adopt the taxi regulations imposed in London.

If you are on the streets of London on a Sunday, keep an eye out for the a man on a scooter, a clipboard on the front. The clipboard contains a list of London's streets and he is memorizing one portion of "the Knowledge" which consists of 468 basic routes and 2,000 main reference points comprising the 600-square-mile London anatomy. The aspirant taxi driver will spend two years cruising around each London neighborhood to absorb "the Knowledge." Then he has to pass examination after examination to satisfy the inquisitors that he has the street smarts to be able to drive a taxi. Seven out of eight fail.

And if he gets a license? A dirty taxi can jeopardize his license.

Oh, to have the same intelligent routine in Boston—home of the dirtiest taxis in the world—and New York, Washington or San Francisco where your driver doesn't yet have a knowledge of the language of the country much less the names of the streets.

Still the problem in London is the crowded streets which with each passing year become more congested. It makes the progress of the taxis less rapid and turns even the reluctant visitor to the more efficient and much less expensive subway system, the Underground or, more colloquially, the Tube.

A total of nine underground lines make up the subway system. Subway maps are everywhere.

What the visitor has to do is to become familiar with the colored maps and, preferably before a journey, make a flight plan.

"Let's see. I go from Sloane Square on the Circle Line, yellow line, one stop to Victoria Station, transfer to the Victoria Line, light blue line, and go two stops to Oxford Circus."

You are charged by the distance you travel. Station directories tell you how much it costs to go to your destination. Machines sell tickets in different denominations, as do the ticket booths.

In underground stations it will save time to have the right change—usually 50p will do it in central London—to drop in a ticket machine. Some machines make change. Otherwise, go to the ticket booth.

You have to feed your ticket to an entry turnstile which spits it back to you. Clutch it in your sweaty hand. You must surrender it at the end of your journey to a ticket taker or pay again.

You can also buy money-saving 1- 7- or 30-day passes.

If you plan a day with more than three bus or tube trips in central London, a "Cheap Day Return Pass" is economical at £ 1.70 (children half that). You can get on and off anything, anywhere, anytime. If a trip beyond the city zones, like to Heathrow and back, is included it will cost a bit more. These day passes cost considerably less than the visitors' "Explorer Pass" but they do have the restriction of traveling after 9:30AM.

Seven-day and longer "Travelcards" (or "Capitalcards" if British Rail travel is required) require a photo. A passport-type photograph will do. You pay a third of what the equivalent five-zone Explorer Pass would cost. The only difference: you need a photo.

Note: A major effort is being made to upgrade the stations and carriages of the underground system. Any particular station might well be in turmoil because most of the work has to take place after the peak traffic hours.

The bus system is more difficult to understand. On arrival forays, I'm too jet-bombed to deal with it unless I am traveling a familiar routing.

Eventually, I can cope. Schedules are posted at every bus stop indicating the routes and numbers of each bus stopping there. Guess it is the small print that makes me think it more difficult. The cost is the same as the underground.

Bus advantages: it gets you above ground where you can see the city life around you, especially from the top deck (front seats reserved for non smokers). The bus offers great solace to a foot-sore visitor, picking you up and letting you off closer to your destinations.

Bus maps are available but we find them difficult to understand.

Unless you have a prepaid pass, the bus conductor will collect the fee en route. However, conductors are being phased out. More and more driver-only buses. Have your money ready to pay the driver when getting on.

You should also know about mini-cabs. If you are going to need extensive transportation especially around the outskirts of London, look in the telephone book yellow pages under mini-cabs.

Dozens of "cars for hire—competitive rates" are listed. Worthwhile to negotiate.

When I was having fittings for my bespoke jacket at W G Child in Wandsworth, I engaged a mini-cab for the round trip. The price was the same as a taxi but it was more convenient to have the "chariot" waiting.

Money

You know that the English pound is no longer in shillings but in pence. One hundred pence to the pound. The coins are 1p, 2p, 5p, 10p, 20p, and 50p denominations. A new   1 coin replaced the £ 1 note.

The pound coin is about the same size as the 5p coin and is a confusing piece of metal despite its thickness. Easy to lose. I bought a pound holder, a spring-fed cylinder, which stores and dispenses pound coins efficiently. Also I carry a change purse because one tends to become overloaded with minor local currency. However, I often found shopkeepers eager to take all of the change, nearly always picking out the pence coins when proffered to them from an upturned palm.

Pound notes are £ 5, £ 10, £ 20 and £ 50.

I don't know how to beat the change of currency dilemma. You do get better rates at banks but, even then, you are not only charged a percentage but a fee as well. Even American Express nicks you in the exchange of American Express travelers cheques.

When you get cash out of an American Express machine with your Amex card, you are charged two percent plus the going exchange rate that day.

If you are going to stay long enough to require a local bank account, be prepared for inept, inaccurate, interminable delays in transactions. Frustration magnified to the zillionth degree.

We dealt with Barclays and it was the closest thing to financial piles one could experience.

Banks usually open at 9:30 and close at 3:30. When they are closed you can cash travelers cheques at the British Travel Centre on Lower Regent Street, at Thomas Cook offices, major department stores and large hotels.

If you are pushed into going to a Bureau de Change, expect to drop an extra pound or two.

Tipping

Ahhh.

A tour bus guide said on a Sunday morning hour-and-a-half tour of London (£ 5), "The question I get asked most by tourists is how much do we tip."

I tip bellboys 50p a bag. If the hall porter has given me a tip on a good horse, he gets a few bob. Otherwise nothing unless he has produced tickets to an impossible show.

A travel writer friend was doing an article on how much you should tip a luxury hotel concierge. She was going to get her information by interviewing the top concierges in London. I laughed and laughed. As if they would tell.

Generally the 15% rule is in order for restaurants where the service charge will be indicated on the bill. See my note under Restaurants. Grrrr.

You don't tip for bar service except at the table.

Taxis take 10% or 15%. With one exception ten years ago, I have never experienced an ungracious taxi driver.

A good barber will take the same. At Harrods I asked for a light clean-up and got sheared. Being as it was Harrods I over-tipped and kicked myself all the way home. Dumb.

You get broad hints by the tour guide or boat guide to take care of Joe, the bus driver. I resent it and don't, except on a long tour. The standard tip is £1 per day on coach or rail tours.

My Sunday tour guide did the same thing.

Information

London Information Centre travel desks are at Heathrow and Gatwick, Victoria Station, Harrods, Selfridges and the Tower of London.

In addition, at Heathrow, as you get on the underground, you receive a free packet of London brochures with maps, theater schedules, etc.

Information booths at Gatwick pass out the same packet.

The London Information Centres offer, besides free literature and counsel, hotel and theater and tour booking bureaus and a bookshop for tourist guidebooks and maps. The Victoria Station office has the most comprehensive bookstore for the visitor imaginable. Any subject about London or Britain is on sale.

The British Tourist Authority has given up its St James's Street address for larger facilities at 12 Lower Regent Street. There you will find free counsel desks, an American Express office, a British Rail ticketing office, hotel and travel reservations agents, and small book and gift shops.

I did a story a few years ago about the amount of free literature available at that time from the BTA offices—10,000 different pieces if memory serves—but the amount has shrunken considerably. A Pub Information Bureau, I was saddened to learn, had also disappeared.

There are Scottish, Welsh and Irish information offices in London.

Guidebooks. What did we buy and use?

The AZ map books are indispensable for getting around London efficiently. We had three. The *AZ London* book of greater London and its surrounding boroughs, the skinnier but bigger print *AZ Inner London,* and the handiest of all, the wallet-sized *AZ Visitors London Atlas and Guide* which, besides maps and street names, carries key data on cinemas, theaters, places of interest, museums and art galleries. A fine little book to carry around and the most practical for day-to-day street prowling. (We wished the publisher had used a more durable binding system.)

I bought a *Fodor's Guide* and a smaller *Fodor's Fun Guide* which were helpful and looked at a *Frommer's* which was not.

Also my library included Bob Kane's *London At Its Best* —which is not the best.

Michelin's London, not easy to read, is a source of detailed information not found elsewhere.

The *Sloane Ranger Directory* which we inherited with our flat was a howl.

Two minor publications by John Wittich, *Discovering London Street Names* and *Discovering London's Inns and Taverns* were nice to have but by no means indispensable.

A useful information book, *The Kings and Queens of England—A Tourist Guide* by Jane Murray was easy to read and did a valiant job of keeping the Edwards and Georges properly separated.

I later bought *The London Encyclopedia*—1029 pages—as a reference book. It is not the thing you want to carry around in your hip pocket but a superb book for history buffs and London aficionados.

The Lady Navigator's shopping library is indicated in chapter 11, "Shoppers' London."

Hotel and restaurant guides are available by the ton—or tonne.

The pocketsized *Nicholson Restaurant Guide* was handy and surprisingly complete.

The Introductory City Tour

We are strong believers in a quick orientation tour of a new city by taking a guided coach tour.

In London the cheapest and quickest city tour is from Victoria Station, a London Transport Official Sightseeing Tour. Go, preferably, on Sunday when the streets are less crowded. The non-stop tour takes an hour and a half and covers 18 miles.

The cost, about £ 5, is a few pence less if you buy it at the London Information Office in the station, but you can also pay the guide at bus-side. Or buy a tour which gives you a sidedoor entry into Madame Tussaud's wax exhibition, avoiding the long lines.

We were excited about the Culture Bus Sightseeing Tour as a way of seeing London quickly and efficiently. There are 37 stops on the route. All the top museums and historic attractions. You hop on and off at any stop that interests you, stay as long as you please, and hop on the next yellow Cultural Bus (614) at special bus stops along the way. Buses run on 30-minute schedules weekdays, every 20 minutes on weekends. Taped commentary en route.

Sounds wonderful. The perfect way to get to off-the-mainline places like the Tate Galleries.

It doesn't work.

The Lady Navigator bought a one-day ticket after 1PM which entitled her to use the pass all of the following day as well. She set off to see EVERYTHING. What she saw was a lot of snarled traffic. As soon as she got within striking distance of a prime destination, she deserted the double-decker ship and walked. Faster. We wouldn't want to be stockholders in the Culture Bus enterprise.

Walks

London is one the world's greatest walking towns.

We thoroughly endorse walking tours, particularly guided walking tours. These may be sometimes too popular for fullest value but even with a too large group, you learn.

You can find the walks for each particular day listed in the weekly events magazine *What's On* or, daily, in the *The Times* "Information Service."

There are walks for every subject, nearly every area: Dickens's London, Shakespeare's London, Roman London, Mediaeval London, Underground London, Fagin's Friends, the Charm of

Chelsea, the Jack the Ripper Murders . . . and that barely scratches the surface.

Costing under £ 3 and taking about two hours, it is a way to become more intimately acquainted with London.

I took eight guided walks of London and at one time hired Colin Oates, a favorite guide, for a couple of exclusive solo walks. The Lady Navigator went off pursuing her own interests including guided museum and gallery tours.

You can do your own self-guided tour of London. You can buy small books on where to go and what to see. Some that we researched are "Off-Beat Walks in London," "Canal Walks in London," "The London Nobody Knows." There are excellent, inexpensive pamphlets such as "London Wall Walk" and even free walking guides like "Wimpy Walks," from the same folk who bring you hamburgers.

We brought with us a taped walk of London and a Walkman but the whole exercise was not worth the time, money or bother.

Media

Information on what is going on in London and the rest of the world is easy to find because London is a communications-intensive city, particularly in print.

You'll find in London the best newspapers in the world and some of the best television.

You'll also find some of the worst. Absolutely penny dreadful.

I can lose an entire morning with *The Times*, the *Guardian*, the *Observer*, the *Independent*, the *Daily Telegraph* and delight in the bright, witty, articulate writing.

The Sunday newspapers can take up the entire day.

The evening tabloids feature a photograph—page one or three—of a stripped lady, one murder, and two scandals. The special delight is bashing royalty. Sickening.

Perhaps sticking pins in the Royal Family sells newspapers to a certain element in England but I heard one call-in radio program where Royalty was a subject and every caller was vehemently opposed to such cheap coverage. Every visitor would agree. The Royal Family, we feel, belongs to us, too.

For a visitor, *The Times*, with its daily Information Service page, its entertainment page and its review of cinema, theater and television is quite valuable. Craig Brown's coverage of the Parliament, when it is in session, is so funny.

The Sunday Times is a paper I could hardly wait to read. Edward Pearce's political column is an example of newswriting at its best. Brilliant writer. For sheer enjoyment, I like columnist Russell Harty who also does an excellent weekly television interview.

British television can be excellent, particularly in the classical dramatic mini-series and documentaries.

The daily fare is not of the same standard. The most popular programs are *Coronation Street* and *Eastside,* evening programs of a soap opera class.

Lots of rerun movies.

Sports coverage includes horse racing, rugby and football—soccer to Americans—in the winter and cricket and tennis in the summer.

The camera coverage is superior in America—more money, more cameras—but the commentators in England are much more intelligent. They have the nice habit of letting the camera tell the story, particularly in tennis, not blabbing incessantly, a common tendency among American announcers who sound as if they are being paid by the word.

For some inexplicable reason, the coverage of the 1987 British Open used an American millionaire sports promoter as one of the announcers. His elocution was irritating and his remarks asinine. Why BBC made such a move when they have the best golf commentators in the world was difficult to understand.

My favorite TV program was an odd *potpourri* Sunday morning with David Frost. In addition to the news broadcast, one or more articulate journalists appeared each week to review the Sunday morning news and newspapers in both straight and humorous forms. High hilarity came from David's reading of jokes sent in by kids and from the best-graffiti-of-the-week. Like the sign "Preserve Our Wild Life" under which someone had written: "Pickle a Squirrel." Finally, there was a serious interview with a leading public character. Fine show. All done with great style.

London radio listeners will tell you that you must tune into BBC4 for the best of British radio. Plays, interviews, essays. BBC3 is the classical music station that costs £40 million a year and gets two percent of the audience.

If you are a reader, you will enjoy the humor of *Punch,* the weekly economic coverage of the *Economist* and the *Spectator,* the house and garden reporting and photography of *Harpers &*

Queens, Illustrated London News and British *Vogue.*

There is also a satirical weekly thing called *Private Eye* but one has to understand the local scene in depth to understand the humor.

Finding One's Roots

Many people return to the British Isles to find the homes of their ancestors.

If you don't have particulars of your English or Irish fore-fathers, the best place to start root finding is the Hyde Park Genealogical Library of the Church of Latter Day Saints (Mormon) on Exhibition Row, almost opposite the Science Museum.

The facilities of the genealogical library are available to the public for a minor (£1.50) charge. Staffed by helpful volunteers. The library is used by 1,000 people a month and 95% of the users are not of the Mormon faith.

The library is a collection point of records of churches, official records and census taking. You can find here, for example, every police officer in the country since 1844.

Records are kept of England, Ireland, Scotland and Wales.

Microfilmed birth and marriage records, alphabetically listed by counties, date back to the 16th century.

Twenty-two machines are available to read microfilmed data.

You have to have some clue as to where to start: a grand-parent's name, a place of birth or marriage, etc.

The librarians are very helpful in redirecting you to other depots of civil registrations and reference sources in London.

The College of Arms on Queen Victoria Street has a complete record of heraldic history if your family's background is an illustrious one.

The Kings And Queens

I bought a graph in the gift shop at Kensington Palace charting the reigns of the royal monarchs and found it a constant reference.

Here is a capsulated version starting after the long reign of Edward the Confessor (1042 to 1066) and the short reign of the last Anglo-Saxon king, Harold, whose rule started and ended the same year when he lost his crown and his life to William I, Duke of Normandy, in the Battle of Hastings in 1066. William I founded the Norman dynasty.

House of Norman Stuart
William I, 1066 to 1087
William II, 1087 to 1100
Henry I, 1100 to 1135
Stephen, 1135 to 1154

Plantagenet
Henry II, 1154 to 1189
Richard I, 1189 to 1199
John, 1199 to 1216
Henry III, 1216 to 1272
Edward I, 1272 to 1307
Edward II, 1307 to 1327
Edward III, 1327 to 1377
Richard II, 1377 to 1399

Lancaster
Henry IV, 1399 to 1413
Henry V, 1413 to 1422
Henry VI, 1422 to 1461

York
Edward IV, 1461 to 1483
Edward V, 1483
Richard III, 1483 to 1485

Tudor
Henry VII, 1485 to 1509
Henry VIII, 1509 to 1547
Edward VI, 1547 to 1553
Mary I, 1533 to 1558
Elizabeth I, 1558 to 1603

Stuart
James I, 1603 to 1625
Charles I, 1625 to 1649

The Commonwealth ruled the country under Oliver Cromwell and later his son, Richard, from 1649 to 1660

Stuart
Charles II, 1660 to 1685
James II, 1685 to 1688
William III & Mary II, 1689 to 1702
Anne, 1702 to 1714

Hanover
George I, 1714 to 1727
George II, 1727 to 1760
George III, 1760 to 1820
George IV, 1820 to 1830
William IV, 1830 to 1837
Victoria, 1837 to 1901

Saxe-Coburg
Edward VII, 1901 to 1910

Windsor
George V, 1910 to 1936
Edward VIII, 1936
George VI, 1936 to 1952
Elizabeth II, 1952 —

Our Thanks

Our stay in London was unsullied with freebies.

No restaurant hosted us. No hotel offered us the royal suite. No official travel organization gave us a free ticket.

If there is a public relations organization whose job it is to massage travel writers, they never laid a hand on us.

The single exception was the round trip ticket to Bath on the Orient Express and that came about because Georj Rafael, a director of the Venice Simplon Orient Express, has one of his four homes in the same compound on Diamond Head where we live.

But we were blessed with the generosity of time and hospitality of many people in London.

To Peter Elmsly, Chris Fulton and the staff at Air New Zealand in London we owe a million thanks for a million kindnesses.

Alan and Marion Ponsford, Brits by birth, who have taken us into their Surrey home so many times, were great sources of knowledge and enjoyment.

Jackie and Patrick Haighton not only introduced us to the Henley Regatta but also to Camberwell, an area of London unknown to most visitors.

Carolyn Daniel, a citizen of the world who helped with the *How To Get Lost And Found In Japan* book, came through again. She assembled a corps of well-traveled inveterate London shoppers with diverse interests and insights, and, over white wine and gourmet chicken salad, filled the Lady Navigator's notebook with tried and true blue shopping tips.

Lord and Lady Brightman, Stevie Ponsford, Jim Croall, Roger and Daphne Lowe, the Ed Sheehans, Donald Ratledge, Tiggy and Neville Trotter, MP, were among those who led us along the way. We are humbly grateful.

Friends at home who also helped included Doris Hackman, the Lee Grays, Jack Ercanbrack, Susan Bourke and the quiet genius, John Whyland.

Bless you all.

INDEX